# A
# HOUSE
# PARTY
# IN
# TUSCANY

TO DADA, MAMA AND CLAUDIA,
THE BELOVED PROTAGONISTS
OF THESE MEMORIES

RECIPES, STORIES AND ART
FROM Arniano

# A
# HOUSE
# PARTY
# IN
# TUSCANY

AMBER GUINNESS

CREATIVE DIRECTION AND PHOTOGRAPHY
BY ROBYN LEA
WITH SAGHAR SETAREH

# CONTENTS

AN INTRODUCTION . . . 9

THE ARNIANO PAINTING SCHOOL . . . 25

HOSTING THROUGHOUT THE SEASONS . . . 37

A NOTE ABOUT COOKING AND INGREDIENTS . . . 61

KITCHEN ESSENTIALS . . . 67

### RECIPES

SPRING . . . 79

SUMMER . . . . . . 121

AUTUMN . . . . . . . . . . . 165

WINTER . . . . . . . 203

SIDES AND STAPLES FOR ALL SEASONS . . . 241

### END THOUGHTS

UNNOTICED TREASURES: DAY TRIPS FROM ARNIANO . . . 272

WINES WE LOVE . . . 276

CONVERSIONS . . . 282

ACKNOWLEDGEMENTS . . . 283

IMAGE CREDITS . . . 284

INDEX . . . 285

AN

# INTRODUCTION

A building site on a barren hill was not what my parents had in mind when they decided to raise a family in Tuscany. Arniano – the derelict farmhouse they bought in 1989, in the then unfashionable southern region of Montalcino – had a roof and windows, but not much else. No electricity, no water, and certainly not the elegant loggias or rococo plasterwork they had hoped to find in their dream *palazzo*. There was not a single shrub or tree in the 30-odd acres of scrubland that fell away from the house on all sides, leaving it proud and exposed on the crown of its own hill. This was where I would spend the first thirteen years of my life.

My parents, Jasper and Camilla Guinness, had decided to find a larger house than the one they were living in at Greve, a small town nestled in a lush, green enclave in Chianti. They had met in Florence in 1982 and moved to Greve before getting married in 1985. In many ways, Il Colto, their previous house, was much more convenient. It was located near the city, in an area populated by all the friends – English and Italian – they had made through their Florentine life. But the house was small, near a main road and, as my mother often recalls, had an inexplicable number of staircases, many of which led to nowhere.

They looked at dozens of properties before settling on Arniano, by which time they had all but given up hope of finding something suitable. A friend had spotted a tiny advert in, of all places, the *Sunday Times*: 'run-down farmhouse on a hill, 30 minutes south of Siena'. So they drove an hour and a half south of Florence, and down the 2-kilometre dirt track that is now so familiar I could almost drive it with my eyes closed. They absorbed the 360-degree views towards Montalcino, a fortress town on a hill, dominated by an even bigger mountain looming behind it, Monte Amiata. And once they had opened all the shutters and realised that the rooms spanned the width of the building, allowing light to come in on both sides, they were sold. They packed up Il Colto, put me, their twelve-week-old baby, in a basket, and moved to this dilapidated shell, much to the shock and dismay of their Florentine friends.

Arniano is an 18th-century farmhouse – a *podere* – where in the past several rural families would have lived together in the upstairs rooms, while the animals lived downstairs. The house is long and wide, with vaulted brick ceilings on the ground floor, and high ceilings with massive wooden beams upstairs. Today, there are mown lawns, rows of cypresses, olive groves, a herb garden and several shaded terraces, but back in 1989 the house sat in the middle of scrubland, every outbuilding tumbling down. The house hadn't been lived in since the 1960s, when, after the war, most rural Italians realised that there was more warmth, comfort and lucrative work to be had in town, and so flocked to the cities. The layout was still geared towards farming, from the time when the ground floor was the domain of cows, pigs and chickens (something I often think about as I lie on the sofa watching *Friends*). My parents undertook the not-underwhelming task of knocking down dividing walls, opening up new doorways and installing plumbing, to turn Arniano into our much-loved family home. This was where they raised me and my sister Claudia, until I was thirteen and Claudia was ten.

I was too young to remember the 'camping' stage of the renovation, when the upstairs sitting room (the nursery, as it is still called, though once it would have been the kitchen) was fitted with a gas stove and a water trough for cooking, which allowed us to move in during a particularly harsh winter. My earliest memories are of builders – characters who would feature for the duration of my childhood and well into my adulthood. The chief of these was Mario, who became a firm friend of my father. He had lunch with us twice a week until long after the works at Arniano were finished.

Mario and his team would come up from the local town every day, to open up bricked-in windows and build the all-important fireplaces. In the natural Italian order of things, all of these men would have been packed off to work by their wives (or mothers) with a lunchtime feast. This would be conjured out of impressively small rucksacks and added to whatever my mother had prepared for them. The meal would be laid out on an old door placed on two wheelbarrows to make a serving table, and then we would all sit down to eat. There is a photograph of everyone seated around a table in the courtyard outside the kitchen on a sunny day, raising their glasses, with me sitting in a high chair and grimacing from under a straw sunhat.

Being Italian, the builders rated babies higher than the Seven Wonders of the World and paid me all the care and attention that solicits complete adoration from a child – and I did *adore* them. Once I could walk, I followed Mario everywhere. I still have a scar above my right eye from the time when I stealthily crept up on him, climbing to the top of a pile of rubble to peer over his shoulder to see what he was doing. So silent was my approach that poor Mario had no idea I was there and was devastated when he brought his hammer up, felt it connect with something and – upon hearing an unearthly wail – realised he had inadvertently hit me in the face with his hammer.

As I grew up, Mario and his cohort would often tell me about that harsh first winter – specifically, the time my mother bathed me in a vat of freezing water. Italians loathe the cold, believing that children especially should never be exposed to it. Unlike the English, they are not hardy. So, when my mother, with no hot water to hand, had apparently seen a trough of frozen water outside, cracked the ice and dunked her baby's head into it, they were absolutely appalled. Whether it was true or not, the builders delighted in telling this story with expressions of typical melodramatic horror.

The day-to-day progress of the house (full-time work, which occurred predominantly between 1989 and 1992, the year my sister Claudia was born) was punctuated by never-ending visits from my parents' friends. There was an open-door policy for anyone who wanted to come for lunch to see the house, as long as they were willing to help paint or knock down a wall afterwards. There is a wonderful picture of my godfather, Tony Lambton – who lived at nearby Villa Cetinale – shirtless, in his signature Ray-Bans, wielding a sledgehammer to knock through one of the bricked-up arched doorways, which now leads from the kitchen to the courtyard.

Aside from being curious about the renovation, these perpetual visits were in large part due to my parents' inherent popularity and their talent for hosting. My father, with his easy manner, quick mind and horror at the sight of an empty glass, was loved for his conversation, his wry smile, and the way he limp-wristedly smoked his Benson & Hedges Gold.

– Through the arch from the
kitchen to the dining room.
The cupboards were designed
by Mama after she found three
matching sets of old windows
in a junkyard. She entrusted
the construction to her friend
Charles Carr. The painting of
yellow peppers was done many
years ago by David MacIlwaine
(whose wife was Rose Gray). It is
much admired, and our painters
often sit in the kitchen doing
studies of it.

– Inside the kitchen cupboards:
Mama's glass and jug
collection, a mixture of things
ranging from glamorous
Venetian and flea market finds
to Ikea buys.

My mother, who is very funny, well-read and engaging, has always been famed as a fabulous cook (she still is, though she claims to have 'hung up her skillet'). She learned the basics after being expelled from school at seventeen. My grandmother had been killed in a car accident when my mother was nine years old, and she was left largely unguided as a young woman in the mid-70s (hence the expulsion), but at some point she realised that cooking could afford her the chance to travel. She went to cook for a summer rental house in the south of France, and then travelled on to California, where she had a close brush with Scientology (happily, she couldn't afford the entry fee) and developed an interest in aesthetics, specifically interiors and furniture. Years later, having met my father while on an antiquing and restoration course in Florence, she embraced their Italian life through assiduous study of Marcella Hazan and Elizabeth David. We still have these old books, dog-eared and filled with her notes, all made in pencil.

The ceaseless stream of visitors was in large part due to my mother's food (as well as her conversation). She has an aversion to anything that isn't aesthetically pleasing, finding it actually upsetting, so tables and food were always a feast for the eye as well as the palate. Even when the house was a building site, and there were only a few sticks of furniture to hand, my mother transformed the nursery into an elegant space, with the simple introduction of a sofa, a few pictures and some well-placed lamps. Meals were curated with the same amount of care as her interiors. Roast peppers were painstakingly peeled and laid out in alternating canary yellow and ruby red on round plates, and finished with perfectly spherical, juicy balls of mozzarella placed at the centre. Broad beans would be shelled into beautiful, blue- or green-speckled Tuscan bowls, accompanied by wheels of fresh pecorino made by our local shepherds. Fresh flowers were cut from the field and put in jugs on the serving table.

Ahead of her time: all forms of single-use plastic were banned, whether they be glasses, plates, cutlery or even toys (we were only allowed wooden toys). And, having the tendencies of a magpie, she was also ahead of the curve with what is now known as 'upcycling'. My childhood was filled with – to me, perplexing – moments of delight from Mama as she spotted a pile of rubbish in a field and bundled her find into the back of the car. By the time she had varnished, restored or reupholstered it, that rubbish would have become an indispensable and much-loved object around the house; there is the wooden cable drum, for instance, found chucked away at a dump near Asciano, which is still to this day a perfectly proportioned side table in our sitting room. And on one famous occasion, when strolling past an abandoned ruin with trees growing out of the collapsed ceiling, Mama crawled under the 'Do Not Enter – Danger' sign and through the overgrown shrubbery to retrieve the silky tatters of an abandoned baldaquin, which she then reupholstered – it still hangs above the bed in what is known as 'The Blue Room'. She dragged us to endless reclamation and junk yards, which we would play in as she searched for hidden treasures, later opening a furniture shop in the village. My mother has a knack for taking an object that most people would consider rubbish and imbuing it with glamour. This knack has also always applied to meals. Whether it be a lunch under the pergola, a picnic in the field, or even a TV dinner served on trays, it will always be stylish if she is in charge.

The kitchen at Arniano – which adjoins the dining room through a large arch – has always been at the heart of life there. My parents put in a fireplace, set at waist height, for cooking on, and my dad would often grill meat or roast chestnuts on the fire. The ceilings in the kitchen are high, and light pours in through two small, rectangular, south-facing windows located high up either side of the fireplace. They were installed at the insistence of my parents' friend, the artist Teddy Millington-Drake, who was very exacting about both gardens and interiors. The only trouble was that the wall where he wanted these windows installed is the end

gable at the south end of the house and essentially props the whole thing up. It is therefore the thickest wall, at over a metre deep, and excavating those two little windows proved to be the most complicated and costly feature of the whole house. My parents railed at the trouble and expense, but persevered at Teddy's insistence. And, of course, he was right – without them, the room wouldn't be nearly so filled with light.

In winter we usually ate by the fire in the kitchen, as by then the other rooms had lost all the heat absorbed during the summer and the stones of the house had grown cold. When we had guests, the house came alive, and I remember elaborate Sunday roasts, complete with Yorkshire puddings, being made in a 'too many cooks' situation by my mother, father and their great friends Adam and Cloe, both fabulous cooks themselves, and very bossy with it. Adam and Cloe were immortalised in the River Cafe 'blue book', with their respective recipes for the exact same spicy sausage pasta sauce – the only difference being that *pasta alla Cloe* takes twenty-five minutes to make, while *pasta alla Adam* takes two-and-a-half hours. Each of them always insisted that theirs was the correct way.

The puddings of the River Cafe became a presiding feature of our house in the spring of 1994. I was five, and my mother had agreed with Rose Gray and Ruthie Rogers to go and work in the restaurant's 'colds section' during the busier summer months that year. In preparation, Mama made endless almond and lemon tarts, and chocolate 'nemeses' from their first cookbook (the aforementioned 'blue book'), and I remember the very indulgent Easter Sunday of that year, when all of the above puddings were served to the dozens of friends and guests who had come to Arniano for a sunny lunch in the garden. I also have a vivid memory of walking hand in hand with Dada down the Thames, months later, on a sunny August day, to visit Mama at work. We walked through the kitchen garden and through the big glass doors to see her before service, and there she was in her chef's whites, standing behind the stainless-steel bar, completely absorbed in what she was doing.

Twenty years later, I walked through those same doors and spent nine months waitressing there, though my real interest lay in the kitchen. Being clumsy to the point of mild dyspraxia, I wasn't a natural waitress and on one occasion managed to drop an entire lemon tart on the floor during service, in front of a packed restaurant (I shudder to think of the waste). But there is a real spirit of encouragement and enthusiasm among the staff there, and eventually two of the very generous head chefs, Sian Wyn Owen and Joseph Trivelli, kindly let me do a handful of shifts in the kitchen. The smells, recipes and food immediately brought back such vivid memories of my childhood in Italy – they reminded me of home, of lunches outside at Arniano, of Dada, Tony, Adam and Cloe, and Rose. It's strange to think they had all died by the time I began my short stint waitressing at the River Cafe.

I think I always realised that, from a culinary point of view, we were lucky. My sister and I got involved from a young age – 'helping' was a favourite pastime, though I now realise we were probably doing anything but. When we were very little, we loved making cakes, a favourite being the very British 'chocolate biscuit cake'.

By the time I was six, I believed our cake-making proficiency was such that we could surprise Mama with a cake. My three-year-old sister peered at me with great scepticism as I mixed unweighed ingredients in a bowl, poured the mixture into the unlined cake tin and put it in the oven at a random heat for an indeterminate amount of time. I was amazed when it came out rock solid and welded to the ruined tin. From then on, 'helping' was always strictly supervised, although still encouraged. Over the years, my mother's knowledge of food had become so ingrained that, after a while, she stopped consulting recipes. She was therefore out of the habit of translating her instinctive cooking into language, and had lost the ability to explain how she prepared things. Whenever I would ask how she had made something, the answer was always the same: 'I don't know. You'll have to watch me do it.' This was usually said in a tone of disbelief at my assumption that she would know how to explain the process of creating whatever she had just conjured up.

If I was watching telly in the days following such a conversation, she would come through from the kitchen and say, 'I thought you said you wanted to learn to make malfatti' (a kind of spinach and ricotta gnocchi; the name literally means 'badly made' – though, needless to say, my mother's never were and so became known as '*benfatti*'). So, I would follow her back into the kitchen, watch, and help where I was allowed.

This ritual carried on for much of my childhood, and when I was twelve I was allowed to make dinner on my own – overseen by the beloved Virginia. Virginia is an Australian artist who was living in Italy and who took care of Claudia and me while our mother was at work, in exchange for somewhere to live. She became part of the family and over the years painted two very beautiful murals at Arniano: the first, in 1992, was a cupboard door on which she intricately created a Renaissance landscape; and the second, in 2010, a magical woodland painted on the walls of the same room, with trees soaring up to the ceiling. Under Virg's watchful eye I made roast chicken with grapes (a Catalan recipe that my mother had learned from a woman in Spain named Josefa) and roast potatoes. I vividly remember the table in the dining room that evening: as ever, lit by candles, and laid for myself, Mama, Dada, Claudia and Virginia, who kindly humoured me and ate the food I had made them. The feeling of pride at having – through what I saw as alchemy – turned ingredients into a meal for the people I loved most in the world is one that I still experience whenever I make a meal for anyone. From that day I was hooked.

Food, and the rituals surrounding it, are melded for me with family, lovely surroundings and nature. My father was a landscape gardener, and he lovingly turned the scrubland that surrounded the house into a garden. It was his obsession, and he cared for it painstakingly, every day. When I think of him, he is sitting on his giant lawnmower – or the orange tractor that was later painted sky blue at the insistence of Claudia and me – shirt off, in his swimming trunks, espadrilles and Ray-Bans, smoking a cigarette under a Panama hat as he mows the lawn or prunes the olive trees in the grove below the house. It was his love of the outdoors that has led me to connect hosting and entertaining with sun-soaked spring days, beautifully curated picnics in the fields and lunches under the beloved pergola that he built with Mario and Adam, which we still use today. For me, food and entertaining are intrinsically connected to my parents, and to the upbringing they gave my sister and me in our house on a Tuscan hill.

It was for this reason that I found going home so painful, following my father's death in 2011 from a short but vicious bout of cancer. No one had been to Arniano for months. Dada had come to England for his treatments, and for his final months we had all decamped to my aunt Catherine's house in Lancashire, where he died, in May. Mama, Claudia and I, accompanied by my father's sister Georgie and her children, went to Arniano a few weeks later, and what we found disturbed us profoundly. The lawn was unmown, the trees unpruned, the ground unswept, and at the bottom of the pool lay a scattering of leaves, branches and dead frogs. We were not prepared for what we saw. We were so wrapped up in the event of his death that we had not foreseen what the physical manifestation of his absence would look like: an abandoned garden.

Over the following three years, we rarely came home. Dada had been so intrinsic to every aspect of life at Arniano that it was inconceivable to be there without him. It was here, at home, that I would run through to another room to look for him and show him something he would find funny, or to point out that the

peonies outside the kitchen were in bloom. He was in the view, in every cypress, in every blade of grass and in the unused tractor – which lay so unused that it was, in fact, eventually stolen.

We all three busied ourselves with our lives: I had started my final year at the University of Edinburgh studying history and Italian; my sister, having had the gargantuan task of completing her A-Levels in the weeks following our father's death, had gone away on her pre-university travels; and Mama was in the final stages of a massive five-year renovation of Villa Cetinale, the home of my godfather, Tony, who had passed away in 2007 – he of the shirtless sledge-hammering twenty years before. We were quietly trying to carry on, accustoming ourselves, each in our own way, to our new reality, the reality that is forced upon you when someone as close as a parent or a husband dies. An event so mammoth that the change of reality is no easier whether you are eighteen and twenty-one, as my sister and I were, or forty, or fifty – or so goes my own theory. Our reaction was to turn away from the place that he, and we, loved so much. I have often thought subsequently how this reaction was the opposite of what it should have been. We saw it as somewhere so tied up with memories of him, and of us as a family, that we didn't have the strength to bear being there without him. When, really, what we should have done is see it for what it was: a monument to him, and to the life that he and Mama had created, so filled with fun, adventure and beauty.

The times we did go there, my chest would ache if someone commented on how lovely the house and garden were; it felt wrong that the compliments were falling on my ears, when they couldn't fall on his. For Mama, cooking and hosting were out of kilter, as she had lost the partner with whom she had done these things for thirty years. Claudia and I were too baffled by the unspoken patterns into which our parents had fallen – which only became apparent to us once he was gone – and were unable to step into Dada's shoes on that front. And so we kept ourselves busy ... and Arniano stood largely unvisited, except for a few weeks here and there, for the next three years.

When I was at university, I had always liked to cook; it never occurred to me that there was any other way to feed myself. And, as only the young can be, I was deeply and earnestly disapproving of the takeaways and the deep-bottomed pizzas that would appear at the door when they were ordered. So I made the food my mother had taught me: chicken with grapes, beef stew, *pasta alla Adam*, malfatti, my dad's scrambled eggs on toast, and desserts from the River Cafe. This brought me so much comfort, and I was aware of the gift that my mother had given me. What was then an interest developed into a passion, which provided me with comfort and distraction. I was manic in grief, studying obsessively, despite being without my main academic support system – my father. It was a way of coping, and of living in denial of what I was really feeling. Having something to do in the hours when I wasn't in the library, something that kept both my mind and my hands fully occupied, was a godsend. As I tried to recreate the food and hospitality of my parents in a kitchen on Leith Walk, I felt closer to home and to Dada.

Friends and food provided solace. When Claudia and I started coming back home, it was with big groups of friends, and there was comfort in trying to recreate the magic that we had learned by osmosis, by watching our parents host the wonderful cast of characters with whom we grew up. After I graduated, I moved to London and started working, trying to find a path in the new reality; I took a job as an assistant in Bryan Ferry's London studio, a wonderful place to work, which afforded much excitement and travel. But really, I was grieving and lost, and soon what gave me solace and made me feel closer to Dada was being at home in Italy. Two-and-a-half years after his death, I knew there was nothing for it, I would have to find a way to process the trauma of losing my father. I quit my job and enrolled in art classes. I supported myself through a mixture of waitressing, working as a cooking assistant on photo shoots and cooking for private dinners. Not surprisingly, being an artist and part-time cook doesn't afford one much financial stability, and I was still unable to spend any length of time in Italy.

I think it was because the only things that seemed to make me feel better were cooking and hosting that I came up with the idea of trying to make a living from them. That would also allow me to spend at least part of the year at home. And so, one day in 2014, in a pub in West London, my painter friend William Roper-Curzon and I came up with the idea of the painting course. We were both looking to spend time in Italy, and to support ourselves while we were there. It seemed the perfect solution – we would run painting weeks at Arniano. William would teach, and I would cook. It would be a chance to spend time at home and to emulate the house-party atmosphere my parents had created, as well as to share the beauty of our family home with others. More on this later, but despite a few hiccups along the way – not least the time when William lost his passport before he was due to fly over from England, leaving me with a group of rather peeved (though well-fed) painters, and no teacher – we have now been running the courses for six years. In that time, we have had some amazing experiences and forged many lifelong friendships with our guests, some of whom return year after year. A few months before our disastrous second art course, when we had no teacher, I met my husband Matthew, a journalist, who has thankfully taken over all the bits of running the courses that William and I don't enjoy and are not well suited to – the logistics. He has become a perfect third to what was a hosting duo.

I don't question that it was a combination of art and cooking that helped me, if not recover from, at least get past, losing my father. Having saved up some money from the first batch of painting courses, I enrolled in a foundation course at City & Guilds, a London art school; here I fell in love with etching, and made prints from memory of the views from Arniano. Dreamlike in quality, and not exactly realistic, they portrayed the very real yearning I felt to be home. Anyone who knows this house well, when they see these etchings, points and says, 'But that's Monte Amiata.' While I was enrolled full-time at art school, I went back to a mixture of evening jobs: cooking for private dinners in London, waitressing and occasionally flying out to Italy to cook for villa rentals.

I was not, and am not, a formally trained chef, but I have in one way or another been cooking all my life. Cooking is one of those practices (like painting or drawing) where you get exponentially better the more you do it, and since beginning to cook in earnest in 2014, I have learned a huge amount. The more you practise, the greater the return. Undoubtedly, my life would have been easier at times if I had gone to chef's school, as there are many things that the self-taught cook needs to confront and figure out for themselves with no help – but I loved my time in Edinburgh studying for my degree, as well as the journey that led me to discover what it was I actually wanted to do. Curiosity, enthusiasm and determination have taken me quite some way, despite my lack of formal training. To this day, I use many of the tips and skills that I observed while waitressing at the River Cafe and learned to do while working my handful of shifts in their kitchen. I am a deft hand at prepping an artichoke, having prepared more of these vegetables for service than I could possibly remember, and I can still retrieve the ink sac from a squid without rupturing it – skills for which I am most grateful. But, on the whole, I am a home cook who makes simple, accessible and tasty meals.

In June of the same year as my stint at the River Cafe, Matthew and I were married in Florence, two years and two days after we met. And five years and a month since we had lost Dada, my sister stood in front of all our friends and family, in her maid-of-honour's speech describing the first Christmas we had all spent together at Matthew's cottage in Wiltshire the year before – how natural it had felt to all be together, and how our family suddenly seemed to be the right number

again. Having spent so much time in Florence planning our wedding, and having a handful of great friends there, Matthew and I decided to embark on a new adventure. He had just left a magazine job to go freelance, and I had finished my course at City & Guilds, so we decided to move for the foreseeable future to Florence. I resigned from my various jobs, and we packed up a car and drove from London to Tuscany, where we have been ever since, spending the majority of our time in Florence, and decamping to Arniano for weekends – to see my mum, or for painting courses.

More than anything else, what has taken me the furthest as a self-taught cook is a love of food and eating, and sharing this with people. I have come to realise that I am more suited to life as a cook for smaller numbers, rather than working as a chef in a restaurant, because I like to connect with and share in the enjoyment of the people I am feeding. If I am cooking for the painting course, this means I sit with them, chat, and partake in the meal, laughing and spilling glasses of wine. At other times, when I am cooking for private clients or villa rentals, this satisfaction comes from hearing laughter and appreciation from the dining table as I stand preparing the dessert in the kitchen.

In 2019, I turned thirty, as did the chapter of Arniano with these Guinnesses at its helm. The stories are endless, the guests innumerable, the house parties legendary, and the sense of home paramount. But always at its heart are Jasper and Camilla, their warmth and hospitality emulated as well as we can, through Claudia and me and our endeavours.

**OPPOSITE**

– The east-facing door that leads from the sitting room to the terrace.

**RIGHT**

– Me on the terrace reaching for a 'Pink Wink' cocktail (p. 85) from the stone table built by Dada and inlaid with reclaimed Sicilian tiles found by Mama.

AN INTRODUCTION

# THE

# ARNIANO PAINTING SCHOOL

– William looking out towards
Montalcino at twilight.

It was over a drink at a pub in West London that William Roper-Curzon and I decided to try to host residential painting holidays at Arniano. William is a painter, who trained in London at the City & Guilds and, later, the Royal Drawing School. I first met him when he was preparing for a large solo show of his drawings to be held in central London, and it was (platonic) love on first speaks.

William is a hilariously funny raconteur and masterful story-teller. He has a seemingly endless arsenal of anecdotes, which have whoever is lucky enough to be with him doubled over with laughter within minutes. Aside from his company, it was easy to fall in love with his dynamic figurative and landscape paintings, all highly expressive, with strong rhythm of line and confident mark-making.

From 2010, William was often travelling on art residencies, searching for exciting places to paint. I sometimes followed to visit, which took me to Scotland, the southernmost tip of Ireland and northern Tuscany. But he also went much further afield, to Buenos Aires, California and New York. These trips, which often lasted months, were usually preceded by a greedy farewell dinner with friends and family, which I would gladly throw for him at my mother's house in London.

It was over our drink in early 2014 that he described Arniano from his perspective as a landscape artist, and made me immediately believe that we should try to share the place I love most in the world with other people. He described what I had never been able to articulate myself – that what makes Arniano special for a landscape painter is the two types of view: 'You have the huge vistas, the 360-degree panorama of the Tuscan hills, which are so rich in opportunity for the painter. But you also have these very intimate scenes, of beautiful plants in the garden, and the structures of the cypress trees planted by your father. It's a mix of formality with raw nature. There is an underlying pink colour that comes through from the earth there, as well as seemingly endless sky. You are so high up that you are soaring above the valleys, and you can look down on everything before it spreads up again towards Montalcino and the mountain.'

William also had a great love for the house, feeling that 'its ability to make anyone feel welcome', as well as the total peacefulness, contributed to an atmosphere conducive to painting. 'It's incredibly quiet, there is no noise, no interruption, and a great sense that you can wander for miles to find any little area to paint. It does take you back in time there – you could be in medieval Tuscany, you would hardly know the difference.'

The concept behind the courses was that we would marry my ability to cook and host with William's talent for imparting his knowledge of and passion for painting. Rather than creating a painting boot camp, the idea would be to ensure that students of all levels could confidently grow into their artistic ability through his charm, sense of humour, enthusiasm and encouragement. While a five-day painting course might not impart the technical ability of Rembrandt to a beginner, it would

– Work in progress: William's
painting of cypresses and the
olive grove with fields beyond.

be enough time to teach our guests to use oil paints, to really look at a landscape in a manner that would make it possible to translate what they saw to canvas. In the case of experienced painters, the course would afford them the time and space to focus on an entirely new view. Either way, we wanted to curate a week in which people could be artistic, appreciate their surroundings and crack on with painting while not having to worry about feeding themselves – hopefully, making them feel well looked after and a bit spoiled along the way.

We decided to do a test run with some of William's family – as he is number eight out of ten siblings, there were plenty to choose from. The week was fun, but chaotic and exhausting, as we had absolutely no help. I cooked, cleaned, made the beds and even modelled for paintings, but we loved it, and it was a fantastic learning curve. From an art perspective, it was a hit, and it was wonderful to see the garden dotted with people immortalising parts of my father's garden and the view that I had always taken for granted.

While we learned so much from our guinea-pig gang, there was still a long way to go. That group had consisted entirely of friends or relations, who knew each other well and so fitted into our house-party format easily enough. We would now have to host up to twelve strangers, who would be eating together three times a day and painting alongside one another every day for a week. Kind and curious friends, relatives and godparents came to support us, and we learned with each course how to improve. But without an established reputation, it is difficult to persuade people to spend a week in an unknown house in the middle of Tuscany, with total strangers, being taught by an as-yet untested art instructor.

We advertised in *The Spectator*, we put flyers up in London art schools and galleries, and we asked the Royal Drawing School to send PDFs of our flyers out with their newsletter, which they kindly did – William being an alumnus and having taught in their foundation year. Finally, by 2016, following a surprise mention in the *Financial Times* and later features in various other publications (including *The New York Times*, *Tatler*, *Vogue*, *The Daily Telegraph* and *House & Garden*), we no longer had trouble filling the house, and have since welcomed guests from all over the world: the US, Mexico, Sweden, Spain, Switzerland and the UK. Best of all, we have made an extraordinary number of truly great friends.

**ABOVE**

– The valley between Arniano and Montalcino, with Monte Amiata looming above, at sunset. The evening light brings with it dramatic shadows and rich colours.

**RIGHT**

– Cow parsley and long grass in the olive grove in spring. The light pouring through the dense but airy olive tree is so tricky to paint.

# THE LANDSCAPE

A peculiar attribute of the landscape surrounding Arniano is the ever-changing light. Early in the morning, there is an extraordinary mist that sits in the valley and interweaves through the hills, allowing just the tops to show above the smoky clouds. These changes bring with them new moods and shadows, drawing our painters to different views and areas of the garden throughout the day. By the evening, everything has altered again, and there are often intense sunsets, bringing silhouettes from the trees and much darker, richer, olive colours.

William encourages our painters to work on two or three paintings at any given time – going back to each one at the same time of day, on each subsequent day, in order to capture the subject in the same light. When the wind picks up, which can happen at around midday and into the early afternoon, he encourages everyone to carry on, professing that 'it is part of painting outside … you have to learn to be in nature, to absorb it – it will make a better picture.' Being a committed outdoor painter, this is also William's philosophy when it comes to painting in the rain – which, on the rare days when we have downpours, perhaps half our guests will heed, while the other half scuttle indoors to draw a still life. 'Sometimes rain is great,' he says. 'Often, if it's raining on you, you will get a fabulous light and these dramatic clouds, and somewhere else in the landscape, a whole drama unfolding in front of you. You learn to be instinctive, to get things down quicker, to try to capture the feeling of being in it and experiencing it.'

An obvious feature of the Tuscan landscape, which begs to be drawn or painted, is the olive trees, which unfortunately are also famously difficult to translate to canvas. 'Olives are hard to paint because they are dense as well as airy,' says William. 'I always tell my students that it's like trying to paint a shoal of fish. It's incredibly difficult. It's a commitment, but once you get into it, and realise that it isn't one mass of leaves the same size, that perspective plays its part – the leaves which are closer to you are bigger, and the further away ones smaller – it's very worthwhile. As with any challenge, it becomes satisfying once you've resolved it, but it's definitely not easy.' Having surmounted that first hurdle of painting at Arniano over the past six years (to the point where he could 'paint olives in my sleep'), William finds that it is the horizon that draws him back again and again. 'Some days you see a ridge, and then others you think, "Oh my god! There's a whole other town I never knew was there. It looks just like a medieval Italian painting." There is a never-ending change of light and endless possibility.'

An important thing to remember when looking at a landscape and composing a view to paint is the foreground. 'You may see a beautiful view and want to paint it, but the whole reason why it's beautiful is what's leading up towards it. People tend to forget about the thing that is right in front of you to help balance it out. Painting is all about balance. A ridge that is miles away, without the surrounding context, doesn't have the same impact as what you are actually seeing.'

# PAINTING WITH OILS

Oil painting has such an illustrious history, and so many famous names are associated with it, that attempting to paint with oils as a beginner can be a much more daunting prospect than it need be. Doubtless, it is a faff. It's messy, the paint takes a long time to dry and you need the right kit as well as space in which to set yourself up. But it also brings a huge amount of freedom and room to experiment. You can change things, work things out, and build up layers of colour and shapes. As William puts it: 'Oils are great because you can fill a large area very quickly, but equally you can wipe or scrape them off if they're not right. Each mark is less of a commitment than with, say, watercolours. The different density of the colours with the mediums means you can make a colour almost transparent, or really thick, and certain colours are more transparent than others. Often the very dark colours, like ultramarine and some greens, are very rich colours, but also very transparent. If you add a warmer colour, they become more opaque and dense. Equally, because there is so much freedom provided by oil paints, there are a lot of things to think about. It can be daunting, but for the better, as you have more to play with and to experiment with, to find out what your style is like.'

As with cooking, painting with oils becomes less daunting every time you do it, as your confidence grows and you get used to the feel of the paints, the brushes and the medium. By the end of the week at Arniano, we always hope that everyone has done something they are proud of, at the same time as having figured out their own way of doing things. William tries to teach in such a way that everyone comes up with their individual style of painting. He disapproves of hard and fast rules, and dislikes the idea of anyone leaving Arniano and simply going on to paint like him. He wants each student to be able to do it on their own, to go home and enjoy it.

The start of the week is focused on finding something that each student is interested in painting. William will walk the students around the garden until they find a subject that captivates them. Quite often, if he sees that a student is good at doing close-ups of plants during the first morning of charcoal drawing, he'll set them up in front of the fig tree with some nice, dark shadows behind, and ask them to paint the pleasing, interlacing fig leaves. Sometimes a student might not want to paint the landscape at all, but would rather stay indoors to paint one of my mother's ceramics. These people are usually those whose knowledge or natural interest lies in design. Even so, this exercise often leads them back into the garden to have a go at landscape, because they feel more confident attempting to paint 'shape' and 'form' outside having had a practice run at capturing a Granada bowl in the kitchen.

Because the guests have just under a week – it is a rarity to have time and space where you can focus purely on oil painting – William's philosophy is that everyone should just get on with it, and procrastinating is sharply discouraged. After an initial morning of charcoal drawing together, to get everyone's eye in and to get them to think about composition, everybody is dropped in at the deep end and told to start painting. Although it's only a week, it's a lot to absorb in a short amount of time, and everyone is exhausted by the end, having done a lot of work.

# STARTING A PAINTING

Before you start painting, you will need the following:

- **a minimum of three round-headed and three flat-headed sable brushes for oils**
- **non-toxic vegetable-based medium, or turpentine**
- **linseed oil**
- **a basic set of oil paints, which includes all the primary colours**
- **a large tube of white, zinc and/or titanium (very useful)**
- **any additional tubes of paint in colours that capture your imagination (we love French ultramarine blue, cerulean blue, lemon yellow, cadmium yellow, yellow ochre, Venetian red, cadmium red, crimson alizarin, burnt umber, raw umber)**
- **primed boards to paint on – you can prime wood boards yourself by coating them with white emulsion, or buy ready-primed from any art store (we order ours from the wonderful art suppliers Zecchi, in central Florence).**

The key to enjoying the process of painting is to set yourself up fully at the beginning, to make sure you are comfortable and to have everything you need. You should also have some cloths for wiping your brushes, and two pots of medium: one pot of pure medium, for cleaning the brushes, and another pot containing half linseed, half medium, to add a little gloss to the paint. Some people prefer a drier finish and omit the linseed – this can also be beautiful. It is entirely down to preference and personal style. Regularly cleaning your brushes is imperative, in order to keep your palette clean and the colours distinct. William is strict about everyone cleaning their brush in-between changing colours – the result of not doing this can be a dreadful grey mush.

The next thing is to make sure that everything is in its proper place. For instance, if you're right-handed, arrange your easel to your left, so that you have your right hand at the view and your palette in front of you (and vice versa if you are left-handed). If everything is in its proper place, then you won't have to keep moving around. Simple, good habits such as these make a huge difference.

Once you are set up, look at the view and decide on a colour palette (a set of dominant colours), before mixing these up using different colours to achieve the one colour you are after. At Arniano, the landscape has a lot of pinks, rich greens, blue skies and sulphur-coloured clouds, but it isn't necessary for the colours to be realistic. It's how colours work next to one another that is interesting, as they can have an amazing effect on each other. If you mix your colours thoughtfully before you start, you can create a tension between them. You can also dive straight in, without having to fastidiously mix as you go along. If William sees that someone is struggling with choosing colours to commit to canvas, he will open one of our art books and choose a painting by, for example, Gauguin and say: 'I want you to make those colours and apply them to this view.' This stops people fixating on capturing the exact colours as they see them, and helps them to learn to play around with colour and to gain confidence.

The best way to get started is by squinting your eyes. You will be able to see the rough shapes within the landscape, as well as the darkness and the light, and how they interact, without being distracted by the details. Once you have determined these elements, quickly block them in. By getting rid of as much of the white on the canvas as possible, you are setting the story. A 'blank canvas', so full of endless possibilities, can actually be upsetting. Once you get some paint on it, it won't freak you out so much, and you can keep building up the detail and begin tweaking.

William believes that the main thing for beginners to overcome is a tendency to get too precious about a painting, which can lead to procrastination. This can be

– William painting in the garden at Arniano. It's amazing to think that none of these trees existed in 1989, when the house was surrounded by barren scrubland.

fatal, as anxiety about what to do, or what not to do, will remove the pleasure from the process. Painting is purely for oneself – a way to feed your own soul, no one else's. When a painter dithers, or hangs back, William will appear with barks of, 'Just slap it on, it doesn't matter.' The beauty is that you can always start a new one if you hate the end result.

William's advice to anyone who is starting out with oil painting is to be brave and to keep doing it, to try to get into the habit of painting as often as you can – every day if that's possible, or even once a week. Be as consistent as you can, and keep looking at the works of other artists, at works that you like for their composition, colour palette or technique. It's not cheating to do that. Quite the opposite. You are doing it for inspiration, to see what clever things people come up with that you really like, and that you would like to emulate.

# HOSTING THROUGHOUT THE SEASONS

When I was twenty-one, I spent a year living in Rome, studying at Roma Tre University as part of my degree from Edinburgh. It was during this time that I really began to understand, as an adult, the joys of seasonality. The term started in October, which meant I arrived just in time for the tuberoses, with their wondrous smell. And, more importantly, the ovoli: small, round mushrooms with a white exterior and egg-yolk yellow centre; hence the name, which translates as 'egg-like'. There were also porcini, the last of the figs, and the year's second crop of asparagus.

Two friends and I lived on Via delle Mantellate, on the border of Trastevere and Gianicolo and – as it happened – on the same street as the inner-city prison. This impressive medieval building spanned the entire street on the opposite side to us, its high walls looming over the roof of the row of houses that our flat was in. Our proximity to Rome's most-wanted was such that, if they felt at all maligned, we would hear them shouting and running metal objects across the bars of their cells. On Sundays, their wives and children would stand beneath our window, which seemed to be a designated point of communication, and shout over the wall to their husbands and fathers. *'Papa, sono Michele, hai ricevuto la mia lettera?'* ('Dad, it's Michele, did you get my letter?') would be answered with, *'Sí tesoro, mi lasci parlare con Mamma?'* ('Yes darling, but please let me talk to Mummy now'), and so on.

Most days, we would wander along this quirky little street, past all the dolled-up wives and girlfriends waiting to visit their imprisoned loved ones, and cross the bridge to the market square of Campo de' Fiori to spend our student loans on whatever delicious produce we could find. We would take our spoils home and feast on salad of raw ovoli (which, being very rare, made a particularly harsh dent in our student loans), thinly sliced and covered in pieces of celery and shavings of parmesan; figs with prosciutto; and fresh artichokes and asparagus, drizzled with olive oil and just a squeeze of lemon. Cheesy favourites were smoked scamorza and burrata, brought up from Campania, not as readily available north of Rome ten years ago as they are now. (I still marvel that burrata is available in our supermarket in Tuscany, let alone when I see it in abundance in England.) When November came, we were horrified to discover the asparagus were over; not only that, but we had to say goodbye to the ovoli, the figs and the best of the summer's tomatoes.

When I was a child, I had been aware that we ate certain things at certain times of year. And that we had to grow our own mint and lettuce in summer – because, until about 1995, the village greengrocer didn't sell them, assuming that everyone grew their own. The shopkeeper would always look incredulous when my mother tentatively asked for salad in July to supplement our meagre crop, and would exclaim: *'Ma signora, non lo cresce nell'orto?'* ('But madam, don't you grow it in your vegetable patch?')

**OPPOSITE**

– Enjoying an *aperitivo* on Mama's daybeds, drinking 'Pink Wink' cocktails and Negroni sbagliati. From left to right: Savannah Alvarez (whose recipe for pasta with spicy Italian sausage is on page 218), Matthew, me and William – who is, as ever, making everyone laugh.

Having spent my teens mainly in London, where everything is readily available all year round, I hadn't really taken notice of what was and what wasn't in season. When at Arniano in the holidays, I was involved in *preparing* food – shadowing my mother when she cooked, but not when she was out buying the ingredients. We teens would mooch around eating *gelati* in the bar while my mum dutifully went to the shops. (For the sake of clarity, a bar in Italy is not the same as the adults-only type we think of, but the focal point of every Italian village, where you go to get your morning coffee, your gelato in the afternoon and your *aperitivo* in the evening.) It was for this reason I hadn't questioned why we were making what we were making. Why were we eating pasta with fresh peas at Easter? Why so much grilled aubergine in July? And come November, why all the fuss about white truffles all of a sudden? My mother knew the answers, but as I had never asked any of these questions when I was young, she hadn't mentioned seasonality.

So, it was during this stint in Rome, when I was on my own for the first time in Italy and left to fend for myself, that I began to understand the joys of seasonal eating. I realised that it was fine to say goodbye for a time to whatever you had been enjoying over the past month or two, because its temporary loss would give way to new pleasures; in the case of that particular November, to new olive oil, white truffles and cavolo nero. And when these waned, we would go on to greet fresh peas, broad beans and baby artichokes, after which summer would arrive and it would be time for aubergine, courgettes, tomatoes, and so on.

I don't think one should be dictatorial about eating seasonally – I often make recipes from across this book, whatever the weather, even if in the wrong season. But I do believe that thinking about what is in season, wherever you happen to be, is a useful starting point for deciding what you are going to cook. And when planning a menu, it is often where I begin, even if I end up mixing dishes from different seasons in the same meal.

Seasonality, as an indicator of what ingredient might be the centrepiece of a meal, is a helpful guide for curating a feast. In a world where our culinary horizons have expanded along with our repertoires, so have our choices, and I find it comforting sometimes to have the limitation of seasonality when pondering the all-important question: 'What shall we have for lunch?' For instance, if I know that asparagus is in season, I might decide to make ricotta and asparagus tart, and from there I might stray from the season and decide to add slow-cooked tomatoes, along with a fennel and orange salad and a plate of finocchiona, to the menu. The oranges may be 'over', and therefore won't be from Sicily, and it might not strictly be summer yet, so the tomatoes may not be the best – but if I remember having seen some in the preceding days at the greengrocer's or the supermarket, I will forge ahead without guilt, because I like the combination of flavours.

By laying out this book seasonally, I do not intend that you should only use certain recipes when the ingredients suit a particular season. Aside from the fact that spring, summer, autumn and winter are a useful way to categorise food, I think that the time of year dictates the *feel* that one might want to give a menu, and also influences how we host.

When it's cold, one wants a cosy and intimate feel, with the biting air outside allowing for time spent in the kitchen to slow-cook beef stew, to boil up some stock, or to roll malfatti by hand. Guests can huddle with a cocktail by the fire, chatting away, before moving through to a cosy, candlelit supper. In spring, when the first outdoor lunches can be attempted, there is a hopeful feel that lends itself to feasts of vegetables, pasta and lamb; these are laid out under the pergola, and consumed amid much joy and contentment, as everyone basks in the first rays of spring sunlight. A cardigan and scarf are probably still necessary, as is a readiness to dash indoors when the inevitable April shower hits.

As the days move on, and the weather becomes more reliable, the temperature rises, and by summer the mood has changed again. Weekend mornings are spent languishing outdoors, reading and lying in the sun for as long as you can bear before moving to the shade to cool off. By midday, the heat is too much, and the cooler respite of the kitchen feels like a blessing, when one can happily spend the next hour assembling a meal to show off summer's finest. A large platter of grilled aubergine dressed in a summer *salsa verde* (green sauce) – at its centre, juicy balls of buffalo mozzarella; grated carrots dressed with oil, basil and lemon; fusilli with generous daubings of homemade pesto; and a plate of home-grown tomatoes, dressed in olive oil and a little salt. All dishes that only require assembling, or minimal cooking, allowing the produce to speak for itself. And all delicious, satisfying and sleepy-making – sending everyone off for a siesta in the shade after lunch or, after an evening feast, to lie on one's back on the lawn, gazing upwards, hoping to catch sight of a shooting star.

With the advent of autumn, everything will suddenly feel re-energised, and a definite back-to-school atmosphere descends on the landscape. It is an important moment for our area, as it means the wine harvest – and the celebration of the bounty it brings. In our village, when I was little, we were always very excited by the *sagra della vendemmia*, the harvest feast, as it meant the arrival of the fair, complete with merry-go-round and dodgems. There would be long tables laid along the main street of the *centro storico*, and you would queue for hours to be given a plastic plate filled with *fagioli all'uccelletto* (cannellini beans cooked in tomato sauce), *patate al forno* (roast potatoes) and some truly delicious grilled meats. The atmosphere was infectious, and definitely affected our mood up the hill at Arniano.

The reason I am recounting these stories is to highlight how the time of year can dictate not only what we eat, but also how we eat. For example, in winter, the fire in the kitchen at Arniano is always roaring, and we dress the table with a plain linen tablecloth and branches of evergreens before sitting down, huddled together, to a meal that is warming as well as delicious – usually something in one pot – in the glow of the candlelight. House parties at this time of year are never longer than a weekend, and we can't really hold our painting courses due to the cold. While one can actually host some of the most glamorous meals at this time of year because of the opportunity to light fires and candles (and for everyone to wear fabulous, warm outfits), this raucous winter merrymaking is not suited to more than two or three nights, given the short daylight hours and everyone's secret desire to spend winter evenings watching telly. Certainly, that is my secret desire – but I don't see it as a reason to abandon aesthetic or culinary standards. Rather, our family tradition is to light the fire in the sitting room and then, having cooked a delicious supper, to lay trays as grandly as we would a dinner setting, bringing through from the kitchen a steaming pot of *stracciatella* (broth with egg and parmesan), or penne with cavolo nero and pancetta, to be consumed silently in front of a movie or box-set.

Spring is the season when Arniano begins to wake again after a short winter, during which my mother and sister are usually in London, and Matthew and I are in Florence, nipping down for the weekend with our hardier friends. It is the season when the house party gets back into its stride, the longer days meaning that the houseful of guests have independence, as well as the chance to mix the indoor and outdoor living that is a particularly charming aspect of life at Arniano.

It is at this time of year that we start welcoming larger house parties, family, friends – and all the wonderful guests who join us for the Arniano Painting School courses.

These are the tricks and rules that I have compiled over the years for times when I am cooking for lots of people and that I apply to any lunch or dinner party, whatever the season. They are the guidelines that make cooking and hosting fun by removing any unnecessary stress when I am preparing for a gathering, and I hope you will also find them helpful in making the proceedings seem effortless.

HOSTING THROUGHOUT THE SEASONS

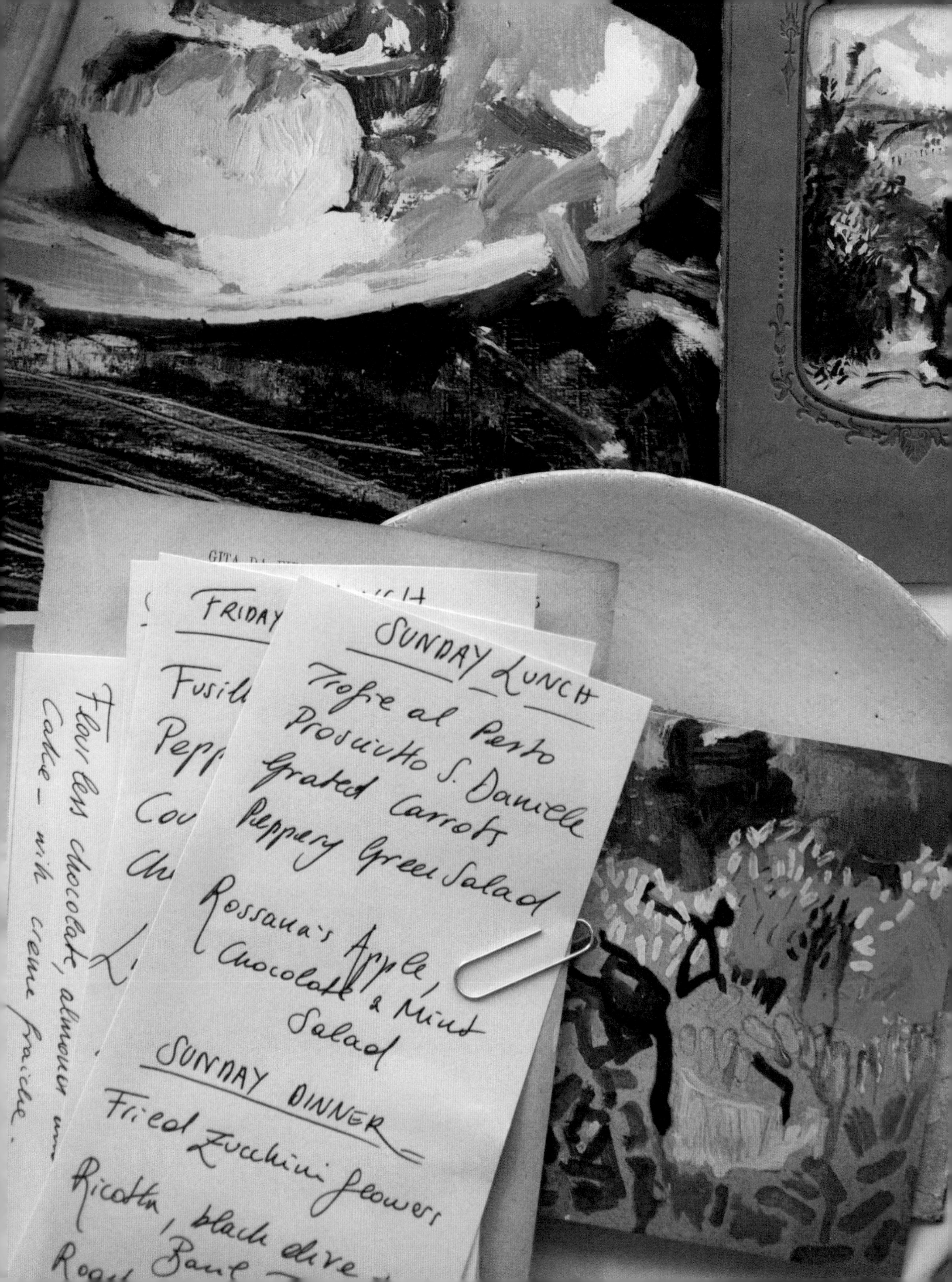

FRIDAY

Fusill

Pepp

Cov

Un

L

SUNDAY LUNCH

Trofie al Pesto
Prosciutto S. Daniele
Grated Carrots
Peppery Green Salad

Rossana's Apple,
Chocolate & Mint
Salad

SUNDAY DINNER

Fried Zucchini flowers

Ricotta, black olive

Roas

Baru

Flourless chocolate, almond an
Cake — with crème fraîche.

# MENU WRITING AND FEAST CURATION

A few years ago, for the sake of ease, and to avoid the brain-racking that I had to do when we first started the Arniano Painting School, I started writing down the menus ahead of the arrival of each group. I would base them on the combinations of dishes that my mother had always served for the array of people who would come for lunch throughout my childhood. She had these committed to memory, and so never needed to write them down, but I found that I did – along with the variations that I had started to make once I had found my culinary feet. These menus, all collated in one folder, have become an invaluable resource, as they allow me to refer back to a meal that was particularly successful and give me inspiration when I'm feeling stuck.

At the end of each of the seasonal recipe chapters to follow, I have suggested a few of my favourite menu combinations. This is how I lay out the menus ahead of having a houseful of guests or painters. I will take a piece of paper, or a notebook, and turn it on its side so it is in landscape format. Then I list the days (for example, six days for a painting course), and each of the meals for those days (Monday lunch, Monday dinner; Tuesday lunch, Tuesday dinner, and so on), and fill the menus in from there, balancing the dishes and keeping an eye on what we had the day before. I also bear in mind any evening meals that I could make in a larger quantity, to be added to lunch the next day; for instance, if I am making roast chicken with grapes, I know that if I pop an extra chicken in the oven, it will supplement any chicken that is left over at the end of the evening and be a delicious cold adjunct to lunch. I think about how delicious it would be with, say:

- **potato and onion frittata**
- **slow-roasted tomatoes**
- **a peppery green rocket salad**
- **a healthy dollop of homemade lemony mayonnaise or aioli.**

This allows me to curate a delicious lunch quite easily, by simply augmenting what I was making anyway the night before.

If a group of friends are coming for the weekend, I will go through the same planning process. I will simply write out the meals from Friday dinner to Sunday evening – or if people are just coming round for lunch or supper, I will pluck out one of the more ambitious and fun menus to make. For any meal, I'll begin with the central dish – based on what I feel like making, and, more importantly, eating – and I will work my way out from there, considering whether to have lots of sides, or a starter plus two or three sides. Will pudding be an elaborate tart, or baked fruit – or, if lunch has been very abundant, might it just be coffee and chocolates?

These menus often evolve. I only really commit in my head to three days' worth of meals at a time, as things might change – as might people's moods. It is also the most amount of time that you can get away with before needing to go to the shops. My least favourite part of hosting is grocery shopping, I suppose because I am often cooking for lots of people and therefore end up having to carry a lot of bags. This is why I find it invaluable to know exactly what I will need over the next three or four days – so I am not constantly having to hop in the car and drive the 9 kilometres to town to buy a bunch of parsley.

OPPOSITE

– My handwritten menus, which allow me to formulate a plan for the week, alongside copies of William's beautiful paintings.

## DIFFERENT MOODS FOR DIFFERENT TIMES OF DAY

Lunches at Arniano tend to be informal feasts, laid out so that everyone can help themselves to a little bit of everything. There will be a central dish – a pasta, a tart or pie, or a frittata – accompanied by one or two salads, a plate of prosciutto, finocchiona or similar, and a variety of vegetables. Dessert might be a custard tart or just a plate of sliced oranges. What these lunches always are is slow and unstressed. There is never a starter, and everything is served at once, allowing everyone to approach the food as they prefer, with plenty of time to help themselves to a spoonful of piping-hot pasta before they tuck into the salads, if they would rather not have more than one thing on their plate. Personally, I like having a bit of everything on there all at once. Neither approach is scorned, and there is time in among the chatting and a glass of Vermentino to feast to your heart's content.

If we are eating outside, the long, narrow lunch table allows for conversation both with your neighbour and the person opposite. In order to save on space on the table, I use a small, inexpensive, metal folding table as a sideboard. All you need is a pretty tablecloth and you have yourself a handy surface on which to lay out your feast – and that people can help themselves from – leaving more room on the table for flowers. Greenery is the preferred table decoration in our house, and at lunch this usually consists of olive boughs, or cut rosemary; if I'm after some colour, I'll plunder the geranium pots and cut a flower per pot, which I combine with the greenery. These bunches are put into small pewter milk jugs that my mother found in a flea market in Florence, and placed along the table at intervals.

The lunch table is always adorned with whatever tablecloth suits the mood and time of year (I adore a tablecloth, and my mother has an amazing collection), as well as white paper napkins (when we have a large number of people for more than one meal, I find the trouble of washing 2 x 12 linen napkins a day is simply not worth it), jugs of water with ice and slices of lemon, small pots of Maldon salt, a black pepper grinder, and a glass decanter of olive oil (these cost very little at Italian houseware stores, and are a wonderful everyday item, as you can fill them with good-quality oil from a larger container).

In the evening, there is a change of tone. Many candles are lit, dresses and clean shirts are donned after a day in dungarees, and, unless it's summer, the fire will be roaring. The table will be decorated simply, with lots of tall candles placed in holders at varying heights along its length to create a pretty sense of movement; these are interspersed with single-stem flowers in bud vases and Mama's pewter jugs. I like the idea of having lots of small, unfussy arrangements, rather than one large, obtrusive one that makes it difficult to talk to someone across the table. At our wedding, my mother placed an array of single pink and red peonies on each table, which looked simple and wonderful. If you happen to be near a good flower market, bear in mind that colourful flowers such as ranunculus, parrot tulips, peonies and dahlias look wonderful as single stems lined along the table, arranged at different heights in small jugs or bud vases. Olive branches (or foraged greenery in general) lined along the middle of the table also look wonderful in candlelight, if you can't get hold of any flowers.

For before-dinner drinks, we'll lay snacks out on the bar – thin slices of good salami, generous pieces of pecorino and giant green olives (there is no need for fancy presentation, just pop these in three separate small bowls that people can pick from) – and Matthew will make martinis or sidecars from *The Savoy Cocktail Book*, a great investment for any cocktail lover. In this atmosphere, I like the delineation of starter, main, dessert – but the starter will always be something simple, which can be made ahead of time or thrown together at the last minute:

PREVIOUS

– A spring feast at Arniano: Spinach and ricotta malfatti with butter and sage (p. 94), a hunk of pecorino *semi-stagionato* and broad beans, Ricotta and asparagus tart (p. 106), Radicchio, cannellini bean and hazelnut salad (p. 246), a plate of prosciutto San Daniele, Artichoke and béchamel pie (p. 101) and Broad beans and pecorino (p. 89).

OPPOSITE

– Preparing to lay the table and pulling out everything that will be needed for the meal: glasses, crockery, drinks, salt, pepper and the all-important olive oil decanter.

soups such as pea and mint, or chickpea and rosemary (made ahead and heated up); or braised artichokes with vinaigrette; artichoke and parmesan salad; or pear, walnut and pecorino salad. Dishes that I can assemble or plate up without noise or stress – possibly while chatting to someone sitting in the kitchen keeping me company and/or helping – before summoning everyone to the table.

Once the first course is finished, everyone is usually happy to help pile up plates and put them on the sideboard ready for the dishwasher, before the main course. I always ask my guests to keep their cutlery, and will have made sure that the plates for the main are already stacked to one side. I'll then carry out the main, either in its cooking vessel or decanted onto a serving plate or bowl, and put it on the sideboard – and everybody helps themselves. Sometimes, I simply put the main and the plates in the middle of the table. If the table is laid and you have everything ready at hand for when you need it throughout the meal (serving cutlery, plates, serving dishes, and so on), a menu of more than one course need not be daunting. Guests *like* the hustle and bustle of a kitchen. Don't be afraid to let them see you putting food on a serving dish, or ladling soup into a bowl for them, it's part of the joy of home cooking. There is no need to stress yourself out with the idea that your guests will be expecting the food to appear as if by magic without your involvement – or as if you had a team of chefs squirrelled away out the back.

# THE KEY TO HAPPY HOSTING: PREPARATION

Over the years, I have noticed that there is one trick to cooking and hosting that has helped me more than any other: *preparation*. As someone who is naturally quite chaotic, I have found that having a menu written out, and knowing what I am going to serve, makes it possible to draw up a plan, and a shopping list, and therefore enjoy the process of cooking and preparing to have guests. The same goes for having everything set up before the guests arrive or descend for drinks o'clock. I know that I will have so much more fun when cooking for big groups if the food prep is (on the whole) done, the ice bucket is full, and an open bottle of prosecco and the ingredients for whatever cocktail Matthew is making are sitting on the drinks tray, along with some delicious titbits. This way, I can avoid having to imitate a jack-in-the-box, jumping up and down to get more ice, snacks or drinks; and if everything is to hand, people can also help themselves to whatever they fancy.

Equally, if I have done all my chopping and general food prep on my own – *con calma*, while listening to music or a podcast – before my guests arrive, I find that cooking and assembling just before dinner is much less stressful and time-consuming. When I worked in an office, I took this to the extreme: if I had people coming over for dinner, I would get up an hour early before leaving for work, so that everything would be prepared for the evening ahead.

However, if you don't have the luxury of time, don't worry, just go easy on yourself and choose to cook something that is straightforward and failsafe; part of the point of cooking for friends and family is for the host to have a nice time too. And if the host is visibly stressed, no one will enjoy themselves. If the host is relaxed, I usually find that everything will fall into place. This is not to say that I am never stressed when hosting a lunch or dinner party. But I do everything in my power ahead of time to make sure that I am as serene as possible, thereby allowing myself to have fun. If I feel stressed or overwhelmed, I do one of two things: either I cut a dish (usually a side, and sometimes the starter; it's only dinner, there's no need to get too attached to the idea of it being perfect, and I can always eat the culled dish over the next few days), or I commandeer one or two of my guests to help. There is no need to be a martyr, and if you feel like you need an extra pair of hands, ask. I find people are always happy to help as long as they are set up in a seat, have a large drink and are given a specific task (most of us hate taking initiative in other people's kitchens). They can then happily crack on with grating parmesan, topping crostini or podding broad beans – plus they are able to chat to you.

# PLACEMENT

Another element to think about ahead of time is *placement*. Assigning your guests a seat might seem overly fussy and formal, and if you are hosting between four and six people I would agree, as conversation tends to be general in smaller numbers. But if you are any more than six, I am a great proponent of telling people where to sit. Writing it out takes two minutes, and it can be fun, as you can imagine what the people you have seated next to each other might talk about, or what common ground they will find. When there is no placement, I find that people tend to sit with whomever they were talking to before dinner (I certainly do) – or are too shy to volunteer themselves as a dinner neighbour to someone they have only just met, but are in fact dying to talk to for whatever reason (as I certainly am). In a world where we are having to make a million decisions all the time, the host taking this small one out of the hands of their guests is a luxury, and it can lead to much more interesting and varied discussions.

# TIMING

Another trick to staying serene when cooking for a big gang is to have an idea (even a vague one) of the *timing* involved in everything you need to get done. Start with the time you want to eat, and work backwards. How long will each element take, and what can you get away with making in advance? Of course, there will always be last-minute cooking to do, pasta to be boiled or salad to be dressed, but having a plan will help make everything feel like it is running more smoothly.

When each dish is ready, put it to one side on a table or a sideboard – keep adding dishes as you complete them, so that you can see everything together. This will allow you to see if anything is missing, or if you need to add an extra salad.

Here are the general rules and order of timing that I follow (in peace, while listening to music or a radio program).

### HOURS AHEAD OF TIME

*Make dessert and set the table*

These are the tasks that can be a nightmare when you are rushed, but a pleasure when you have plenty of time. In my less experienced days, I often made the mistake of waiting until an hour before lunch before preparing a dessert that needed time to chill – which then obviously didn't have time to set. Or I would start to make pastry while surrounded by friends and family who were trying to talk to me, and then I would go red with stress as my pastry got too hot and ended up being impossible to roll out.

The same goes for setting the table. If this hasn't been done before people arrive, it adds an aura of chaos. It also scuppers the opportunity to be creative with flowers or greenery, as you rush to make it look like you are ready and your guests welcome.

I now try to do these things first. I will make dessert early in the morning, or even the night before. If this isn't possible, I will make a very easy dessert, or just chop some fruit to set to one side. Then I will lay the table before I crack on with preparing the main meal.

## TWO HOURS AHEAD

### *Prep salads, veg and meat*

Next, I will start chopping and preparing the ingredients for the starter and main. If we are having salads, I will throw these together to dress later. If I am serving meat, I will take it out of the fridge, season it generously with salt, then cover and leave it to one side to come up to room temperature while I chop my veg. Once all the ingredients are ready, I move on to cooking, whether it be making a pasta sauce, a béchamel for the filling of an artichoke pie, or using the vegetables to make a *soffritto* as the base for soup or ribollita. Anything that can be reheated later, I will make and set to one side, ready to heat up just before we sit down.

## ONE-AND-A-HALF HOURS AHEAD

### *Put meat into the oven*

If we are having roast meat (with the exception of slow-roasted lamb, which takes three hours), the meat will go into the oven about an hour and a half before everyone arrives. This allows for more cooking time if needed, plus resting time while everyone is having drinks.

### *Tidy up kitchen, stock bar, organise crockery (and change outfit)*

Once all the cooking feels under control, I will have a general tidy up and wash and put away whatever I'm not using. Again, this helps in the battle against chaos. Next, I will make sure that there is ice, wedges of lemons or lime, snacks and an open bottle of wine or prosecco on the bar. I will also pile up the plates for the second course and for dessert, and get out all the serving dishes I will need, before heading upstairs to change.

## HALF AN HOUR BEFORE EVERYONE ARRIVES

Back downstairs. I check on the meat to see whether it needs basting, put the prepared veg in the oven and, if we are having pasta, pop the salted pan of water on to boil. Once this is done, I put on a playlist, light the candles and make myself a large drink.

# A NOTE ABOUT COOKING AND INGREDIENTS

# 'A SORT OF CARBONARA'

This book does not claim to be made up of entirely original Italian recipes, as Italian cooking has been developed and discovered and written about extensively since long before I was born. I was reminded of the impossibility of laying claim to expertise in Italian food just the other day, when my parents' dear friends, Alessandro and Caterina, a Florentine couple living just south of the city, retold me the story of my mother's carbonara. Many years ago, my mum had assiduously studied what she thought was the best recipe for *pasta alla carbonara*, before cooking it for Alessandro, Caterina and my dad. When they sat down to lunch, everyone was full of praise for the tastiness of the dish, although my mother became very deflated when Caterina exclaimed: 'This is delicious! What is it? A *sort of* carbonara?'

This story sums up the specificity and nuance of Italian cooking, which is why I would describe this book as a collection of recipes that have always played a part in our life at home, that my mother made, and that she insisted that my sister and I learn. They have become part of the fabric of our home life and our hosting. As I look through the recipes and think about the common thread that binds them, I realise that they all exemplify a fundamental principle of Italian home cooking. Which is that simplicity – and keeping ingredients as close to their original form as possible – leads to the most delicious and rewarding food. The beauty of Italian cooking is that it is not about fancy sauces or preparation techniques. Rather, it is about bringing out the best in what you are cooking, through patience, *constant tasting* and the development of flavour – sometimes using nothing but some olive oil and salt.

# TASTING AND PATIENCE

There is no trick more useful in cooking than remembering to taste what you are making at every stage. This is how you really get to grips with ingredients, learning how their flavours and textures develop and change with cooking, seasoning or dressing. It is also how you can make a plate of food that you, personally, will find truly delicious, as you will have adjusted it to suit your own palate. For example, my sister doesn't like celery, so when she makes breadless ribollita (which you will find in the winter recipes in this book), she lessens the celery called for in the recipe and ups everything else. The change is hardly perceptible to anyone else, as she has not omitted the celery, just included enough to keep the character of the dish. But to her, this adjustment makes the dish infinitely more delicious.

Patience is the second most important thing that I have learned over the years, something that was certainly not my strong point when I was at university. But patience and time are what make dishes feel like they were prepared with love and care. Marcella Hazan, the doyenne of Italian cooking, wrote that the patient and gradual cooking of a *soffritto* is the most important step, as you are allowing the flavour to deepen and develop early in the process; this principle of patience should be applied to the first stages of cooking in any recipe. I have found this supremely helpful and most definitely true: you can always taste when these early stages have been rushed – you just don't feel that any love has been put into the preparation.

# VEGETABLES AND MEAT

While I am not a vegetarian, I have certainly been swept up in the general move towards lower meat consumption over the past decade. I adore a delicious plate of veal with green sauce, or roast chicken, or beef stew, and would struggle to give up prosciutto, salami or pancetta, but vegetables play the central role in the food I cook. One of the well-known attractions of cooking in Italy is the inspiration provided by a visit to the local market or greengrocer. Stalls and shops are crammed with rainbow displays of fresh seasonal produce, bought by weight and entirely free of cellophane packaging. Part of the excitement of such a visit is the element of surprise, which teaches one to be curious and resourceful. So, if you see some particularly fresh peas in the farmers' market, you might look up the best way to cook these. The same goes with courgettes, which may suddenly become cheap and plentiful; as anyone who has grown courgettes will have asked themselves: how am I going to make the abundance of this one vegetable varied and mouth-watering?

> The produce in this book is based on the Italian seasons. But produce that is ready in spring in Italy may not be so until the summer in England (broad beans, for example). Use the recipes depending on what is in season where you are.

It is partly this delight in simple, fresh ingredients that has led to a shift in my own eating habits, whereby I prioritise vegetables over meat – and partly that I simply like eating vegetarian dishes for, say, half the week, and mixing in meat for the other half. Even then, it might only be that I add crispy pancetta to a plate of penne with cavolo nero, lending a salty and moreish note that elevates the dish. But the central player is the cavolo, not the bacon. I have also found that dishes that happen to be vegetarian often end up being the more delicious and indulgent – the crowd pleasers – usually including some form of cheese, and often pasta, which happen to be two of my favourite things.

When I do cook meat, it is to make something truly special. The meat recipes in this book are the dishes that I really love, and that I would find it difficult to live without. I don't say this to be in any way sanctimonious or to imply that this is how everyone else should eat, or even that I always eat this way, but simply to explain why you will only find a handful of meaty mains in this book.

Now that I consume much less meat, when I do eat it, I try to make sure that I am shopping with conscious intent to find the best I can afford. I am aware, from having lived in the UK for a long time – where good-quality anything is incredibly expensive – that I am lucky to have an inexpensive family-run butcher in the village, whose organic farm is 7 kilometres down the road. They are able to tell me all about the provenance and life of the chicken or beef that I am buying. This is what the Italians call shopping 'a kilometro 0', when the food you are buying has travelled hardly any distance to get to your plate. It's a privilege that is usually a bonus for anyone living in the countryside.

I changed my buying habits around meat when I was living in London. As a student in Edinburgh, I had bought the cheapest meat I could find, on an almost daily basis (a false economy). But when I moved to London, I started buying better quality meat, more infrequently. The supermarket had always seemed big and impersonal to me, but I realised that if they had a meat counter, I could chat to whoever was manning it about the produce. Chatting with your butcher about the quality and provenance of meat is often rewarding – you will probably learn something interesting, and I hope that stores will be encouraged to source produce that is good quality and as local as possible if they feel their staff are being questioned about it. If I am in London, and there is no meat counter in a store, I will read the label and have a look at where the meat is from: France, okay ... Britain, even better. I do the same in Italy, when I find myself in an area without a good butcher.

When I eat meat, I want to get as much flavour out of it as possible. So, to make the meat as tender and mouth-watering as it can be:

- **remove it from the fridge and bring it up to room temperature before cooking**
- **cover it generously with salt at least an hour or two before roasting**
- **leave it to rest for at least half an hour after you have removed it from the oven.**

Something as simple as roasting a piece of topside beef with some olive oil and white wine will be elevated to delicious heights by these few simple steps.

# KITCHEN ESSENTIALS

Everyone has their kitchen staples, the ingredients and condiments that occupy a permanent position in the larder or fridge and form the basis of each person's individual style of cooking. Here – in my order of importance – are the items that are always found in the larder at Arniano and that I make sure I have on hand wherever I live. With these ingredients as a backdrop, I find you can bring the best out of whatever fresh produce you are lucky enough to get your hands on.

## MY LARDER

### EXTRA VIRGIN OLIVE OIL

I get through a lot of olive oil. I not only cook with it, but also generally eat it on toast and use it to dress salads, and so on. As a basic oil for cooking, I buy Filippo Berio or Farchioni Il Casolare. They are widely available and perfectly delicious, while not being so precious that I worry about using them up.

### 'VERY GOOD' EXTRA VIRGIN OLIVE OIL

This is a luxury worth splashing out on (particularly if you can get your hands on the new olive oil pressed every year in November). Good oil will elevate your food and turn the simplest salad or grilled vegetable into a delight, with minimal effort. Always check the label to see when the olives were harvested: olive oil should be consumed within eighteen months of the harvest. Use extra virgin olive oil for the final stages of cooking, for dressing, for drizzling and for sauces – such as Green sauce (p. 254) or Lemony aioli (p. 255) – or just to have on a piece of toast rubbed with fresh garlic and sprinkled with sea salt. I am spoilt living here in Tuscany, as we have an olive press, Frantoio Etrusco, at the end of the road. When our scanty home-grown supply runs out, I buy directly from them; they also sell their oil online and ship internationally. Other wonderful oils include the Sicilian Zisola, and the Tuscan Fonterutoli from Marchesi Mazzei, also available online at affordable prices.

## PEELED PLUM TOMATOES

Knowing I have tinned tomatoes in the cupboard (an assortment of 400 g and 800 g tins) makes me feel safe, as I know that a delicious and frugal way to augment a dinner for many is always at hand. When possible, I opt for whole plum tomatoes over the pre-chopped ones, as they have more flavour and it takes a second to mash them up in the pan. These tomatoes are the base for most of the soups I make, as well as for my pasta sauces. They are more flavoursome and a little more acidic than fresh tomatoes, and pair so well with a variety of other flavours.

### TO MAKE A SIMPLE TOMATO SAUCE
(*Salsa di pomodoro*):-

For two people, simply heat a little oil in a pan with a garlic clove, a pinch of salt and a few leaves of basil until gently sizzling. Add 400 g tinned tomatoes, then half fill the empty tin with water, swirling it around to pick up all of the remaining tomato, and add the tomatoey water to the pan. Allow to simmer for half an hour before removing the garlic clove – you can either use it as is, on pasta, or add a little chilli to make *Pasta arrabiata*.

### TO MAKE A DELICIOUS AUBERGINE PARMIGIANA (*Melanzana alla parmigiana*):-

Use the (chilli-free) Tomato sauce recipe above to smother grilled aubergine, layered with mozzarella and fresh basil leaves. Bake in the oven at 200°C/180°C fan-forced for 40 minutes.

## CHILLI FLAKES

I am never without a pot of chilli flakes, as I find that this spice allows me to liven up even the simplest vegetable. Notably, I find that chard, cabbage and most greens benefit from cooking *in padella* ('in the pan') with a little garlic and chilli. I also know that I can make one of my favourite meals, Spaghetti with garlic, oil and chilli, with little fuss and expense, as long as I have those four basic ingredients.

### TO MAKE A SIMPLE SPAGHETTI WITH GARLIC, OIL AND CHILLI
(*Spaghetti aglio, olio e peperoncino*):-

Put a large pan of salted water on to boil for the pasta. Put two crushed garlic cloves per person, a pinch of chilli and some oil into a frying pan and bring to a gentle sizzle over a low heat. Very slowly, bit by bit, keep adding a little more oil (about 70 ml for two people). The oil should be hot enough to infuse with the garlic, but not hot enough to fry it – if the oil is getting too hot, remove the pan from the heat every so often. When the salted water is at a galloping boil, put the spaghetti on to cook, allowing 100 g of pasta per person. Add a pinch more chilli to the garlic, oil and chilli mixture, season with salt and freshly ground black pepper, then remove from the heat. Halfway through cooking the spaghetti, add a ladleful of the pasta water to the garlic, oil and chilli, and set the frying pan over a low heat to bubble away. When the pasta is done, toss it through the garlic and oil, and add some chopped parsley if you have it, along with some grated parmesan.

## BALSAMIC GLAZE

This is more widely available than very good balsamic vinegar, and I think more delicious than the acidic and watery balsamic generally offered up on the tables of most Italian restaurants. I have only ever tasted the traditional balsamic vinegar (which is aged for twenty-five years) once, when I was in its birthplace of Modena; it is delicious, but very expensive, which is why I opt for lemon juice or balsamic glaze day-to-day. If you feel like splashing out on a 20+ years aged balsamic – which is like a sweet black tar, to be used sparingly – Villa Monodori is widely available. They also have a less swanky organic balsamic vinegar, which is delicious and not outrageously expensive. If you can't find a balsamic glaze, you can make your own version.

### TO MAKE BALSAMIC GLAZE:-
Mix 70 ml of balsamic vinegar with 2 tablespoons of honey.

## CHICKPEAS

I always have a pack of dried chickpeas, as well as 360 g and 700 g jars of ready-cooked chickpeas, in my store cupboard. In Italy, it is possible to buy ready-cooked *ceci giganti* (giant chickpeas) in glass jars. These are my favourite, as they have a wonderful texture and flavour, being larger and plumper than the tinned variety – but I have never seen them outside of Italy (if you do find them, I would recommend buying a few jars for the larder). When I don't have access to these, I find that tinned chickpeas from the supermarket are absolutely fine, though a little tougher and less tasty. You can make delicious soups with them (for example, Chickpea and rosemary soup, p. 178), or add them to a salad if you need to make a meal more abundant, or use them to whip up some homemade hummus. Having said that, you will get much more flavour from the dried variety, which are undoubtedly a faff, but all the more tasty.

> **TO COOK DRIED CHICKPEAS:-**
>
> Soak overnight with a teaspoon of bicarbonate of soda in a bowl filled with enough water to just cover the chickpeas. Add some herbs (sage, bay leaves and parsley work well), and two to three garlic cloves. Once the beans have doubled in size – after about 8 hours – drain and rinse the chickpeas, and put them in a pan filled with enough cold water to cover them by 1 cm. Bring the pan to the boil, and simmer for 15 minutes – at the end of this time, foam should be forming on the surface of the water. Drain and thoroughly rinse the chickpeas. Return them to the pan and once again cover them with cold water, adding two to three garlic cloves and a whole sprig of rosemary. Bring to the boil and simmer for about 1 hour, until tender. Drain, rinse and set aside until needed.

## CANNELLINI BEANS

I love the creaminess of these white beans, and always have some tinned cannellini in the cupboard to chuck into Breadless ribollita (p. 212) or to add to a Radicchio, cannellini bean and hazelnut salad (p. 246). Annoyingly, the tinned beans don't work so well for the Tuscan stalwarts *fagioli al fiasco* (beans dressed with oil, garlic and rosemary) or *fagioli all'uccelletto* (beans in tomato sauce – rather like posh baked beans); for these dishes it is necessary to give dried cannellini the same treatment as dried chickpeas.

## PUY LENTILS

These dried legumes are inexpensive, with virtually no use-by date. I like to have a couple of packets of lentils in the cupboard in case I have to unexpectedly cook for a crowd. As I always have an onion and some cloves lying around, I put these in with the dried lentils when boiling them. If I have any pancetta, I will make Balsamic-glazed lentils (p. 249). I have turned to this dish (on several occasions) when, expecting to cook for ten, I found I was cooking for twenty. And once when I was expecting to cook for thirty and found I had to feed seventy.

## '00' FLOUR

This variety of flour is the more finely milled type that Italians use for cakes and pasta-making. I don't bake much bread but do like making pastry, cakes and pasta, so this is the flour I always have on hand. '00' is less 'floury' than plain flour or strong flour and is therefore more efficient for making sauces like béchamel, and for use as a coating when browning beef for stews, as it cooks more quickly. It can be substituted with plain flour.

## ANCHOVY PASTE

Coming in a satisfying tube that looks like old-fashioned toothpaste, anchovy paste (*pasta di acchiuge*) is a staple in many of my Italian friends' fridges. I always have it on hand to make Green sauce (p. 254), as it adds a delicious and necessary depth of saltiness to the sauce (and is quicker than using whole anchovies). It's also very useful for slow-cooking meat. You can, for example, add anchovy paste to a marinade for lamb shoulder; after a long, slow cook, the flavour will be one of intense, savoury saltiness, rather than fish. I have seen anchovy paste in lots of places outside of Italy, including in standard UK supermarkets, so you should be able to find it easily. Being an hour and a half from the sea, Tuscans from our area have traditionally resorted to cured fish, as opposed to fresh, in their cooking. Salted anchovies and cod, as well as anchovy paste, represent the few seafood additions to a very meat-based cuisine, illustrating how hyper-local cooking is around these parts. My husband and many of our friends also love to have anchovy paste spread on buttered toast.

## CAPERS

Capers (*capperi*) are the mustardy-flavoured flower buds of the caper bush, which grows out of crevices in rocks and buildings throughout the Mediterranean. When I'm in Rome, I love the sight of these plants creeping up the walls of ancient churches. The shrubs have attractive rounded leaves and pretty white flowers, and the capers are picked when they are still tight little buds. My larder is always stocked with a jar of brined capers stored in vinegar; these capers last forever if you keep them in the fridge once you've opened them. I use them for Green sauce (p. 254), to pep up a plain pasta or to cook with flaky white fish. Having said that, the larger capers stored in salt rather than vinegar are the best, as the salt interferes less with the flavour of the caper, making them more complex and interesting. Whenever I go to Salina, an island off the north coast of Sicily, I buy a pack. So proficient is the island at growing capers that they host the 'Caper Festival' every June, complete with a dazzling fireworks display. The first drawback with the salted capers is that they need rinsing and soaking for at least ten minutes, otherwise they are far too salty. And the second is that they go off. This means I buy them less often than capers in vinegar, as I always like to have some in the fridge.

## MAILLE DIJON MUSTARD

Not strictly speaking Italian, but I find this essential for Green sauce (p. 254), as well as for my homemade Lemony aioli (p. 255). I also include a small bowl of this mustard when serving Roast beef with green sauce (p. 109) or Slow-cooked lamb shoulder with garlic, herbs and lemon (p. 112), for an optional fiery kick.

## WHOLE NUTMEG

This spice has a delicious flavour – nutty and almost creamy. When freshly grated, it gives a decadent depth to béchamel sauces that are used in pies or in lasagne; it can also be added to ricotta and a variety of pasta recipes, lending a little 'warmth' to many a dish.

## OLIVES

I always stock jars and tins of Nocellara olives from Sicily, Cerignola olives from Puglia, and black olives stuffed with red pepper, so I can rustle up a last-minute *aperitivo* if we have guests, or if I suddenly find I don't have time to make anything more elaborate to nibble with drinks. I find their briny saltiness a perfect accompaniment to prosecco and most cocktails, particularly when paired with some pecorino and salami.

## DRY PASTA

I always have a stock of dry pasta in the cupboard. It is hugely versatile, cheap – and never goes off. Dry pasta is made of durum wheat, semolina and water, which means you can use it to quickly rustle something up if you have an unexpected vegan joining you for dinner (when you have made roast veal). When it is cooked properly, it can be a wonderful vehicle for vegetables.

I feel like dry pasta sometimes has a bad rep outside of Italy. Until quite recently, this was particularly the case in the UK, where often it was overcooked and reduced to a glutinous mass before being dressed with a very one-dimensional, undeveloped sauce that hadn't been cooked for long enough. Today, dry pasta is having a moment back in England, following the realisation that, in fact, with the right pasta and the right sauce (which needn't be complicated, but may require patience) a good plate of pasta can be an utter joy, even if cooked on a large scale.

Factory-made, dry pasta is not inferior in any way to fresh. They are just different, both in texture and flavour. Fresh pasta, being made with eggs and flour, is much richer and more filling, while dry pasta is compact and chewy. Personally, I prefer dry pasta, but there are some occasions when only fresh will do, such as when having Homemade tagliatelle with spring peas (p. 98), or when you manage to get your hands on a fresh white truffle.

The trick with dry pasta is to buy the fractionally more expensive brands. This advice is not based on supermarket snobbery – rather, it has to do with the method of making the pasta in the factory. During the drying process, a good pasta will be baked slowly, at 70°C, and it will also be allowed to cool slowly. This all takes time and slows down production. Those pasta manufacturers looking to churn out as much pasta as they can, as quickly and cheaply as possible, will accelerate every stage of this process – the pasta is baked at higher temperatures and dried out quickly at higher temperatures. You can tell a poorer quality pasta by its colour and feel. If it is a darker, umber colour, rather than a pale gold, then it was dried at a higher temperature to speed up production, affecting both the flavour *and* the predictability of boiling time – making it very easy to end up with a disastrous plate of overcooked pasta. A good-quality dry pasta will have been shaped using bronze cutters, which give the pasta a rougher, more textured surface (which is what you're after). With cheaper brands of pasta, the dough will have been passed through machines fitted with teflon-coated cutters, which give the surface of the pasta a very smooth finish. This is the enemy of the marriage between pasta and sauce; nothing will cling to this teflon-cut pasta with its even surface. My go-to pasta brand is De Cecco, as it is widely available, inexpensive and consistent in its cooking time, but other good brands include Rummo, Barilla and La Molisana.

Another misconception about dry pasta is that all shapes go with all sauces. In fact, there is complete rhyme and reason to the pairing of a specific shape with a particular sauce. As a rule of thumb, lighter sauces, where the flavour is carried predominantly by olive oil (as with Spaghetti with garlic, oil and chilli, p. 70) or by a simple, fresh tomato sauce, need the lighter touch of thinner, more delicate pasta shapes such as spaghetti and linguine. Whereas hardier sauces, containing butter, cream or meat (as in Pasta 'alla Savannah', with spicy Italian sausage, p. 218), call for the sturdier shapes – preferably those with cavities, such as penne, conchiglie and tortiglioni, which will naturally scoop up the richer sauces. I like to have a variety of these in my cupboard, so that I can pair the appropriate shape with whatever sauce I feel like having.

- **SPAGHETTI:-** I use De Cecco no. 12. Cooking time 9 minutes. See Spaghetti with datterini tomatoes and basil (p. 141).
- **PENNE RIGATE:-** Cooking time is longer than that of other pastas – 10 minutes for al dente. See Penne with cavolo nero and pancetta (p. 217).
- **CONCHIGLIE:-** Cooking time 9 minutes. See Pasta 'alla Savannah', with spicy Italian sausage (p. 218).
- **FUSILLI:-** De Cecco makes fusilli with tight spirals (no. 34), which carry the sauce very effectively. Cooking time 9 minutes. See Fusilli with Sicilian almond pesto (p. 140).
- **ORECCHIETTE:-** Cooking time 9 minutes. I like to toss orecchiette through some green veg, such as brussels sprouts or broccoli.

**TO COOK DRY PASTA:-**

The trick is to (vigorously) boil the cooking water in a pan that seems impossibly large for your needs. More water means more space for the pasta to cook and expand, and this prevents the pasta sticking together and cooking unevenly. Add a fistful of salt to the water so that it seasons the unsalted pasta; don't be alarmed by the amount of salt you are putting in – most of it will go down the kitchen sink when you drain the pasta. Assume that the pasta is done about 2 minutes before the time given on the packet. Always retain some of the pasta's cooking water in case you need to loosen the sauce; you don't want it to be too dry. Whenever possible, transfer the pasta directly from its pan of boiling water to the sauce (whether the sauce is in a pan or a serving bowl), using tongs for long pasta such as spaghetti, and a slotted spoon for short pasta such as penne and fusilli. Draining the pasta in a colander risks drying it out. An exception to this rule is conchiglie, which carry so much water in their shells that, even if you drain them, they won't dry out. However, it isn't always practical to move the pasta straight from the cooking water to the sauce, particularly when serving large numbers of people. In this case, you may need to use a colander because of the volume of pasta you are cooking – which makes retaining a mugful of the pasta's cooking water all the more important.

– In most areas of Tuscany, and Italy generally, there is a touring food market that visits a different town or village every morning from Tuesday to Saturday. Here you can find the best purveyors of cheese and cold cuts; sellers such as the charming Giacomo degli Innocenti (pictured below) will cut off hunks of parmesan or pecorino from enormous wheels to ensure you are taking home the freshest cheese possible.

# IN THE FRIDGE

## PARMESAN

I am *never* without a hunk of parmesan in the fridge. Along with tinned tomatoes, it is one of those staple ingredients that make me feel safe, knowing that I will be able to conjure up something to eat even in a world crisis ... such as a pandemic. Parmesan, nutty and salty in flavour, is integral to all the food I cook, because – like good oil – it has the ability to lift a seemingly mundane plate of food and make it luxurious, with very little effort. Vegetable stews, roast vegetables or the plainest pasta dish can all be transformed and elevated by a little freshly grated Parmigiano Reggiano. While it is expensive (and when one thinks of the time it takes to make and mature it, that seems fair enough), if stored properly a large hunk of this cheese can last you a long while. It is a DOP (denomination of protected origin) product, coming from a specific area of Emilia-Romagna, made by an exacting process and aged for a minimum of twelve months. Always grate it fresh, at the last possible minute. It is also completely delicious eaten on its own in small chunks.

## PECORINO TOSCANO

This sheep's cheese is typical of our area – I always have a quarter of a wheel of either a *semi-stagionato* (semi-matured) or *stagionato* (extra-matured) pecorino if we have people over. Sheep are a part of everyday life at Arniano, as they graze in the fields surrounding the house, so it is nice to taste and share their product. Pecorino is wonderful as an *aperitivo*, a snack to have with drinks before dinner. The *semi-stagionato* is a bit softer and milder, and goes well alongside a bowl of olives and some carbohydrate like *taralli* (crunchy fennel seed 'pretzels' from Puglia) or *grissini* (breadsticks). The *stagionato* is hard, stronger and nuttier, and is delicious on a pre-dinner cheese board with walnuts and a few slices of pear – a versatile and useful cheese to have stored away ready for entertaining. Outside of Italy you can usually find delicious pecorino from most high-quality cheesemongers, and online from Prezzemolo e Vitale or Eataly in the UK and US.

## RICOTTA

Ricotta is a by-product of pecorino: the re-cooked whey of the milk that separates out in the cheese-making process. I love that this wonderful ingredient was developed as a way to use up as much of the leftover liquid whey as possible. I always have a tub or two of ricotta in the fridge, as it is so versatile. Its mellow flavour means that it pairs well with almost all fruit and veg, and can be used in both savoury and sweet cooking. Sicilian cuisine makes particularly good use of sweet ricotta (cannelloni fillings, cassata cakes, and so on). I know that if there is ricotta in the fridge, I can bake it whole with just a little oil and salt, or eat it on toast – or use it for more complicated and impressive recipes such as Spinach and ricotta malfatti (p. 94), Baked ricotta with olive oil, tomato and basil (p. 182) or Ricotta and asparagus tart (p. 106). Good, fresh ricotta, which we can buy locally from the shepherds who make pecorino, is great (and delicious for lunch), but I find that UHT ricotta, which is available in supermarkets, works best for most of the recipes I make. In my experience, Santa Lucia ricotta requires less draining and has a smoother texture than other brands. Always drain ricotta of any excess liquid in a sieve over the sink before using.

## PROSCIUTTO CRUDO

*Prosciutto* is the general Italian word for ham, and *crudo* means 'raw'. Prosciutto di Parma refers to the raw, cured variety from the region of Parma. Prosciutto di San Daniele, which is similar in style, is considered to be a slightly superior variety. Italians refer to both these DOP cured hams as *dolce* ('sweet') – as opposed to *salato* ('salty'), which is the saltier, more rugged style typical of Tuscany. San Daniele is a little more expensive than Prosciutto di Parma, but all the more silky and delicious: the meat is very lean and salty, while the fat is sweet and almost velvety. San Daniele goes beautifully served with grilled or boiled artichokes and a tiny drizzle of oil. Prosciutto di Parma is even sweeter and fattier, and has a little more chew. Whenever we have a painting course, I will go to the deli to have a few *etti* (*un etto* = 100 g) of one of these hams sliced up and wrapped in parcels, as a plate of prosciutto makes a delicious addition to any lunch.

---

### BOILED ARTICHOKES WITH PROSCIUTTO:-

See page 91 for instructions on how to prepare artichokes. You will need to put your prepped artichokes into lemony water as you go, so that they don't turn brown. Once all the artichokes are ready, pour half the lemony water into a large lidded pan, together with a pinch of salt. Make sure that enough water remains in the bowl to keep the artichokes covered. Bring the salted, lemony water to a rolling boil, then pour in the rest of the artichoke water, along with the artichokes. The water will come back to the boil after about 5 minutes – cover with the lid and leave to bubble away for 15 minutes. The artichokes are cooked when you can pierce the stalk with the end of a knife. Drain, then serve hot or at room temperature dressed in a little oil and salt. Arrange on a platter with prosciutto (preferably San Daniele), simply accompanied by bread and cheese, or serve as a side to a wider feast.

---

## FINOCCHIONA

A Tuscan salami infused with fennel seeds (its name comes from the Italian word for fennel – *finocchio*), finocchiona originated in Florence during the Renaissance. As wild fennel grew all around the city, fennel seeds were easy and cheap to come by, thus circumventing the need to season salami with black pepper – which was more popular, but prohibitively expensive. Finocchiona is no longer the poor man's option and is served as a dish on its own with artichokes or cheese. Here in Tuscany, it comes in enormous logs, which sit behind the deli counter. It is bought by the *etto*, and should be cut in paper-thin slices. I love adding an enormous plate of finocchiona to a spring lunch of salads and Artichoke and béchamel pie (p. 101). Served alongside pasta, it lends a salty note of protein to a feast of many dishes. Another of my favourite ways to serve finocchiona is to lay slices out on a plate and top them with artichokes preserved in oil – simply buy a jar, or make your own. I have seen more modestly sized discs of Italian finocchiona available in the UK from Natoora, and it can be purchased online in other countries.

# A FEW THOUGHTS ON ...

## BREAD

While Tuscany is famed for its cuisine, most people who visit are baffled by the seemingly inexplicably bland bread. *Pane toscano* is a white sourdough, made with no salt. It has a crunchy crust and very dense, chewy crumb. The story goes that the historical expense of salt, and the fact that it was highly taxed, led Tuscans to omit it from their bread dough – but there is also a more palate-led explanation, which is that the plainness complements Tuscan cooking and ingredients. Tuscan prosciutto is particularly salty, so the unassuming pieces of bread that you eat with it serve to balance your mouthful. In northern Italy, where the bread is undeniably tastier and the prosciutto is *dolce*, the opposite is true. The fact that Tuscan bread isn't made with strong bread flour means that it can be used when stale. This explains why it features in historic peasant dishes such as *ribollita*, a stew-like soup made with bread and vegetables (I give a recipe for a breadless version on page 212), *panzanella* (a tomato and bread salad) and *pappa al pomodoro*, a bread and tomato soup – the *pane toscano* soaks up the liquid in a pleasing way and is springy rather than slimy. I see why anyone who hasn't been brought up on this bread would think it a weak link in Tuscan cooking, but for those who *were* raised on it, it is the perfect vehicle for Tuscany's peppery olive oil, tomatoes and beans. It is also delicious toasted, spread with lashings of butter and Marmite.

## SALT

My favourite salt is Maldon salt. I love its natural flavour and its crystalline texture, which makes it uniquely satisfying to crumble between your fingers into the dishes you are preparing. It is less 'salty' than fine salt, or appears to be, and it takes longer to dissolve – another reason why it is important to taste as you go when you are cooking, to check how the flavours and seasoning are developing. Conversely, I always use fine salt to season cooking water, precisely because it is 'saltier' and dissolves more quickly. Whatever salt you use, the main thing is to know it well, to be aware of how it will season your dish and to adjust the quantities accordingly.

## EGGS

Wherever possible, I always use organic, free-range (usually medium-sized) eggs, or the best that are available. I love eggs and cook with them often. A glorious, intensely yellow yolk is a wonderful thing to me and is usually the result of the hen having outdoor space and not being given feed that is laced with hormones. So, as obvious as it sounds, the better the hen is treated, the more delicious the egg. Eggs in Europe all have a serial number printed on the shell: the first number of this code indicates how the hens are raised, starting at '0' and going up to '3'. (I always open the box to check the number. You have to be quite beady about the distracting terms that are used on the packaging – they can be misleading.) '0' means that the eggs are from chickens that are given organic feed and raised with at least 10 square metres allowed for each hen, while '1' indicates 2.5 square metres per chicken. '2' and '3' mean that they are sad eggs from battery farms, the worst case being that the farm keeps twenty-five caged hens per every square metre – so I don't buy them.

I always make sure that any eggs I am cooking or baking with are at room temperature; if they have been kept in the fridge, take them out an hour or so before using. Unless I specify otherwise, all the recipes in this book use medium-sized eggs.

## OVEN TEMPERATURES

Everyone's oven is different. Yours may be more or less powerful than mine, so please think about what you know of your oven, and adjust temperatures by 20 °C in either direction as you see fit. When cooking in someone else's kitchen and using an unfamiliar oven, I have occasionally ruined something I was roasting by sticking rigidly to the settings of my oven at home. At Arniano, I use an electric fan oven, which as a general rule is more powerful than a conventional oven.

## SERVINGS

Most of the recipes in this book serve six people. This is because if you are four, you can usually polish off a bit more, and if you are any more, you can easily double the quantities to twelve. If you are eight or ten, you can eat whatever is left the next day or, in lots of cases throughout the book, freeze it for a later date.

# SPRING

## PRIMAVERA

There is a common misconception that Tuscany is hot year-round. Friends often ask in February: 'Have you opened the pool yet?' 'No,' I shiver, poking the kitchen fire, dressed in fingerless gloves and a woolly hat. From Arniano, you can drive ninety minutes and be skiing. Tuscan winters are dry and frosty – and while they can be bitingly cold, they are usually short and certainly don't feel as interminable as those in Britain. It is because the seasons are so pronounced here that the arrival of spring is utterly joyous. It sneaks up on you. One day in March we will be making the usual trip to the wood store with the wheelbarrow to keep the fires going, looking at the garden's bare branches, beautiful in their way – the next day, the sun will suddenly make a bold appearance. A tentative lunch outside will then be attempted, held under the pleached lime tree that my dad trained to fan out over the kitchen courtyard. The lime provides shade all summer, but at this time of year it is still leafless, allowing the sun to warm our faces.

By degrees, the light changes. You start to notice the hum of bees and the tense buds on every bush, waiting to burst into life. The wisteria at the end of the house explodes into a wispy violet trail; my father's favourite peonies come out in all their blousy, hot-pink glory, to last precisely one week; and the creeping *Rosa* 'Cooperi' climbing the south wall blooms with such an abundance of pale white flowers that we have to scale a ladder to cut it back, so that the light can get in through the high windows. Suddenly, you find yourself leaving the kitchen doors open to let in the spring air and listening out for the call of the nightingales. Walks don't require such serious wrapping up, and towards the end of March you might spot the first wild asparagus. This is a very exciting moment. Having seen the first dark-green shoot, usually thrusting up at the base of an olive tree, your eye is then constantly scanning the ground every time you go out. What would have been a pounding hike a few weeks ago is now a slow meander, as your eyes dart about, searching for these tender green prizes, to be plucked and taken home to toss in a pan with great knobs of butter.

At Arniano, spring means the opening up of the house and the arrival of a constant flow of people. We start thinking about the annual family gathering at Easter, when the house is packed with aunts, cousins, and friends of my mother and sister from London – as well as old friends who live locally. Meals are long and filled with laughter, usually leading to a siesta, and then a walk. Soon after the Easter weekend, we welcome our first painters, in preparation for which I start visiting the local food markets and speaking to the vendors about what produce is having a good year. 'How is the pea crop? Has there been enough rain for broad beans? How long until the artichokes come to an end? Is the cavolo nero over? Do you have any of the last of the Sicilian oranges?' I start to think specifically about dishes that I know some of our returning painters like, and plan the menus accordingly.

The colour of spring is green. Looking out from Arniano, everywhere is a riot of brilliant greens, so exciting to capture on canvas. In the kitchen, I love to welcome back old friends like broad beans, asparagus and fresh peas with their crisp pods. Outside, it is still cool enough to enjoy walking in the hills – or to stand in the garden at an easel with no discomfort or danger of overheating, just the pleasant tingle and smell of the sun on your skin. It is a season of change, of course, and good weather is never guaranteed. We might have summer and winter all in one day. But whether eating inside or out, all our meals at this time of year are bountiful, a smorgasbord, and I often like to serve several of the recipes that you will see in the following pages as part of a single meal.

# 'PINK WINK' COCKTAIL

This drink was invented by Sam, a friend I made in Rome. Sam's family live in the mountains north of Lucca, and this is their customary celebratory drink - which is now a beloved feature of cocktail hour at Arniano. You can prepare jugs of this cocktail a few hours before serving. If you are in Italy, it is very common to find *bibita gassata al pompelmo* (sparkling grapefruit drink) in 1-litre bottles; this is as good as - and much more economical than - tins of San Pellegrino.

**PREPARATION:- A few minutes**

**SERVES 6**

1 bottle dry prosecco

990 ml (3 tins) San Pellegrino Pompelmo

60 ml Campari

Pour all the ingredients into a large jug, mix with a cocktail spoon until the drink takes on a pastel-pink colour, and keep in the fridge until drinks o'clock. Serve in cocktail glasses.

If you are making individual drinks, fill each glass with roughly one-third prosecco and two-thirds fizzy grapefruit. Leave room to top up with enough Campari to turn the drink pink.

*Crostini con baccelli, menta e ricotta*

# CROSTINI WITH BROAD BEANS, MINT AND RICOTTA

To me, broad beans are *baccelli*, which is what we call them in Tuscany; everywhere else in Italy they are known by the 'correct' name of *fave. Baccelli* is actually the collective term for the pods of legumes, but I like that the Tuscans have adopted this more romantic-sounding word – when I was small, I thought it was just an odd way of saying 'little kisses'. These crostini are fresh and green, and to my mind they sum up spring. You can make them with ricotta or cream cheese, depending on what you have – both versions are delicious.

**PREPARATION:**- 10 minutes, plus 45 minutes podding and double-podding the broad beans (20 minutes podding if done with friends)

**SERVES 6**

1.5 kg broad beans (about 250 g once podded) or 250 g frozen podded broad beans

6 slices white sourdough (preferably a little stale), cut 1 cm thick

2 tablespoons olive oil – plus extra, for drizzling onto the crostini

A large handful of mint leaves, roughly chopped

Salt

Freshly ground black pepper

100 g ricotta or 100 g cream cheese

1 teaspoon lemon zest

Preheat the oven to 120 °C/100 °C fan-forced.

If using fresh broad beans, remove them from their fleshy outer pods and put them into a bowl.

Bring a large pan of water to the boil. Prepare a bowl of water with ice cubes for refreshing the beans (fresh or frozen) after boiling.

To prepare the fresh broad beans, transfer them to the pan of boiling water (retaining the bowl of icy water) and blanch for 5 minutes. Drain, then refresh the beans in the icy water. Drain the beans again. Nick the skins using your fingernail – the skins should slip off easily to reveal the bright-green, tender beans inside. As you pod the beans, put them in a bowl. Leave them to one side until you are ready to assemble the crostini.

If you are using frozen broad beans, boil them for 3 minutes rather than 5, then refresh and pod as described above.

Cut the bread to your preferred size before you put it in the oven. Once toasted, the crostini will crumble if you try to cut them. Arrange the bread slices on a baking tray and toast them in the oven for 5–7 minutes, until golden and completely dry. Turn the slices over halfway through, so that they dry evenly. Remove the crostini from the oven and set to one side until ready to serve.

Toss the beans with the olive oil, the mint leaves, a pinch of salt and a few grinds of black pepper.

Drizzle the crostini with a little oil and lightly sprinkle with salt, before spreading each one with some of the drained ricotta or cream cheese and spooning the dressed broad beans on top. Sprinkle over the lemon zest and serve immediately.

*Baccelli e pecorino*

# BROAD BEANS AND PECORINO

Broad beans are a glorious and ubiquitous sight in Italy from early April to mid-May. I am always filled with the joy of spring when I see them on the menu at a particular restaurant in Florence, as their appearance is usually accompanied by the first sun-dappled lunch outside.

At their best, the pods containing these sweet and crunchy jewels are firm and crisp, with a velvety inside. Friends bring large brown bags of them when they come round for an *aperitivo* – the ultimate hostess gift. The beans are dumped unceremoniously in the centre of the table, alongside a piece of pecorino for people to hack at. Everyone absentmindedly pods and gossips, the cheese and beans washed down with a glass of wine. The type of pecorino will be dictated by where you are: each region – whether that be Tuscany, Lazio or Sardinia – will serve this dish as described, accompanied by its distinctive style of pecorino.

Podding young, fresh broad beans is uniquely satisfying: as you simply snap off the top, run your thumb down the very convenient seam that travels the length of the pod, and – again using your thumb – ease out the large, green pearls. You can eat young broad beans raw, without double-podding; that is, without having to remove the bean's skin.

When I am not eating *baccelli* straight from the pod at cocktail hour with friends, I like to serve them pre-podded as a sort of salad, with cubes of pecorino, a drizzle of oil and generous grinds of black pepper.

**PREPARATION:– A few minutes**

**SERVES 4-6**

**250 g podded broad beans, double-podded if the beans are large**

**200 g young pecorino, cut into 2 cm cubes**

**1 tablespoon very good olive oil**

**Lots of freshly ground black pepper**

Put all the ingredients in a serving bowl, toss them together and serve immediately.

---

**VARIATION:–**

If you have a large batch of older pods, I suggest eating them on toast with some mint and mozzarella. Prepare the broad beans by blanching and double-podding, as in the recipe for Crostini with broad beans, mint and ricotta (p. 86).

*Insalata di carciofi, parmigiano e rucola*

# ARTICHOKE, PARMESAN AND ROCKET SALAD

One of my favourite restaurants in Florence makes this to order, and I often watch the owner prepare it at the bar, dousing it with fresh lemon juice and oil, which makes it irresistible. Raw artichokes are a particular, if delicious, thing. The flavour and texture are hard to describe, at once tender but chewy, sweet but woody ... and a little bitter. Artichokes pair beautifully with very bitter leaves, such as large-leaf rocket, and with the nutty saltiness of parmesan shavings. In Italy, it is quite normal to eat artichokes uncooked, and the greengrocer will always ask when you are buying them whether you intend to eat them cooked – or raw, as *pinzominio*. When buying artichokes that will be eaten raw, choose those that look most like an unopened flower bud. When you tear away the tough outer leaves, the interior leaves should be firm and compact. If you can find tender little baby artichokes (*carciofini*), even better – just use twice as many of them.

Here in Italy, in addition to the globe artichoke – which is actually much more common outside of this country – there is a glorious, spiky variety from Sardinia. Literally known as *spinoso* ('spiky' in Italian), it is green with flashes of purple, and has terrifying-looking spikes at the tip of its leaves. I recommend that you prepare this dish using the Sardinian variety if at all possible.

This salad merits being eaten as a starter in its own right, as it is made up of a few tasty elements. I scoop up the lemony oil at the end with a fresh piece of bread.

**PREPARATION:– 15 minutes**

---

**DELICIOUS WITH:–**

Wonderful served before Homemade tagliatelle with spring peas (p. 98) or as a side to accompany Roast beef with green sauce (p. 109).

---

**SERVES 6**

2 lemons (1 lemon half for lemony water, 1 lemon half for preparing the artichokes and stalks, and juice of 1 lemon for dressing the salad)

4 large Sardinian spiny artichokes or 8 baby artichokes (*carciofini*)

250 g large-leaf rocket

50 ml very good olive oil

Salt

12 long shards of parmesan (use a potato peeler to shave thin slices from a piece of parmesan)

Freshly ground black pepper

### PREPARING THE ARTICHOKES

Fill a bowl with cold water, squeeze the juice of half a lemon into it, and drop the half lemon shell into the water. You will put your prepped artichokes in this lemony water to stop them oxidising and turning brown.

To prepare the artichokes, start by tearing off the tough outer leaves (the ones that feel rough in your hands, and that your digestive system is not up to processing). Then, using a potato peeler, peel away the dark green skin from the stalk so that you are left with lighter green flesh, the colour of fresh peas. Rub the newly exposed, tender flesh with the other lemon half to stop it oxidising. Chop the tops off the artichokes (about 4 cm below the spikes), then quarter your prepared artichokes lengthways. Remove the hairy 'choke' with a paring knife.

Keep the artichokes in the lemony water until you are ready to make the salad, to stop the cut edges turning brown.

### ASSEMBLING THE SALAD

Put the rocket in a large, shallow serving bowl.

Take an artichoke from the lemony water and gently wipe with a clean tea towel to remove any excess moisture. Put the artichoke cut side down on a chopping board and slice lengthways, as thinly as possible, while still retaining the shape of the artichoke. Add the slices to the bowl of rocket as you go. Working quickly, slice the rest of the artichokes.

Add the juice of 1 lemon to the artichokes and rocket and toss. Add the olive oil and a generous pinch of salt and toss again. Top the salad with the shards of parmesan as a garnish, and season with a little black pepper.

Serve immediately.

*Zuppa di piselli e menta*

# PEA AND MINT SOUP

Pea and mint soup is a staple of my cooking repertoire. I adore its thick, hearty and almost meaty consistency, as well as its vibrant green colour and sweet flavour. While I adore the all-too-brief period when fresh peas are in season in early spring - when I can devour plates of Homemade tagliatelle with spring peas (p. 98) - frozen peas are in fact punchier in flavour. When I have made this recipe with fresh peas, it becomes a very subtly flavoured soup, the colour of a pale-green olive - delicious, in its way, but not the vibrantly sweet soup my mother has been making since I was little. This soup is very easy to prepare, but the result is sophisticated and guaranteed to get people asking what the secret is. The quantities I have given here are for a starter, but it is filling enough to serve as the main course at dinner if you and your guests have had a particularly hefty lunch. By chance, it is vegan - and when I made it for a vegan client one summer, he loved it so much that he flew me out to his family home for Christmas just so I could make it for him again.

**DELICIOUS WITH:-**

I like to serve this before a hearty main course of Pasta 'alla Savannah', with spicy Italian sausage (p. 218), Spinach and ricotta malfatti with butter and sage (p. 94) or a simple Roast beef with green sauce (p. 109).

**PREPARATION:- 15 minutes**
**COOKING:- 30 minutes**

**SERVES 6**

**5 tablespoons olive oil – plus extra, to serve**

**Leaves from 10 mint sprigs, roughly chopped**

**1 whole mint sprig, stalks and leaves**

**2 large red onions, finely chopped**

**Salt**

**1 kg frozen peas**

**500 ml vegetable stock (made from 1 organic vegetable stock cube dissolved in 500 ml boiling water)**

**Freshly ground black pepper**

**2 tablespoons very good olive oil – plus extra, to serve**

**Parmesan, finely grated, to serve**

Gently fry half the olive oil, half the mint leaves and the whole sprig of mint in a wide, heavy-based pan over a low heat. Move the mint leaves around the pan with a wooden spoon, allowing the mint to infuse and flavour the olive oil.

Once the oil is gently sizzling, remove the whole mint sprig and add the chopped onions, together with a pinch of salt, stirring thoroughly to ensure the onion is coated in oil. Increase the heat to medium and cook until the onion is translucent (about 3–5 minutes), then add the peas. Stir until they start to turn bright green and no longer look frozen. (There's no need to defrost them first as they will cook in the pan.)

Add the rest of the chopped mint leaves to the pan. Mix through, then allow the ingredients to cook for 1 minute or so before adding enough stock (or water) to just cover the peas. Simmer for 15 minutes.

Once the peas are cooked and tender, remove the pan from the heat. Add a large pinch of salt, lots of pepper and 2 tablespoons of good-quality olive oil, then transfer the soup to a blender or food processor. Gently pulse and blend until you have a textured, substantial soup – blending it too much will make it overly thin. A good way to achieve the right texture is by processing the soup in two batches, making sure that you evenly distribute the peas with the liquid.

Transfer the soup back into the pan and gently reheat.

Serve hot, or at room temperature, and top each bowlful with a sprinkling of parmesan, a good amount of pepper and a drizzle of olive oil.

*Malfatti con burro e salvia*

# SPINACH AND RICOTTA MALFATTI WITH BUTTER AND SAGE

Malfatti are one of the first things that I can remember my mother making for us. They were always considered a huge treat, as they require some time – and meditative patience. Also known as *gnudi*, meaning 'naked' in Italian, these ricotta and spinach 'gnocchi' are basically the same as the filling for ravioli, and are naked by dint of not being encased in pasta. In nearby Siena, they are known as *malfatti*, or 'badly mades', as there is a danger they will disintegrate while you are cooking them (which can be dispiriting) if you have skipped any of the basic steps in preparation. Never so when made by Mama; her friend Beatrix always jokingly calls them *benfatti* ('well mades') when a plate is served up to her at Arniano. But as long as you obsessively dry the spinach of all their excess water and allow the mixture to rest in the fridge, you will have the pleasing sight of these pillowy dumplings floating to the top of your boiling water, ready to be fished out and dressed as you wish. In the winter, I like them dressed in tomato sauce, but the rest of the year I love the fragrant indulgence of serving them with melted butter and sage leaves, along with a liberal sprinkling of Parmigiano Reggiano.

**PREPARATION:-** 30 minutes, plus 1 hour resting and 30 minutes shaping (less time if the shaping is done with friends)
**COOKING:-** 10 minutes

**MAKES 42 MALFATTI, ENOUGH FOR 6 AS A MAIN (7 PER PERSON)**

**FOR THE MALFATTI:-**

400 g fresh spinach or 250 g frozen spinach, thawed

25 g mint leaves, finely chopped

500 g ricotta

Salt

Freshly ground black pepper

½ whole nutmeg, finely grated

80 g parmesan, finely grated – plus extra, to serve

2 large eggs

75 g '00' flour – plus extra, for dusting

Olive oil, to serve

If using defrosted spinach, put this directly onto a clean tea towel and wring out to remove as much moisture as possible.

If using fresh spinach, wilt the leaves in a wide, high-sided pan over a medium heat, gently tossing with tongs as they cook down. If there isn't enough space for all the spinach initially, add it in batches. After a few minutes, when the spinach is bright green and has wilted into a manageable amount, remove the pan from the heat.

Leave the spinach to cool for 5 minutes or so and then transfer to a sieve over the sink. Squeeze out as much moisture as possible, either with your hands or by placing a small plate on top of the spinach and pressing down hard. Once you have removed as much excess moisture as you can, put the drained spinach on a clean tea towel and wring out the last of the water. This helps prevent the malfatti falling apart while they are boiling.

Add the mint leaves to the spinach, and chop finely. Set aside to cool completely.

Put the drained ricotta in a bowl. Add a generous pinch of salt, a few grinds of pepper, the grated nutmeg and parmesan, and combine using a fork. Taste for seasoning and adjust as necessary. Mix in the spinach and mint, and beat in the eggs. The ricotta mixture will be quite liquid because of the egg. Gradually stir in the flour, a tablespoon at a time.

Put the malfatti mixture in the fridge for at least half an hour, to rest and firm up.

**140 g unsalted butter**

**Salt**

**A handful of sage leaves, stalks removed**

Generously dust a clean surface with flour. Flour your hands, too, so that the mixture doesn't stick when you are shaping the malfatti. Dust a large plate or baking tray with flour (this needs to fit in your fridge; alternatively, use several smaller plates and baking trays), and keep this next to you as you work, ready for your shaped malfatti.

Using a teaspoon to measure your malfatti (the equivalent of about 20 g), scoop up some of the mixture and drop it onto the floured surface. Roll it in flour, before picking it up and gently rolling it between the palms of your hands to make a ball about 3 cm in diameter. Place the ball on the floured plate or tray. Repeat, until you have about 42 small balls. Make sure they don't touch, as they will stick together. Put the tray of malfatti in the fridge for at least 30 minutes (or up to 24 hours if you are serving them the next day), to rest and firm up.

Put a very large pot of salted water on to boil over a high heat.

While the water is coming up to a boil, prepare the sage butter. Gently heat the butter, with a pinch of salt and the sage, in a wide pan over a low heat. Stirring occasionally, allow the butter to slowly melt and infuse with the sage. Once the butter is lightly sizzling, remove the pan from the heat and put it to one side while you cook your malfatti.

When the water reaches a hard, galloping boil, cook the malfatti in batches. Gently drop the malfatti into the water one by one, making sure not to overcrowd the pan. They will initially sink to the bottom, but will happily bob to the surface when they are done – this usually takes 1–2 minutes. If they don't appear on the surface, gently nudge them with a wooden spoon to make sure they have not stuck to the bottom of the pan.

When one batch has floated to the top, use a slotted spoon to fish out the dumplings and transfer them to the pan of sage butter, before adding a fresh batch of malfatti to the boiling water. As you wait for each new batch to boil, gently turn the cooked malfatti in the sage butter to ensure they are thoroughly coated.

Once all the cooked malfatti have been transferred to the pan of sage butter, gently heat them through over a low heat. Put them onto a serving dish, drizzle with a little olive oil and sprinkle liberally with parmesan before serving.

**VARIATION:-**

Instead of sage butter, dress the malfatti in a simple Tomato sauce (p. 70).

**DELICIOUS WITH:-**

I love serving malfatti as the main course following a warming bowl of Pea and mint soup (p. 92), or a Pear, rocket, pecorino and walnut salad (p. 175). We have been known to serve them as a starter at Arniano when everyone is really hungry. They are lovely as the starter for something that is not too rich; for example, Roast beef with green sauce (p. 109), along with Mama's roast cherry tomatoes (p. 251) and Peppery green salad (p. 244). Make sure dessert isn't anything too sweet or dense, as the malfatti themselves are rich – I often make Cardamom poached pears (p. 232) as the final course. A bowl of your favourite dark chocolates would also be heaven.

*Tagliatelle con piselli freschi*

# HOMEMADE TAGLIATELLE WITH SPRING PEAS

This dish is buttery, sweet and delicious. If you happen to come upon some fresh garden peas in spring, make this recipe immediately! And if you can't find spring peas, it is just as delicious made with frozen peas - although it won't be quite as delicate and sweet. In general, I prefer dry pasta, but in this instance, fresh makes all the difference. Making pasta may seem time consuming, but it is fun if done with friends. If you are preparing it on your own, it can actually be quite soothing and meditative. You will need a pasta machine to prepare the tagliatelle - I use a KitchenAid pasta attachment, which makes life very easy.

MAKING THE PASTA:- 1½ hours
COOKING:- 35 minutes

SERVES 6

FOR THE PASTA:-

600 g '00' flour – plus extra, for dusting and for coating the pasta

6 eggs

Semolina, for coating the pasta

FOR THE PEAS:-

4 tablespoons olive oil

1 white onion, finely diced

Salt

1 garlic clove, peeled and crushed

400 g fresh, shelled spring peas or 400 g frozen peas

Freshly ground black pepper

1 teaspoon caster sugar

100 g unsalted butter

75 g parmesan, finely grated – reserve half for serving

MAKING THE PASTA

Skip this step if you have found some good, shop-bought, fresh tagliatelle.

Tip the flour into a large bowl. Make a well in the centre and crack the eggs into it. Using a fork, start swirling and breaking up the eggs, slowly and gently incorporating some of the flour as you do so. After about a minute you can start to be less cautious and bring together all the flour and the eggs.

Once you have a rough, combined dough, tip it onto a floured surface and begin kneading. Using the heel of your palm, push the dough away from you, then use your fingers to bring it back towards you while allowing the dough to fold over itself. Knead for 15 minutes, until you have a lovely, smooth pasta dough (not wet and sticky, but not crumbly). Alternatively, knead the dough in an electric stand mixer with the dough hook attached.

Cover the dough in cling film, then put it in the fridge and leave it to rest for 20 minutes to an hour. This allows the gluten to relax, thereby making it easier to run the dough through your pasta machine.

Remove the dough from the fridge and divide it into six smaller pieces, gently rolling each one into a ball. Keep one piece aside, ready to process in the pasta maker. Cover the other pieces in cling film and put them to one side until you are ready to run them through the pasta maker.

Take the ball of pasta dough and flatten it out to a disc, about 2 cm thick. Run the disc of dough through the widest setting of your pasta machine ten times, turning the sheet of dough 90 degrees and folding it in half (rather like closing a book) every other time as you run it through. The pasta should now feel smooth and silky. Next, run it through each of the following settings, finishing with the thinnest setting – the dough should be thin enough to see your hand through it. Dust the sheet of dough lightly with flour and semolina, then put it to one side. Repeat this process with the remaining five balls of pasta dough.

Trim each sheet into neat rectangles, roughly 25 cm long and as wide as the pasta machine. Dust each one with a little flour and semolina so that the sheets don't stick together.

Change the setting on your pasta machine to 'tagliatelle' or 'fettucine' (depending on your model), then run the sheets through. Gently scoop the tagliatelle up with the palm of your hand as it comes through the machine. Hang the pasta over the back of a chair, and/or any available handles in your kitchen (or on a drying rack) and leave for 10–15 minutes.

While the pasta is drying, dust a large plate or baking tray with semolina. Transfer the dry tagliatelle to the plate or baking tray, coat with the semolina and twist into neat, loose piles (the semolina helps to further dry the pasta and will prevent clumping during cooking). Sprinkle some more semolina over the pasta – this will fall to the bottom of the pan when you cook the tagliatelle. Put the pasta to one side until you are ready to cook it.

### MAKING THE SAUCE AND ASSEMBLING THE PASTA

In a heavy-based pan (I use a cast-iron skillet), gently heat a drizzle of olive oil, enough to lightly coat the bottom of the pan. Add the onion with a pinch of salt and gently fry over a medium heat for a few minutes. Once the onion has begun to soften, stir in the garlic. Allow to sizzle for a few moments, then add the peas, stirring to make sure they are coated with the oil.

Add enough cold water (about 350 ml) to come to about 1 cm above the peas. Season with a generous pinch of salt and a few grinds of black pepper. If using fresh peas, cover and cook for 15–20 minutes, or until the peas are tender. If using frozen peas, cook for 5 minutes.

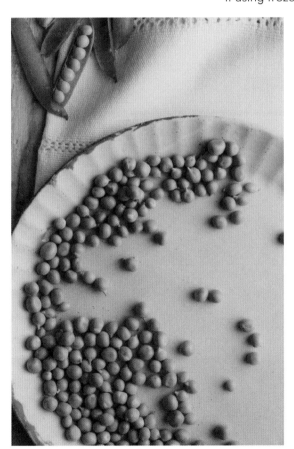

Turn the heat down to low. Add a teaspoon of sugar and a pinch of salt, then add the butter, stirring until it melts and amalgamates with the peas' cooking water. Cook for a further 5 minutes.

Put a very large pan of well-salted water on to boil. Once the water is at a lively boil, gently drop the pasta into the pan and then immediately stir with a wooden spoon. Cook the tagliatelle for 1–2 minutes. Being fresh, the pasta will cook very quickly.

Increase the heat for the pan of peas to medium. Using tongs, fish out the pasta and add it to the pea mixture, along with a ladleful of the pasta water to bring it all together. Stir the tagliatelle through the peas and switch off the heat. Once the pasta is fully coated in the sweet, buttery liquid, toss with half the parmesan, before serving with another liberal sprinkling of parmesan.

I serve this dish directly from my skillet, but feel free to transfer the dressed pasta to a serving dish. Eat immediately.

SPRING

*Torta di carciofi e besciamella*

# ARTICHOKE AND BÉCHAMEL PIE

I first tried artichoke and béchamel pie at a dinner that Matthew and I were invited to when we first relocated to Florence. It was huge fun, and kind of our hosts to ask us, given that we had just moved to the city. We were the youngest there by about twenty years, and the evening was impossibly glamorous. I will always remember that dinner, not just for its splendour, but because the *primo*, or starter, was *torta di carciofi e besciamella*. So enamoured was I with this dish that I foolishly had seconds - knowing full well that this was an Italian dinner at a Florentine's house, and there was bound to be a *secondo* appearing at any moment. There was, but I had no regrets about not being able to eat the main course, so delicious was the first. Not knowing our host well enough to ask him for the recipe, the next day I went to the market in Santo Spirito, bought a huge number of artichokes - and everything else I would need for a few trial runs - and took them back to our tiny kitchen. Then I set about tinkering and trying to recreate what we had eaten the night before. This recipe is the result of these tinkerings (or, rather, it is version six). If you can get hold of Sardinian *spinosi* artichokes, all the better, as the flavour and texture are wonderful. But the pie will work just as well with globe.

This dish may sound like it takes a long time to make, but remember that you can do it in stages. Prep the artichokes, and then leave them in a bowl of lemony water for a few hours while you do something else. Or prepare both the artichokes and the béchamel, and leave them overnight in the fridge before filling the pie case. You can also make and refrigerate this pie (no more than) two days ahead of time, then reheat it in the oven before serving. It also freezes really well for up to a month once cooked, so you can pull it out of the freezer in the morning to defrost, before putting it back in the oven for 20–30 minutes at 200°C/180°C fan-forced to warm through and crisp up for dinner.

PREPARATION (INCLUDING COOKING AND RESTING):-
2 hours 45 minutes
BAKING:- 30 minutes

## FOR THE ARTICHOKES:-

1 lemon, halved
(one half for lemony water,
one half for rubbing the
exposed artichoke flesh)

4 large Sardinian spiny
artichokes or globe artichokes

30 g unsalted butter

2 tablespoons olive oil

Salt

Freshly ground black pepper

## FOR THE BÉCHAMEL:-

500 ml full-fat milk

50 g unsalted butter

50 g '00' flour

30 g parmesan, finely grated

Cayenne pepper

¼ whole nutmeg, finely grated

Salt

Freshly ground black pepper

## FOR THE PASTRY:-

2 discs (or 2 rectangular sheets)
of ready-rolled puff pastry

1 egg, lightly beaten,
for egg-washing

## PREPARING AND COOKING THE ARTICHOKES

Fill a bowl with cold water, squeeze the juice of half a lemon into it, and drop the half lemon shell into the water. You will put your prepped artichokes in this lemony water to stop them oxidising and turning brown. Prepare the artichokes as described on page 91. Quarter the prepared artichokes lengthways.

Melt the butter in a frying pan (choose one with a lid) over a medium heat, then mix in the olive oil, salt and pepper.

Once the butter and oil are starting to sizzle in a pleasing way, add the artichoke pieces and two ladlefuls of the lemony water that they have been sitting in. Partially cover the pan, and leave the artichoke to gently cook for 10 minutes, turning occasionally.

Switch off the heat and cover the pan completely. Leave to cool while you get on with your béchamel.

## MAKING THE BÉCHAMEL

Put the milk in a pan and set it over a high heat. When it is on the edge of boiling, remove it from the heat.

Meanwhile, in another pan, make the roux (the mixture of flour and fat that is used to thicken the sauce). Melt the butter in the pan over a medium heat and then gradually add the flour, a tablespoon at a time, stirring constantly with a wooden spoon. You want the flour and butter to amalgamate and sizzle, creating a paste. Once amalgamated, the mixture should come away from the sides of the pan.

Add a ladleful of the hot milk to the roux, along with the parmesan, a pinch of cayenne, some finely grated nutmeg, and salt and pepper. Remove the pan from the heat and stir the lot together until smooth. Gradually add the rest of the milk, bit by bit, stirring constantly. To prevent lumps forming, make sure the mixture is completely smooth before each addition of liquid.

Once you have added all the milk, set the pan over a low heat and bring it back up to a simmer, stirring constantly. The sauce should now become thick and creamy. Remove the pan from the heat and taste for seasoning, adjusting as necessary. Add the artichoke pieces and their cooking liquid to the béchamel, gently folding them into the sauce.

Allow the mixture to cool to room temperature, then pop it into the fridge for at least an hour, so that it is cold when you fill your pastry. This will help you avoid the dreaded, unappetising stodge that is 'soggy-bottomed' pastry.

Preheat the oven to 240 °C/220 °C fan-forced.

Line a 20 cm cake tin with baking parchment. Unroll a disc or rectangular sheet of puff pastry and place it over the cake tin. Gently press the pastry down into the tin to form the base and sides of your pie. The pastry should be sitting flat and even against the sides of the tin, so that that none of your filling escapes. Stab the bottom of the pastry all over with a fork. Using a pastry brush, coat the bottom of the pastry case with a thin layer of egg wash. Spoon your cold filling into the pastry-lined tin.

Unroll the second disc or rectangle of pastry, trimming off any excess so that it will sit comfortably on top of the filling. Carefully place the pastry over the top of the pie and pinch the edges of the two layers of pastry together to seal in your filling. If necessary, cut away any remaining excess pastry.

Brush the top with egg, and make four 'leaf-shaped' cuts with a sharp knife, in a loose cross shape, to allow steam to escape. Put the pie in the oven and bake for 30 minutes. It is ready when the top is crisp and golden.

Remove the pie from the oven and allow it to rest for 15–20 minutes before serving, so that the béchamel isn't too liquid and everything is the perfect temperature when you dig in.

DELICIOUS WITH:-

This dish is hearty enough on its own, so I would serve it with something refreshing, such as a Peppery green salad (p. 244), which cuts through the rich decadence of the pie. I also love it with boiled potatoes and mint, or Charred roast potatoes with lemons (p. 265), or even a simple plate of finocchiona or prosciutto.

# CARCIOFI

 Artichokes in England mean a very particular variety - globe. They are usually boiled whole and eaten leaf by leaf, the tender base of each leaf becoming a vehicle for melted butter or peppery vinaigrette; this is followed by an unwieldy performance involving tearing away the final leaves and slicing the heart from the 'choke' with a straight cut, before using a butter knife to retrieve the heart. It is the French way of turning the preparation of the vegetable into the meal itself. In Italy, *carciofi* are associated with a plethora of varieties and cooking methods, and the artichokes are generally prepared *before* serving, with only the edible parts making it to the table.

The flavour of artichokes is difficult to describe – all at once they are bitter, nutty and sulphurous, with a sweet aftertaste. They contain a chemical that makes everything taste sweet afterwards, even water, and it is this chemical (cynarin) that makes them difficult to pair with wine – though personally I've never minded wine with artichokes.

Many people see the preparation of artichokes as an obstacle to their enjoyment, or even to their consideration for inclusion in a home-cooked meal, and in the past I would have agreed. But once you master this ritual – sometimes time consuming, but not difficult – you can enjoy this hugely versatile vegetable, and the variety of ways to eat it, with the same abandon as the Italians. You will find instructions for preparing artichokes on page 91.

Artichokes like the cold and have a wonderfully long season in Italy, only disappearing from shops and restaurant menus entirely when the temperature rises between mid-May and late October. One of the most enjoyable meals I have eaten in the past few years was, in fact, a very simple artichoke-based one. It was prepared for us just before the end of the season, by vegetarian friends who live in a farmhouse with their five children about half an hour south of Florence. Matthew and I drove out to see them for dinner one evening in spring. The roses creeping up the side of their house

were in full bloom, a subtle riot of pinks and whites under an April sunset. Our hosts had prepared and boiled a cauldron's worth of artichokes. They drained them, and brought them to the table in said cauldron, serving them alongside a bottle of good olive oil, half a wheel of a hard (*stagionato*) pecorino and some fresh bread. We each had a plate, which we piled high with artichokes and hunks of cheese, dousing the artichokes in oil, and eating them with the cheese and bread. This meal may sound humble, but it was in fact one of such bounty that it is not easily forgotten. To prep so many artichokes must have taken at least an hour, and the combination of the nutty greenness of the hot, freshly boiled artichokes with the saltiness of the cheese was unbeatable. (I've given instructions for preparing boiled artichokes on page 76.)

There are many artichoke varieties in Italy: the Romanesco, or '*mammola*' from Lazio, the 'Tondo di Paestum', the Sicilian '*violetto*', and the '*spinosi*' from Sardinia, to name but a few. The little violet-and-green baby artichokes (*carciofini*) are wonderful thinly sliced and eaten in a salad, or – once suitably prepared – boiled whole in lemony water with bay leaves, and served with potatoes and lamb. The Sardinian *spinose* – often mistrusted due to the rather frightening-looking talons at the ends of their leaves – are my favourite, and are perfect for an artichoke and béchamel pie, or simply boiled and served up with cheese and bread. Or you could combine the British/French tradition with the Italian, and eat them boiled, with a vinaigrette; with the preparation ritual removed, you can eat them with a knife and fork, dunking each mouthful of artichoke into the mustardy sauce without worrying that you are going to swallow a choke or chew on an indigestible leaf.

The Romans have a dab hand with an artichoke – if you go there, eat a dish of *carciofo alla Giudea* ('Jewish-style artichokes'), featuring artichokes that have been deep-fried whole and flattened between two plates. Glorious, but best left to the restaurant's deep-fat fryer rather than made in a home kitchen. My favourite restaurant at which to eat these, Da Giggetto, in the Jewish quarter of the city, plants a man at the entrance, surrounded by boxes of artichokes. He will sit there all day with his paring knife, preparing the artichokes, wielding his knife in a circular motion as though he were whittling a piece of wood.

In eastern Sicily, where the volcanic minerals from lady Etna ensure that vegetables abound and taste as nowhere else, little informal food stalls pop up by the side of the road whenever a particular crop is in full, bountiful production. I was once there in early spring, in time to see little open-sided trucks selling artichokes priced at €3 for 5 kilograms – a bargain unheard of in Florence, let alone London.

However, the best and most widely available artichokes are from Sardinia, so I long to go and see what bargains can be picked up there during the season.

Another fabulous combination is *prosciutto crudo dolce* (Parma ham, or prosciutto San Daniele) served with artichokes that have been boiled and then braised, or even simply with good-quality *carciofi sott'olio*. These are bottled artichokes that have been poached in vinegar and then covered in oil and various seasonings – my favourite variety includes whole peppercorns and bay leaves. The best I have ever eaten are from a farm called Fattoria S.Anna, near Bolgheri, on the Tuscan coast. I highly recommend popping in if you are in the area. I buy jars and jars of these and keep them in the cupboard at home, to be eaten on their own as an antipasto or to be placed on top of thinly sliced finocchiona or prosciutto.

In ancient Greek myth, Cynara (which is also the Latin name for artichoke) was a mortal woman with whom the god Zeus fell madly in love. Such was his passion for the beautiful Cynara that he deified her and brought her to live on Mount Olympus. Unfortunately, when he found out that she had been sneaking off to visit her family, his rage was such that he cast her out and sent her back to earth as an artichoke. All I can say is, poor Cynara, but thank goodness for her homesickness.

---

**A FEW CARCIOFI RECIPES:-**

- Artichoke, parmesan and rocket salad (p. 90)
- Artichoke and béchamel pie (p. 101)
- Artichoke risotto (p. 224)

---

**ABOVE**
– Artichoke block print by Hugo Guinness.

*Torta di ricotta e asparagi*

# RICOTTA AND ASPARAGUS TART

This dish is always a hit with the painters on our courses. I first devised it as something that I could quickly rustle up to feed many mouths at lunch. Making two or three of these tarts takes hardly any more time than making just one, and with the addition of a salad and some prosciutto you have yourself a feast in a mere half-hour or so.

**PREPARATION:- 15 minutes**
**BAKING:- 20 minutes**

**MAKES 1 TART,
ENOUGH FOR 6 PEOPLE**

500 g asparagus

1 rectangular sheet of ready-rolled puff pastry

2 eggs (1 egg for the ricotta mixture and 1 egg, lightly beaten, for egg-washing)

250 g ricotta

Salt

Freshly ground black pepper

Chilli flakes

¼ whole nutmeg, finely grated

1 tablespoon olive oil

20 g parmesan, finely grated

Zest of 1 lemon

Preheat the oven to 220 °C/200 °C fan-forced.

Remove the tough ends from the asparagus stalks by gently bending each spear from the base – the inedible part of the stalk will snap off.

Unroll the pastry onto a rectangular baking tray lined with baking parchment. Prick the pastry all over with a fork, brush generously with egg wash, and put it in the fridge for 10 minutes while you prepare the ricotta mixture.

Put the drained ricotta in a bowl and break it up using a fork. Add a generous pinch of salt, some grinds of black pepper, a pinch of chilli flakes and some finely grated nutmeg. Mix everything together using the fork, and taste to check the balance of seasonings.

Add the olive oil, beating it in with the fork until it is fully incorporated into the ricotta. Mix in the parmesan and lemon zest, and add another pinch of salt and a grind of pepper. Taste for seasoning, adjusting as necessary (you might like it with more nutmeg or black pepper – it's entirely up to you), and beat in one of the eggs.

Retrieve the pastry from the fridge. Being careful not to cut right through, use the tip of a sharp knife to score a line 5 cm in from the edge of the pastry, all the way around – a neat, raised crust will form as the pastry cooks. Spoon your ricotta mixture into the centre of the pastry (without straying onto the edge you have scored with the knife), and smooth it out evenly with the back of the spoon.

Turn the baking tray so that the longest edge is facing you. Arrange the asparagus on top of the ricotta, in packed, neat rows extending across the width of the pastry. You may need to arrange some of the spears top to toe, if their shape so dictates. And if some of the asparagus are too long or too bent, just chop them up and place them wherever you see any exposed ricotta.

Bake the tart for 20 minutes, until the edges of the pastry are raised and golden.

Remove the tart from the oven, slide it onto a large serving plate and serve immediately.

**DELICIOUS WITH:-**

Radicchio, cannellini bean and hazelnut salad (p. 246), a plate of finocchiona or prosciutto, or Slow-roasted San Marzano tomatoes (p. 250).

*Rosbif con salsa verde*

# ROAST BEEF WITH GREEN SAUCE

*Rosbif* is what the Tuscans call roast veal or beef, a reference to the British tradition of roast beef. I have no idea how this name made its way into the Italian lexicon, particularly as the Tuscans know full well how to cook a piece of meat beautifully. If you are buying meat from a butcher in Italy, and would like the perfect cut for your Sunday roast, ask for *rosbif*, and they will give you a glorious red-plum-coloured piece of veal (*vitellone rosbif*). In the UK, I ask for 'topside'. This dish is my mother's failsafe main for a crowd. She likes it because whether we are fifteen people, or thirty, she can make it ahead of time - as long as the sides are hot, it doesn't matter if the beef is room temperature.

PREPARATION:- **A few minutes (after bringing beef up to room temperature)**
COOKING:- **55 minutes**
RESTING:- **Minimum 30 minutes**

**SERVES 6**

**800 g to 1 kg topside of beef or *vitellone rosbif***

**Salt**

**Freshly ground black pepper**

**75 ml olive oil**

**A handful of sage leaves**

**Leaves from a handful of rosemary sprigs**

**2 garlic cloves, left unpeeled, gently squashed with the edge of a large knife**

**350 ml dry white wine**

**Green sauce (p. 254), to serve**

Take the beef out of the fridge 2 hours before cooking, to bring it up to room temperature. Put the beef in a roasting tray and lightly coat all over with a layer of salt and black pepper. Cover the meat with a tea towel.

Preheat the oven to 220 °C/200 °C fan-forced.

Drizzle a little oil into a heavy-based pan, bring the heat up to high and brown the beef all over.

Put the sage, rosemary and whole garlic cloves into the roasting tray, and sit the browned beef on top. Drizzle the rest of the oil over the beef, followed by the wine. Roast in the oven for 25 minutes, basting the meat occasionally with the pan juices. If the pan looks like it is drying out, add a little water.

Turn the oven down to 200 °C/180 °C fan-forced and cook the beef for another 20 minutes for medium-rare.

Remove the roast from the oven and check to see how well it is cooked. Either slice a piece off the end to check the colour, or press on the top: medium-rare will feel soft but springy. If the beef is still too red for your taste, return it to the oven for another 5–10 minutes. Once you have removed the meat from the oven, allow it to rest for at least 30 minutes before eating. (Alternatively, allow it to cool completely, wrap it in cling film or foil, and put it in the fridge to serve at room temperature the next day.)

Pour the cooking liquid into a little bowl or jug, and set aside to cool completely.

Slice the beef as thinly as you can, ideally to about 1.5 mm (roughly the thickness of an English penny). Arrange the slices on a serving dish and drizzle with the cooled cooking liquid. Serve with a bowl of green sauce.

**DELICIOUS WITH:-**

My mother always serves this dish with Balsamic-glazed lentils with pancetta and cloves (p. 249), her Roast cherry tomatoes (p. 251) and a Peppery green salad (p. 244). It is also wonderful with Roast potatoes with garlic and rosemary (p. 262). This meal deserves an exciting dessert, something like Custard and berry tart (p. 116), or Maria's marmalade, mascarpone and almond tart (p. 196).

*Frittata di patate e cipolle*

# POTATO AND ONION FRITTATA

This was another of the dishes taught to me by my mother as an early introduction to cooking. My mother's frittata is much more akin to a Spanish tortilla than a traditional Italian frittata, as it is deep sided rather than thin and, most crucially of all, it is flipped. As a teenager, I was proud of having mastered it, given that I initially found the idea of flipping a frittata halfway through cooking very daunting. This particular recipe should be used as a guideline in terms of timing, as everyone's pan, stove and apparatus for inverting will be different. Don't be discouraged if you don't produce a beautiful, golden frittata on your first attempt - the flavour will still be delicious. Frittatas - like horses and soufflés - can smell fear, and the minute you think you won't be able to flip the piping hot mass of eggs, potato and onion neatly, you invariably can't.

This serves four generously, or six at a stretch - with lots of sides - but if we are more than four, I always make two frittatas (I simply double the quantities and divide the mixture before cooking). I try to make the frittatas ahead of time, as they are delicious at room temperature; they can also be easily reheated.

PREPARATION:- 20 minutes, plus 10 minutes resting
COOKING:- 25 minutes

SERVES 4-6

500 g waxy potatoes, peeled
1 large white onion
Salt
100 ml olive oil
6 eggs
Freshly ground black pepper

Cut the potatoes in half lengthways, then cut into half-rounds, each about 3 mm thick, making sure all your slices are of a consistent thickness. Set the potato aside in a bowl large enough to hold the onion slices in the next step.

Cut the onion in half lengthways, then cut into slices about 3 mm thick (basically, the same thickness as the potato slices). Add the onion slices to the potato and toss with a generous pinch of salt.

Pour the olive oil into a wide (20 cm or 24 cm) frying pan and set over a medium heat. Check that the oil is hot enough by putting a piece of onion in the pan – when this starts sizzling, carefully add all the onion and potato. Fry for 10–15 minutes, stirring two or three times to make sure everything is cooking evenly.

Using a slotted spoon, transfer the cooked potato and onion to a colander set over a bowl, to collect the oil. (Leave any remaining oil in the frying pan, and set the pan to one side, as it will be used later in the cooking process.) Once drained, put the potato and onion in a bowl to cool a little. Pour the oil collected from the cooked vegetables back into the frying pan and keep to hand.

Crack the eggs into a bowl and gently whisk to break up the yolks. Season generously with salt and pepper, then pour the beaten egg over the potato and onion, gently mixing with a wooden spoon so that the egg completely coats the vegetables. Set aside and allow the flavours to develop for 10 minutes.

DELICIOUS WITH:-

This is one of my all-time favourite lunches when served with Lemony aioli (p. 255), Slow-roasted San Marzano tomatoes (p. 250) and Peppery green salad (p. 244). If you feel the need to augment for a hungry gang, I would add a large plate of prosciutto San Daniele or finocchiona with *carciofi sott'olio* (artichokes preserved in oil) and a Radicchio, cannellini bean and hazelnut salad (p. 246).

Bring the frying pan containing the oil back up to a medium heat. When the oil starts to gently sizzle, add the egg, potato and onion mixture, making sure the sliced vegetables are fully submerged. Leave to cook for 5 minutes, occasionally running a spatula around the inside edge of the pan to loosen the sides of the frittata.

For the next part of the process, you will need a flat plate that is wider than the frying pan. Remove the pan from the heat and take it over to the sink, in case of any spillage. Place the plate over the top of the pan. Holding the pan by the handle with one hand, apply pressure to the plate with your other hand, and flip the pan over to invert the frittata onto the plate. You should have a lovely, golden frittata. Push the frittata to one edge of the plate and gently slide it back into the pan. Cook over a medium heat for a further 5 minutes. When it is ready, invert the frittata back onto the plate, and leave it to rest for 10 minutes before serving.

This dish is equally delicious served either piping hot or at room temperature.

*Spalla di agnello al forno con aglio, erbe e limone*

# SLOW-COOKED LAMB SHOULDER WITH GARLIC, HERBS AND LEMON

This was the first thing my husband ever cooked for me. As we ate, with Matthew describing the marinating and slow cooking, the forethought and the length of the process involved in making it for me, he had me hook, line and sinker. I still love this dish, because it's so flavoursome - and, as I now know, actually relatively easy to make. The key to this dish is the lemon juice, which cuts through the fattiness of the lamb shoulder. It is also imperative to seal in the juices as efficiently as possible, so that they don't escape and evaporate during the long, slow roasting. The recipe originally comes from my husband's mother, a very good cook, who uses oregano as the main herb. I have adapted it slightly to feature rosemary and thyme, which grow more abundantly here at Arniano.

PREPARATION:- 15 minutes, plus at least 2 hours marinating
(the lamb can also be left to marinate overnight in the fridge)
COOKING:- 4 hours

**SERVES 4**

1.2–1.5 kg lamb shoulder

Salt

Freshly ground black pepper

10 garlic cloves, peeled and halved lengthways

70 ml olive oil

Leaves from 2 rosemary sprigs, finely chopped

Leaves from a handful of thyme sprigs

Juice of 3 lemons

---

**DELICIOUS WITH:-**

I love to serve Charred roast potatoes with lemons (p. 265) and Greens 'in the pan' with garlic and chilli (p. 258) alongside the lamb. And to finish, a delicious Berry clafoutis with Amalfi lemon cream (p. 199), or just coffee and chocolates.

---

Find a rectangular roasting pan big enough for the shoulder, and position with the longest edge facing you. Lay two long sheets of foil (long enough to wrap around the lamb) across the narrow width of the roasting pan, slightly overlapping them to prevent any juices escaping as the meat cooks. Stand the foil up along the sides of the pan, ready to be folded over the lamb to form a sealed parcel. To prevent the meat sticking to the foil, place a long sheet of baking parchment lengthways across the base of the foil-covered pan.

Season the lamb generously with salt and pepper. Using a very sharp knife, and being careful not to cut straight through the meat to the other side, make 10–15 incisions all over the lamb. Stuff each incision with half a garlic clove. Put any additional garlic at the bottom of the pan with a pinch of salt, and sit the lamb on top.

Drizzle the oil over the lamb, then add the rosemary and thyme and rub it all over the meat with your hands. Pour over the lemon juice, allowing it to run into the incisions. Add 50 ml water to the pan, then bring the edges of the foil up and over the lamb, and seal. Cover the pan with another layer of foil. Leave to marinate for a minimum of 2 hours, or in the fridge overnight.

Preheat the oven to 140 °C/120 °C fan-forced.

If you have left the lamb to marinate in the fridge, take it out 1 hour before cooking so that it comes up to room temperature.

Roast the lamb for 3½ hours, until very tender, checking occasionally to make sure the juices haven't escaped from the parcel. If they have, carefully unseal the foil, add a little more water and lemon juice, then reseal. At the end of the roasting time, remove from the oven and turn the heat up to 200 °C/180 °C fan-forced. Unwrap the parcel and fold back the foil, then baste the meat with the juices from the pan. Return to the oven and roast for 20 minutes until browned. Remove and leave to rest for 30 minutes before serving on the bone with the juices.

*Torta caprese al cioccolato e pepperoncino*

# FLOURLESS CHOCOLATE, ALMOND AND CHILLI CAKE

Chocolate with chilli is one of my favourite flavour and sensation combinations, and one that I don't find nearly enough in shops or restaurants. Here I have paired it with the nutty indulgence of a *torta caprese*, the famous flourless cake from Capri. The quantities of spice in this recipe are optional, and you are free to omit the chilli if you prefer - it will still be a delicious cake. The amounts given are for ready-ground spices. If you intend to grind your own whole dried chilli, be aware that it is much more powerful than store-bought chilli flakes and you will need to halve the quantity.

**PREPARATION:- 20 minutes**
**BAKING:- 30 minutes**

**SERVES 8**

25 g cocoa powder

1 teaspoon cayenne pepper (or to taste)

Salt

200 g ground almonds

½ teaspoon chilli flakes (or to taste)

100 g blanched whole hazelnuts

200 g dark chocolate, broken into pieces

3 eggs, separated

200 g caster sugar – plus 1 tablespoon for whisking egg whites

200 g unsalted butter, melted

Crème fraîche or pouring cream, to serve

Preheat the oven to 200 °C/180 °C fan-forced. Butter a 20 cm cake tin and line with baking parchment.

In a small bowl, mix together the cocoa, cayenne pepper and a pinch of salt. In a separate large bowl, mix the ground almonds with the chilli flakes. Put the hazelnuts, chocolate pieces, and the combined cocoa and cayenne pepper in a food processor. Blitz to a rough texture – don't grind the mixture too finely. Add this to the ground almonds and chilli flakes, and set aside.

Using hand-held electric beaters, whisk the egg yolks with the sugar until thick and pale. Use a wooden spoon to mix the egg yolks and sugar in with the chocolate and nuts, and then add the melted butter – this will help the mixture come together.

Whisk the egg whites until they form stiff peaks, adding a tablespoon of sugar halfway through whisking. Using a clean metal spoon, gently fold the egg whites into the chocolate and nut mixture, bit by bit.

Pour the mixture into the cake tin and bake for 30 minutes. At the end of this time, check the cake using a skewer. If it comes out covered in chocolate, return the cake to the oven for 5–10 minutes. If the cake tester comes out clean(ish), remove the cake from the oven and leave it to cool in the tin for at least an hour before serving. Serve with a dollop of crème fraîche or pouring cream.

*Crostata di crema e frutti di bosco*

# CUSTARD AND BERRY TART

**PREPARATION:-** 1½ hours, plus 2 hours chilling
**BAKING:-** 25 minutes

**SERVES 8**

**FOR THE PASTRY:-**
2 egg yolks
2 tablespoons ice-cold water
60 g caster sugar
Salt
240 g '00' flour
140 g unsalted butter, chilled and diced

**FOR THE CRÈME PÂTISSIÈRE:-**
400 ml full-fat milk
1 vanilla pod
4 egg yolks
100 g caster sugar
Zest of 1 lemon
25 g '00' flour
10 g cornstarch

300 g raspberries or wild strawberries (or a mixture of berries of your choice), to serve

To make the pastry dough and blind bake the pastry case, follow the instructions for Maria's marmalade, mascarpone and almond tart (p. 196).

While your pastry case is cooling, make the crème pâtissière (essentially a thick, flour-based egg custard) by putting the milk in a small saucepan. Split the vanilla pod in half lengthways and scrape the seeds into the milk, discarding the pod. Bring the milk to boiling point and remove from the heat immediately, setting it to one side to cool a little.

Whisk the egg yolks with the sugar and lemon zest in a large bowl until very thick and pale – this will take about 2 minutes using an electric mixer or hand-held electric beaters. Whisk in the flour and cornstarch.

Whisk the hot milk into the egg yolks and flour, then pour the mixture back into the pan. Over a medium heat, continue to whisk until it comes to the boil. Turn down the heat and cook for another 1–2 minutes, whisking constantly until the custard has cooked and thickened. At this point, the custard will hold the shape of the trail left by the whisk. Remove the pan from the heat to a cool surface, and keep mixing for a few more minutes. Allow the crème pâtissière to cool before assembling your tart.

Spoon your room-temperature crème pâtissière into the cooled pastry case, spreading it evenly with the back of the spoon. Put the filled tart in the fridge for 30 minutes to firm up.

Once the custard has set, retrieve your tart from the fridge. Starting from the outer edge, lay the berries in a circular pattern on top of the custard, working your way to the middle. I do this with wild strawberries or whole raspberries, but you can use whatever berries you have available and arrange them in any pattern you wish. Allow the tart to cool in the fridge for a few hours before serving.

# SPRING MENU

### MENU 1

Artichoke and béchamel pie . . . p. 101

Radicchio, cannellini bean and hazelnut salad . . . p. 246

Broad beans and pecorino . . . . . . . . . . . . p. 89

A plate of prosciutto San Daniele

Boiled new potatoes with mint

Coffee and chocolates

❀❀❀

*(Serve all at once, for everyone
to help themselves)*

❀❀❀

### MENU 2

Potato and onion frittata . . . p. 110

Slow-roasted San Marzano tomatoes . . . . . . . . . . . . . . . . . p. 250

Buffalo mozzarella with grilled aubergine and summery green sauce . . . p. 137

Peppery green salad . . . . . . . . . . . . . . . . . p. 244

Lemony aioli . . . p. 255

Maria's marmalade, mascarpone and almond tart . . . p. 196

### MENU 3

Crostini with broad beans, mint and ricotta . . . p. 86

Slow-cooked lamb shoulder with garlic, herbs and lemon . . . . . . . . . . . . . . . p. 112

New potatoes with baby artichokes . . . p. 263

Chard wilted in a pan and dressed in lemon and oil . . . p. 258

Radicchio, cannellini bean and hazelnut salad . . . . . . . . . . . . . . . . . p. 246

Custard and berry tart . . . . . . . . . p. 116

### MENU 4

Ricotta and asparagus tart . . . p. 106

A plate of finocchiona and prosciutto San Daniele

Radicchio, cannellini bean and hazelnut salad . . . . . . . . . . . . . . . . . . . . . p. 246

Slow-roasted San Marzano tomatoes . . . . . . . . . . . . . . . . . . . p. 250

Peppery green salad . . . . . . . . . . . . . . . p. 244

Flourless chocolate, almond and chilli cake . . . p. 115

## A FEW FAVOURITE SPRING DINNERS

**MENU 1**

**TO START**

Artichoke, parmesan and rocket salad . . . . . . . p. 90

**TO FOLLOW**

Spinach and ricotta malfatti with butter and sage . . . . . . . . . . . p. 94

**TO FINISH**

Flourless chocolate, almond and chilli cake . . . . . . . . . . . . . . . . . . . . . . . . . . . . . . . . . . . . . p. 115

**MENU 2**

**TO START**

Pea and mint soup . . . p. 92

**TO FOLLOW**

Roast beef with green sauce . . . p. 109

Balsamic-glazed lentils with pancetta and cloves . . . p. 249

Baked endive and radicchio . . . p. 259

Peppery green salad . . . p. 244

**TO FINISH**

Custard and berry tart . . . p. 116

**MENU 3**

**TO START**

Broad beans and pecorino . . . p. 89

**TO FOLLOW**

Roast pork loin with wine and herbs . . . p. 192 (variation)

New potatoes with baby artichokes . . . p. 263

Baked endive and radicchio . . . p. 259

**TO FINISH**

Lime and basil ice cream . . . p. 154

**MENU 4**

**TO START**

Crostini with broad beans, mint and ricotta . . . . . . . . . . . p. 86

**TO FOLLOW**

Homemade tagliatelle with spring peas . . . . . . . . . . . . . . . . . . . . . . . . . p. 98

**TO FINISH**

Roast peaches with bay and Grand Marnier cream . . . . . . . . . . . . . . . . . . . . . . . . p. 158

**OR**

Cardamom poached pears . . . . . . . . . . . . . . . . . . . . . . . . . . . . . . . . . . . . . . . . . . . . . . . . . . p. 232

*(depending on what fruit is available at the store)*

# SUMMER

ESTATE

As the warmth of spring begins to give way to a fierce heat at the start of summer, outdoor living becomes the norm at Arniano. The sun, a comfort on one's skin during spring, is suddenly fierce – and too strong to sit in for any great length of time without using a high-factor sunscreen. The days in June are wonderfully long as the summer solstice comes and goes, and it is the start of evenings spent chatting on the terrace, sitting or lying on the iron daybeds designed by my mother, with drinks placed on the stone table built by my father. The hills, which for a time have still retained the brilliant green of spring, rapidly turn the colour of burnt sienna as the grass and meadows are scorched by the sun. The ground becomes hard and cracked underfoot, and the thick, hot air smells of herbs and drying wood. After a long absence, the invisible cicadas begin their incessant creaking as the temperatures rise in June, marking the beginning of the comforting soundtrack of summer, their cacophony of croaks becoming more insistent as the sun gets hotter.

Spending any time outside in the garden during the day means finding a shady spot in which to languish, while trying one's best to get on with whatever work or life admin is required (or, when time allows, to read a good book or chat to house guests). Relief from the heat can always be sought indoors, as the thick stone walls of the house keep it mercifully cool. When the midday sun is at its least forgiving, stepping into the kitchen to assemble lunch is like crossing over into a cool oasis.

Early rising is important if you are to get anything done, particularly the food shop, or a visit to the market, where the stalls are a riot of colour. Enormous watermelons, the length of my arm, are sold in chunks – the vendor wielding a rather alarming machete as he asks you how much you would like. Peaches, nectarines and plums dot the displays like tempting sweets, and deep red cherries are out in all their glory – expensive, but delicious and moreish. All the summer vegetables that have a familiar, year-round 'version' – aubergines, courgettes and tomatoes – suddenly triple or quadruple in variety, and you find yourself spoilt for choice. As well as the deep purple aubergines that are always available, there are round, violet-coloured ones from Sicily (much sweeter and more flavoursome), and albino ones, the colour of pale eggshell – as well as stripy aubergines that seem to be a cross between both of these. The same goes for courgettes. In addition to the usual long, dark-green courgettes, there are round, pale-green ones, others that are canary yellow and some that are stripy white and lime, as well as a uniform pale-green variety – all with the typical yellow flower sprouting from their base, perfect for deep-frying or whacking in a risotto. Tomatoes, of course, are a whole other thing in the summer, so much more flavoursome and wonderful at this time of year when compared with what we buy in winter. Their superiority at this time means you can blend and juice them to make a simple but exquisite chilled soup, *Acqua di pomodoro* (literally, tomato water). Again, the colours, sizes and shapes available in summer vary hugely, and I've been told the more misshapen the tomato, the tastier it is.

I like making pasta for lunch in the summer. It's always a hit if people are staying, as pasta has the ability to make people happy – and why come to Italy if not to eat pasta in the sunshine? Most of the pasta sauces I prepare at this time of year only require cooking for as long as it takes the pasta to boil; or they are uncooked, more like salads. It's all about minimising time spent over a hot stove, and included here in this season's recipes are the pasta dishes that I find perfect for entertaining without ending up in a hot fluster.

Meals at this time of year are a smorgasbord of salads: courgette carpaccio, the famous caprese, prosciutto with the first figs, and a delicious pasta or savoury tart showing off the best of the summer veg – all dishes that can be thrown together without too much fuss or any hot-making movements. Any tarts that are made are always prepared with shop-bought pastry, as trying to grapple with homemade pastry in these temperatures is a sure-fire way to inspire summer madness.

Cool drinks are a must, and jugs of sparkling water laced with mint and lemon are a mercy. As is cool, crisp, dry white wine, and on an indulgent day I might even imitate my favourite restaurant in Positano by pouring the wine into a jug in the morning and adding chunks of fresh, ripe peaches. The fruit-laced wine will then be perfectly cold in time for lunch under the pergola, overlooking the now honey-coloured landscape that shimmers in the heat rising from the ground.

Being located on a remote hill, in a UNESCO World Heritage site, where no new buildings can be constructed, we are lucky to have very little light pollution, and with this comes an almost endless view of the night sky littered with stars. By August, the main after-dinner activity is to lay cushions on the lawn – by now, brown and spikey from the long periods of dry heat and no rain – and watch for shooting stars, a common sight at this time of year.

In June and July, Italians battle through the heat during the week, going to work and getting on with life, even when there are weather warnings of heatwaves telling them to stay indoors. This is the norm, and all are used to it. The business of life does not diminish with the heat – though many people will nip to the coast to swim in the sea at the weekends. August, though, is a different story. This is the month in which no one is reasonably expected to work, and every Italian is to be found at the beach. Family businesses, which for eleven months of the year are open six days a week, almost all close on 1 August, and the family will take a well-deserved month off. Ferragosto, a national holiday celebrated on 15 August, is sacrosanct, and in inland regions you will struggle to find a restaurant, newsagent, pharmacy or any other type of shop open the week preceding or following this day. Around Arniano, restaurateurs have realised the potential footfall of tourists visiting Tuscany in August, and so have capitulated by moving their month off to September or October – but fifteen years ago, it would have been difficult to eat out if you were staying in the area. Personally, I find it too hot to leave the compound, the only exception being to drive ninety minutes south-west to the beach for a refreshing swim in the Mediterranean.

**OPPOSITE**

– The hall table, adorned with olive branches and other greenery foraged from the woods. Dada's Panama hat sits under a framed painting by Phyllipa Gulden.

*'La Bomba'*

# WATERMELON COCKTAIL

'La Bomba' was my father's signature party trick in the 70s and 80s. His friends still talk to me about it with a smile, then a grimace, then a shake of the head, describing it as a drink to be made 'only when one has nothing to do the next day'. I think this is because, as with all fruit punches, the sweetness of the watermelon when chilled makes the alcohol content seem much less than it really is, giving the impression that you are sipping on an innocent glass of juice. Making a Bomba is quite a performance, but offers a nice excuse to get into the cool of the kitchen. By the time my sister and I were old enough to drink, my dad only had a few opportunities to show us how to do it - but we still make it every summer for friends and guests.

The name 'La Bomba' comes from its similarity to an underwater mine: my dad would drive holes in a circle around the top of the watermelon and stick straws into them so everyone could take a sip simultaneously. Although I love this look, I don't use plastic straws, and I find that cardboard ones disintegrate. My sister got around our single-use plastic phobia by buying a wonderful contraption, essentially a keg tap for watermelons, which makes the whole presentation even more theatrical. If you don't have one of these marvellous but slightly one-dimensional-in-usefulness pieces of kit, you can make do by lifting the lid and using a ladle.

PREPARATION:- 45 minutes, plus 2 hours chilling

**MAKES 15 COCKTAILS**

**1 large watermelon (should yield about 3 litres of juice)**

**200 ml good-quality vodka (or to taste)**

**150 ml good-quality dark rum (or to taste)**

**150 ml crème de banane (banana liqueur) (optional)**

**Mint sprigs, to serve**

Using a sharp knife, trim about half a centimetre from the bottom of your watermelon, so that it can stand upright without toppling over. Be careful not to cut into the red flesh.

Stand it upright. Using a sharp knife, cut a zigzag pattern all the way around the top to create a lid – the zigzag cuts will stop the lid sliding off. With each cut, make sure the knife goes right through the skin and deep into the red flesh so that you will be able to lift the lid off easily.

Once you've gone all the way around, lift off the lid. With a large spoon, scoop out the flesh into a separate bowl. Once you have an empty shell, blitz the flesh in batches in a food processor to make a pulp. Strain the pulp through a fine mesh strainer, using the back of a spoon to help force the juice out. Once you have a large bowl of lovely, strained juice, discard the pulp and pips. In the same bowl, combine the watermelon juice with the vodka, rum and crème de banane.

If you are using a watermelon keg tap, this is the moment to install it in the empty shell as per instructions.

Fill the watermelon shell with the cocktail, pop the lid on, and put it in the fridge to chill for 2 hours. Serve the chilled cocktail in glasses with ice and a sprig of mint.

*Frittura di fiori di zucca, salvia e mozzarelline*

# FRIED COURGETTE FLOWERS, SAGE LEAVES AND MINI MOZZARELLAS WITH LEMON ZEST

Fried courgette flowers and sage leaves is a classic and well-loved dish in our region. As is the case for anything deep-fried, really. A restaurant near us even serves pieces of deep-fried bread dough as an appetiser. Deep-frying is undoubtedly a faff – but whenever I serve this *frittura* at our painting courses it is always such a hit that I try to make it for at least one *aperitivo*. I usually allow one courgette flower per person, simply to cut down on the time I spend at the fryer, but if you are more patient than I, or have a deep-fat fryer fit for purpose, then feel free to make as many as you like. As an appetiser this dish is quite rich, which is important to bear in mind when planning the rest of the menu. Although it might sound heavy for a hot summer's evening, there is something lovely about drinking a cold glass of wine outdoors while crunching on a fried courgette flower.

PREPARATION:- 15 minutes
FRYING:- 25 minutes

**SERVES 6**

**FOR THE BATTER:-**

150 g '00' flour

200 ml fizzy water, chilled

100 ml beer, chilled

1 teaspoon olive oil

Salt

6 large courgette flowers (if only small flowers are available, increase the number)

18 sage leaves (feel free to add more leaves)

12 (7 g each) mini fior di latte mozzarellas

30 g '00' flour

Salt

1.5 litres vegetable or sunflower oil, for deep-frying

Maldon sea salt, to serve

Zest of 2 lemons, to serve

Chilli flakes, to serve (optional)

### MAKING THE BATTER

Sift the flour into a metal bowl. Add the water, beer, olive oil and a generous pinch of salt and gently whisk together until you have a smooth, amalgamated batter. Put the batter in the fridge to rest for 10 minutes while you prepare your other ingredients.

### PREPARING AND DEEP-FRYING THE COURGETTES

Gently prise open the courgette flowers and pinch out the stamen. If the stalk is very long, trim it back to about 3 cm from the base of the flower. Set the flowers aside in a bowl. Put the sage leaves in a separate bowl.

Drain the mozzarella balls and dry them thoroughly with a clean tea towel. In a bowl, mix the flour with a generous pinch of salt. Toss the mozzarella balls in the flour and then set them aside until you are ready to deep-fry.

Pour the vegetable oil into a deep, heavy-based saucepan set over a high heat and allow the oil to come up to deep-frying temperature. This will take about 10 minutes – do not leave the oil unattended during this time.

While the oil heats up, place a layer of kitchen paper on a large serving plate in preparation for draining the batches of *frittura*. The paper will soak up any excess oil. Retrieve the batter from the fridge and set the bowl alongside the other ingredients.

To check that the oil is hot enough for deep-frying, drop a small amount of batter in the oil – if it begins to sizzle, you can start frying. Start by deep-frying the sage leaves. Take each one by the stalk and dip it into the batter, so that the leaf is fully submerged. Give it a shake to remove any excess batter, then gently drop the coated leaf into the oil. Allow the sage leaves to fry for 30–40 seconds on each side, until they are a light golden colour, turning them with tongs or a slotted spoon. Make sure to fry in batches and take care not to overcrowd the pan.

Once each batch is ready, use tongs or a slotted spoon to carefully transfer the leaves to the serving plate lined with kitchen paper. Lay another sheet of kitchen paper over the sage leaves, in readiness for the first batch of deep-fried courgette flowers that will be placed on top.

Dip the courgette blossom in the batter, shaking off any excess, and gently pinch and twist the ends of the petals so they don't open out when frying. Deep-fry the courgette flowers for 60–90 seconds on each side (slightly less time if the flowers are small), until they are a golden colour. Give the flowers a light shake as you remove them from the pan, to allow any excess oil to drip off. Transfer them to the serving plate, covering each batch of deep-fried flowers with a sheet of kitchen paper.

Dip the floured mini mozzarellas into the batter and gently drop them into the oil. Fry for 50–60 seconds before transferring them to the serving plate. Don't fry for any longer than this, as their batter 'jackets' will slip off. Cover each batch of deep-fried mozzarella balls with a sheet of kitchen paper.

Once you have fried all your ingredients, remove the kitchen paper layers from the serving plate. Season the *frittura* generously with Maldon salt, and scatter with the lemon zest and (if using) chilli flakes. Serve immediately, or within 30 minutes of frying, along with a chilled glass of wine or prosecco, a pile of napkins and a group of good friends.

*Acqua di pomodoro con basilico e mozzarella di bufala*

# TOMATO 'WATER' WITH BUFFALO MOZZARELLA

This dish is a special one for me, as it was served as the appetiser at our wedding. Five years on, people still speak to me about it and long to know how to make it. It affords the opportunity to enjoy the holy trinity of flavour combinations - tomatoes, basil and mozzarella - in a chilled soup format, which is refreshing and delicious while also being a little different. The *Acqua di pomodoro* will keep in the fridge for up to five days - and it freezes well too. Blending the tomatoes for several minutes means you can skip the arduous task of peeling them, though if you have the patience (which I don't) feel free to add this step by scoring a cross at the top and bottom of each tomato and pouring a full kettle of boiling water over the tomatoes in a deep saucepan. Then drain, and peel the tomato skin away from the cross.

**PREPARATION:- 30 minutes, plus at least 2 hours chilling**

**SERVES 6**

**3 kg large, juicy tomatoes (the tastiest you can find – ask your greengrocer)**

**Salt**

**A handful of basil, leaves and stalks – plus extra leaves, to serve**

**3 large (125–150 g each) balls of buffalo mozzarella, to serve**

**Olive oil, to serve**

Roughly chop the tomatoes and put them in batches into a high-speed blender or food processor, blending for 3–5 minutes until thoroughly liquidised. Remove the blended tomatoes to a bowl as you go.

Pass the pulp through a Mouli, placed over a bowl – if you don't have a Mouli, sieve the puréed tomato flesh through a mesh strainer, pressing down with the back of a spoon to help extract the liquid. Repeat the Mouli or sieving process to make sure that all of the pulp is left behind. Discard the pulp. You should be left with about 1.5 litres to 2 litres of *Acqua di pomodoro*. Add two generous pinches of salt and a handful of basil. Put it in the fridge to chill for at least 2 hours, until ready to serve.

Retrieve the *Acqua di pomodoro* from the fridge and remove the basil. Pour two ladlefuls into each serving bowl and put a quarter of a mozzarella ball in the centre of each bowl. Top with a few basil leaves, a drizzle of olive oil and a pinch of salt.

---

**DELICIOUS WITH:-**

This soup is a fabulous starter on a warm summer's night. Follow with cold Roast beef with green sauce (p. 109), served with some roast potatoes and a summery salad such as Courgette carpaccio (p. 134). Alternatively, you could serve it before a plate of pasta, such as Fusilli with Sicilian almond pesto (p. 140), or its northern counterpart, Trofie with pesto and cherry tomatoes (p. 138).

*Insalata di pesche, mozzarella e menta*

# PEACH, MOZZARELLA AND MINT SALAD

**PREPARATION:–** 10 minutes

**SERVES 6**

3 peaches, ripe but firm

2 large (about 150 g each) balls of buffalo mozzarella

250 g rocket

A handful of mint leaves, roughly chopped – plus extra whole leaves, to serve

60 ml olive oil

½ lemon

Salt

Cut each peach into quarters, remove the stone and slice each quarter into four slivers. Set to one side while you prepare the rest of the ingredients. If you are preparing the peaches ahead of time, squeeze some lemon juice over the slices and keep them in the fridge for up to 2 hours, until you are ready to assemble the salad.

Drain the mozzarella and roughly tear the balls into small pieces. Pat with a tea towel or kitchen paper to remove any excess moisture.

In a large salad bowl, gently toss the peaches, mozzarella, rocket and mint with the oil, a squeeze of lemon and a generous pinch of salt. Taste for seasoning and adjust as necessary. Top with whole mint leaves and serve.

**DELICIOUS WITH:–**

This rich salad is wonderful served as part of a wider meal, with a plate of prosciutto, Grated carrots with lemon and basil (p. 245) and Courgette carpaccio (p. 134), or as a starter before Spaghetti with datterini tomatoes and basil (p. 141). Finish off with some Lime and basil ice cream (p. 154).

*Carpaccio di zucchini*

# COURGETTE CARPACCIO

A fresh and pretty salad, ready in 10 minutes. You can keep the carpaccio in the fridge undressed for a couple of hours, and toss it with oil and lemon juice just before serving. If I can find them, I like to make this with green and yellow courgettes for an assortment of pleasing colours.

**PREPARATION:– 10 minutes**

**SERVES 6**

**3 large courgettes (a mix of yellow and green, if possible)**

**3 tablespoons olive oil**

**Juice of ½ lemon**

**Salt**

**Freshly ground black pepper**

**A few mint leaves, roughly chopped, to serve**

**Zest of 1 lemon, to serve**

**Chilli flakes, to serve**

Using a potato peeler, peel a long strip all the way down the side of one of the courgettes, to form a flat 'base'. Put the courgette cut side down on a clean chopping board – it should sit there without rolling onto its side. Holding the courgette in place on the board with one hand, use the potato peeler to peel away ribbons of courgette, putting these into a serving bowl as you go. This process will get trickier towards the bottom of each courgette – you will be left with about a centimetre that you aren't able to slice using the peeler. Don't worry, simply set this piece aside to chop up later. Repeat with all the courgettes.

Take the courgette ends and use a sharp knife to slice them lengthways into fine matchsticks, for added texture. Put them into the bowl with the ribbons. You can pop your prepared courgettes in the fridge, undressed, until ready to serve.

In a bowl, mix together the oil, lemon juice, a generous pinch of salt and some grinds of black pepper. When it is time to serve the carpaccio, toss the courgettes with the dressing, and top with the mint, lemon zest and chilli flakes.

> **DELICIOUS WITH:–**
>
> These refreshing ribbons go well served alongside Grilled chicken breast with lemon and thyme (p. 147), Buffalo mozzarella with grilled aubergine and summery green sauce (p. 137) and Linguine with lemon, ricotta and basil (p. 143).

*Melanzane alla griglia con mozzarella e salsa verde estiva*

# BUFFALO MOZZARELLA WITH GRILLED AUBERGINE AND SUMMERY GREEN SAUCE

On a boiling August day, there is nothing I enjoy eating so much as aubergine and mozzarella. The bitter nightshade flavours of the aubergine, combined with the milky yet sour mozzarella, make this a 'meaty' but refreshing lunch dish. My favourite aubergines are the violet spheres that grow in Sicily. These have all the texture and deliciousness of the more common dark purple aubergine, while being milder and sweeter in flavour.

The dressing is my mother's summery version of a green sauce; it is less punchy than the usual Italian *salsa verde*, as it omits the anchovy.

I love the sourness of buffalo mozzarella, but if you prefer to pair your grilled aubergine with something creamier, feel free to substitute burrata. I sometimes add courgettes to the dish - if you would like to do this, cook them in the same way as the aubergine.

PREPARATION:- 10 minutes
GRILLING:- 30 minutes

**SERVES 4-6**

**4 large aubergines**

**4 tablespoons olive oil – plus extra, to serve**

**Juice of ½ lemon**

**A handful of basil leaves, finely chopped – plus extra, to serve (optional)**

**A handful of flat-leaf parsley leaves, finely chopped**

**1 teaspoon capers, finely chopped**

**2 garlic cloves, peeled and crushed**

**Salt**

**2 large (150–200 g each) balls of buffalo mozzarella**

Slice the aubergines evenly into thin discs, about ½ cm thick. This will be much easier if you give your knife a really good sharpen beforehand. If your knife wobbles and you cut some uneven slices, or a few come out as half-discs, don't worry – they will still taste delicious, and you can hide them underneath their prettier counterparts when you lay them out on a serving plate.

Set a chargrill pan over a high heat and wait for the pan to get piping hot. When you can feel heat radiating from the metal, put as many aubergine discs in the pan as will fit in one layer and leave them to grill. This process requires patience, as you need to do it in batches. The beauty of grilling is that you don't need any oil to cook the vegetables (whether they be aubergines or courgettes).

After about 5 minutes, check the underside of the aubergine, using a pair of tongs to lift up the slices. Once there are deep black stripes etched into the bottom of the discs, flip them over and cook for 2–3 minutes. When the other side is suitably blackened and a little charred, transfer the aubergine slices to a plate, and cook the rest in batches.

While the aubergine slices are grilling (and continuing to keep an eye on them), make the dressing. Put the olive oil and lemon juice in a bowl, and add the finely chopped basil, parsley and capers, the crushed garlic and a pinch of salt. Stir together, then taste and adjust the seasoning and acidity as preferred.

Move to a serving dish and start by placing the grilled aubergine slices around the outer edge of the plate, then keep arranging more discs in a circular pattern, slightly overlapping them, working towards the centre of the plate. Of course, this has no effect on the taste – I just like how it looks.

Place the drained whole balls of mozzarella in the centre of the plate of aubergine and, if you like, garnish with a basil leaf. Douse the aubergine thoroughly with the dressing. Drizzle some good-quality olive oil over the whole dish before serving.

# TROFIE WITH PESTO AND CHERRY TOMATOES

While I know that pesto is a world-famous sauce, I eat it so regularly myself, and serve it so often to crowds of delighted guests at Arniano, that it would be a pity to skip it here for the sake of originality. It is also a fantastic dish to serve to large numbers of people - you can pre-make a big batch of pesto and pour it over large quantities of pasta - and as part of a broader meal, as it goes with lots of things. *Pesto alla senese* features chopped raw cherry tomatoes added to the traditional sauce. Although I can't remember whether the following recipe is an 'official' Siennese variation, this is what it has always been called in our house. Trofie are pleasing short twists of pasta from Liguria, but you can of course use any short pasta shape. I also love fusilli with this pesto.

**PREPARATION:- 10 minutes**
**COOKING:- 10 minutes**

**SERVES 5-6**

150 g basil leaves, stalks removed

50 g pine nuts

2 garlic cloves, peeled

Salt

150 ml olive oil

100 g parmesan, finely grated – plus extra, to serve

500 g trofie (or your preferred short dry pasta)

250 g cherry tomatoes, halved

Put the basil leaves, pine nuts, garlic, a pinch of salt and the olive oil in a food processor. Blitz until you have a runny paste. Transfer to a bowl. (You can freeze your pesto at this stage, before adding the parmesan.) Using a spoon, mix the grated parmesan through the paste until thoroughly combined. Taste for seasoning, adjusting as necessary. If it looks a little dry, add another drizzle of oil, and stir again. This pesto sauce will keep in the fridge for up to 3 days, but is most vibrantly green when used fresh.

Bring a large pan of salted water to a vigorous boil. Add the trofie or your preferred pasta and cook until al dente.

When the pasta is almost ready, spoon the pesto into a large serving dish or bowl. Using a slotted spoon, transfer the trofie to the serving dish and mix the pasta through the pesto, pouring over half a ladleful of the pasta cooking water if the pesto needs any help to thoroughly coat the pasta. Toss the cherry tomato halves through the pasta and serve immediately, with extra grated parmesan on the side.

---

**DELICIOUS WITH:-**

Buffalo mozzarella with grilled aubergine and summery green sauce (p. 137) and Peppery green salad (p. 244).
A bowl of *pasta al pesto* also goes very well with a large platter of good-quality finocchiona served alongside.

# FUSILLI WITH SICILIAN ALMOND PESTO

Another delicious raw pasta sauce – this time the Sicilian take on pesto, from the province of Trapani. I first had this dish on the Aeolian island of Salina and now often serve it to our guests at Arniano on a hot summer's day.

**PREPARATION:– 10 minutes, plus 30 minutes resting**
**COOKING:– 10 minutes**

**SERVES 5-6**

100 g blanched almonds

Salt

100 g basil leaves, stalks removed

2 garlic cloves, peeled

120 ml olive oil – plus extra, to serve

100 g cherry tomatoes

40 g parmesan, finely grated – plus extra, to serve

500 g fusilli (preferably De Cecco no. 34)

Put the almonds and a pinch of salt in a food processor and blitz until roughly chopped. Transfer the nuts to a bowl and set aside.

Put the basil, garlic, olive oil, tomatoes and a pinch of salt in the food processor and blitz until the mixture becomes smooth and velvety. Add this to the bowl of almonds and fold it through, along with the parmesan and another drizzle of oil. Set aside and allow the flavours to amalgamate for at least half an hour.

Toward the end of this time, cook the pasta. Bring a large pan of salted water to a galloping boil. Add the fusilli, stirring to stop the pasta sticking together, and cook until al dente.

When the pasta is almost ready, spoon the pesto into a large serving dish or bowl. Using a slotted spoon, transfer the fusilli to the serving bowl, adding a little of the pasta cooking water if the sauce needs loosening. Toss the fusilli through the sauce, add another tablespoon of the cooking water, drizzle with olive oil, top with some grated parmesan and serve immediately.

# SPAGHETTI WITH DATTERINI TOMATOES AND BASIL

This is my go-to dish when I want to rustle up a tasty meal for a group, big or small. The short, gentle cooking allows the tomatoes to retain a little of their acidity, just when they are on the edge of losing it and becoming entirely sweet.

**PREPARATION:–** 10 minutes
**COOKING:–** 15 minutes

**SERVES 5-6**

600 g datterini tomatoes or a mixture of various cherry tomatoes (if you can find some yellow ones, they are delicious to mix through as well)

Salt

4 tablespoons olive oil – plus extra, to serve

A generous handful of basil leaves

500 g spaghetti (preferably De Cecco no. 12)

Parmesan, finely grated, to serve

Place a medium-sized frying pan next to the chopping board where you will be halving your cherry tomatoes. As you halve them (using a serrated knife), pop them straight into the pan before moving it to the heat – this will save you washing up another bowl.

When all the halved tomatoes are in the pan, add two generous pinches of salt and pour the olive oil over the tomatoes. Using your hands, roughly tear up the basil leaves (discarding the stalks) and put them directly into the frying pan. Gently mix the basil in with the tomatoes, oil and salt. Set the pan over a medium-low heat and cook the tomatoes for 5–10 minutes, allowing them to virtually 'melt' into the oil. Stir the sauce occasionally, and very gently, ensuring that you don't squash too many of the tomatoes. At the end of the cooking time, some of the tomatoes should have disintegrated into a liquid sauce, with others retaining their shape. Take the sauce off the heat and taste, adding another pinch of salt and a drizzle of oil if needed.

While the tomatoes are cooking, put a large pan of salted water on to boil, ready for the pasta. Once the water has come to a galloping boil and the tomatoes are ready, tip the packet of spaghetti into the boiling water. Wait a few seconds and then give the spaghetti a good stir to ensure the pasta doesn't stick together. Cook until al dente.

When the spaghetti is ready, use tongs to transfer the pasta, as well as a little of the pasta cooking water, to the pan of tomatoes. Once all the spaghetti is in the pan, mix it into the tomatoes so that each strand is slick with the sauce, and drizzle with a little fresh olive oil. Transfer to a serving bowl, top with a generous grating of parmesan and serve.

*Linguine con limone, ricotta e basilico*

# LINGUINE WITH LEMON, RICOTTA AND BASIL

**PREPARATION:- 10 minutes**
**COOKING:- 10 minutes**

**SERVES 5-6**

500 g linguine

Juice of 2 lemons

150 g parmesan, finely grated – plus extra, to serve

75 ml olive oil

250 g ricotta

Zest of 4 lemons (use unwaxed Sicilian lemons if possible)

Freshly ground black pepper

Salt

A handful of basil leaves, roughly torn (stalks removed)

Bring a large pan of well-salted water to a lively boil. Add the linguine and cook until al dente.

While the pasta is cooking, put the lemon juice, 50 g parmesan and the olive oil in a bowl and beat together with a fork. Once thoroughly mixed, move the mixture to a serving bowl large enough for the pasta.

In a separate bowl, use a fork to mix the drained ricotta with the lemon zest, the rest of the parmesan, lots of black pepper and a pinch of salt.

Once the pasta is done, use tongs to transfer the linguine to the serving dish and toss it through the lemon juice, parmesan, oil and half a ladleful of the pasta's cooking water. Add the ricotta mixture and basil leaves, and toss through. Add more cooking water if the pasta looks dry. Top with a little extra grated parmesan and lots of black pepper. Serve immediately.

*Penne con pomodorini, cipolla e ricotta*

# PENNE WITH CHERRY TOMATOES, ONIONS AND RICOTTA

A refreshing, versatile summer pasta, which is essentially a warm salad.

**PREPARATION:– 10 minutes**
**COOKING:– 15 minutes**

**SERVES 5-6**

½ red onion, sliced into half-moons

1 teaspoon white wine vinegar

500 g cherry tomatoes (a mix of red and yellow, if you can find them)

1 garlic clove, peeled and very thinly sliced

Salt

200 g ricotta

80 g parmesan, finely grated – plus extra, to serve

Freshly ground black pepper

100 ml olive oil

500 g penne rigate

Soak the sliced onion in a shallow bowl of cold water and vinegar for 15–20 minutes. This will make the onion sweeter and less overpowering.

Put a large pan of well-salted water on to boil.

Chop all of the tomatoes in half and put them in a large serving dish or bowl. Add the thinly sliced garlic, sprinkle with salt, toss to combine and set aside.

Put the drained ricotta and parmesan in a mixing bowl. Season with salt and lots of black pepper to taste. Pour half the olive oil over the ricotta and use a fork to roughly combine.

Once the water is at a lively boil, add the penne rigate and cook until al dente. A few minutes into cooking the pasta, pour the rest of the oil over the tomatoes in the serving bowl and toss through to combine. Drain the onion slices, pat dry with some kitchen paper and add them to the tomatoes and garlic. Using a slotted spoon, transfer the penne to the serving bowl and toss the pasta through the tomatoes, garlic and onion. The hot pasta will cook the tomatoes slightly. If necessary, mix in a tablespoon of the pasta cooking water to loosen the mixture. Add a generous pinch of salt and lots of black pepper.

Leave the penne and tomatoes to cool for a couple of minutes, then mix the ricotta and oil through the pasta. Add a generous drizzle of oil, grind a little more pepper over the pasta, top with grated parmesan and serve.

*Scaloppine di pollo al timo e limone*

# GRILLED CHICKEN BREAST WITH LEMON AND THYME

I have always loved the Italian way of eating chicken. These thin mouthfuls are elegant and appetising, and much less daunting than an entire chicken breast. In Italy, it is possible to buy ready-sliced thin pieces of chicken breast, something that I tried to replicate in the UK in my youth by simply hammering a whole breast with a meat cleaver - chicken mince, anyone? Slicing the chicken into thin *fettine* may sound daunting, but is in fact supremely easy. This dish is a fabulous centrepiece to any lunchtime feast, as it pairs well with all vegetables and is light enough to serve among lots of other dishes, including pasta.

**PREPARATION:-** 5 minutes, plus 1 hour marinating
**COOKING:-** 10 minutes

**SERVES 6**

**800 g chicken breast**

**80 ml olive oil (for coating and frying the chicken) – plus extra, to serve**

**Salt**

**Leaves from a handful of thyme sprigs**

**1 lemon, sliced into thin discs**

**Juice and zest of 1 lemon**

**Freshly ground black pepper**

Using a sharp knife, remove any excess fat from the chicken breast. Then, starting from the side of the breast, slowly slice the chicken in two, slicing horizontally through the breast and lifting the top half back as you go (so you can see where your knife is cutting). Be careful not to head off at an angle and slice diagonally. Once you have two chicken pieces, repeat the process for each of the halves, so that you are left with four thin slices of chicken, each between half a centimetre and 1 cm thick. Repeat with each chicken breast. You could also ask your butcher to do this for you.

Lightly drizzle the bottom of a large plate or roasting dish with a little olive oil, then add the chicken pieces, turning them a few times to make sure they are all evenly coated in the oil. Sprinkle the chicken with salt and the thyme leaves, again turning the pieces to make sure that the seasoning is evenly distributed. Place the lemon slices on top of and underneath the chicken, gently squeezing the lemon so that a little juice coats the meat. Cover with cling film and leave to marinate in the fridge for an hour. Remove from the fridge and allow to come back up to room temperature for 10 minutes, before patting each piece of chicken dry with a kitchen towel so they can brown in the pan.

Lightly coat a chargrill pan or frying pan with oil using a pastry brush (alternatively, you can use a piece of kitchen roll dipped in oil), and set the pan over a high heat. Once the pan is hot, add your first piece of chicken – it should hiss as it hits the metal. You want a short, quick cooking process, which doesn't allow the chicken to dry out.

**DELICIOUS WITH:-**

On a hot summer's day, this is fabulous with Grated carrots with lemon and basil (p. 245), or served to follow a starter of *Acqua di pomodoro* with buffalo mozzarella (p. 130), alongside Mama's roast cherry tomatoes (p. 251), Peppery green salad (p. 244) and Roast potatoes with garlic and rosemary (p. 262).

Don't try to move the chicken around before it has had time to turn a lovely golden brown and release from the pan – otherwise it might tear or stick. When the sides of the chicken start to become opaque and lighter in colour (which usually takes 2–3 minutes), turn the chicken over and cook for a further 1–2 minutes. Once the chicken is done, transfer it to a clean plate and carry on cooking the rest of your chicken pieces in batches. Once done, grill the lemon slices for 1 minute on each side.

Before serving, drizzle the chicken *scaloppine* with a little more olive oil and a squeeze of lemon, and top with the chargrilled lemon slices, zest and black pepper.

*Crostata di pomodorini, timo e mascarpone*

# CHERRY TOMATO, THYME AND MASCARPONE TART

**PREPARATION:- 10 minutes**
**COOKING:- 35 minutes**

**SERVES 6**

**1 rectangular sheet of ready-rolled puff pastry**

**1 egg, lightly beaten (for egg-washing)**

**150 g cherry tomatoes**

**Salt**

**Leaves from a small handful of thyme sprigs**

**100 g mascarpone**

Preheat the oven to 220 °C/200 °C fan-forced.

Unroll the puff pastry and place it on a baking tray lined with baking parchment. Using the tip of a sharp knife, and being careful not to cut straight through the pastry, score a line 1 cm in from the edge of the pastry, all the way around – a neat, raised crust will form as it cooks. Using a pastry brush, egg-wash the pastry and prick all over with a fork. Place the pastry in the fridge while you prepare your tomatoes.

Slice the tomatoes into very thin discs using a serrated knife. Put them in a colander over the sink, so that any excess liquid drains away. Sprinkle the sliced tomatoes generously with salt and half the thyme leaves, and toss through until evenly seasoned. Leave the tomato to sit in the colander for 5 minutes.

Retrieve the pastry from the fridge. Lay the tomatoes out on some kitchen towel and pat dry to remove any excess moisture, before arranging the slices on the pastry base in neat, flat rows, without straying onto the 1 cm edge that you have scored with the knife. Using a teaspoon, neatly dollop small mounds of mascarpone at intervals all over the tomatoes. Sprinkle with the remaining thyme leaves and more salt.

Bake the tart for 10 minutes, then check to see if the pastry has risen. If it has, open the oven and carefully pierce any risen air pockets with a cake tester or the end of a knife to allow steam to escape. Bake for another 10–15 minutes, until the mascarpone is starting to brown on the top and the crust looks crunchy and golden. Remove the tart from the oven and move it to a cooling rack. Allow to cool for 10 minutes before moving to a serving dish.

Serve warm or at room temperature.

**DELICIOUS WITH:-**

This tart is rich and indulgent, and goes perfectly with Courgette carpaccio (p. 134), Grated carrots with lemon and basil (p. 245) and Peppery green salad (p. 244).

# PECORINO TOSCANO

If I close my eyes and picture the view from Arniano, one constant feature in the landscape is sheep. There is always a flock grazing in the lush pastures across the valley, a patch of white against the brilliant, bright green. They are moved from field to field every day by the Sardinian farmer and his six *maremanni* sheepdogs – great, grizzly, white, Tuscan polar bears, which stay out all night to protect the herd from wolves. When the shepherd moves the sheep, he often uses the white dirt road that connects us to the outside world. This means that, if our timing is off, it can take us half an hour to get to the end of the drive, following behind the scraggy herd at sheep's pace in the car. It's always better to meet them head on, when they divide either side of the car and, for a few moments, you find yourself surrounded by a sea of bobbing, woolly heads.

In this part of Tuscany, sheep mean cheese. Their milk is used to produce *pecorino*, literally 'of the sheep', from the Italian word for a sheep, *pecora*. This ancient, round cheese is thought to have originated in Sardinia, although there are now several varieties found throughout Italy. It comes in a range of flavours and textures, and it's important to appreciate the differences. There's the milky and delicate pecorino *fresco*, so wonderful with tender, young broad beans, a grind of pepper and a drizzle of oil. Or the chewy and mellow *semi-stagionato*, usually discernible by its tangerine-coloured rind, which is delicious eaten on its own. Then there's the hard and intense *stagionato*; matured for thirteen months, this pecorino calls for an accompaniment of slices of pear, walnuts, a drizzle of chestnut honey and a large glass of Rosso di Montalcino.

Pecorino production in Tuscany dates back to the Etruscans. This explains why there is so much pecorino around Arniano, which sits on the site of an Etruscan stronghold. Our local village, a tiny, walled hamlet, even has a museum for Etruscan artefacts found in these hills.

Growing up in Tuscany, I had always taken pecorino for granted. When I moved to England as a teenager, I assumed that, come spring, I would still be feasting on broad beans and fresh pecorino. Not so. Which is why, when I was at university in Edinburgh,

I would come home in the holidays and stuff my suitcase full of as many wheels of pecorino as Ryanair would allow (in those days, that was quite a lot, as the cabin allowance was more generous). It is only when you miss a thing that you really think about how special it is. I had never taken in the fact that we had some of the finest local producers of pecorino right on our doorstep.

While this cheese is made throughout Italy, it is generally acknowledged that southern Tuscany boasts the finest quality pecorino. Pienza, the name of the pretty hilltop village about half-an-hour's drive from us, is synonymous with pecorino, and the town's main street is packed with picture-perfect cheese shops selling wheels of the stuff, in every form you could possibly think of. There are stacks of wheels maturing in hay, or fig leaves, or walnut leaves, or covered in peppercorns. We often take the painters to Pienza on a jaunt; this perfect chocolate box of a fortress town is a sight to behold, complete with battlements from which you can ogle one of the most beautiful views in Tuscany, the Val d'Orcia. The town's ancient cathedral hangs precariously over a cliff, so precariously in fact that there is a crack across the marble floor, caused by the land on which it sits lurching downwards. No visit would be complete without a visit to Marusco e Maria, a cheese shop that sells a fiery, chilli-infused pecorino that I am particularly partial to – I like to serve it as an *aperitivo* with drinks in the evening. The spice makes it dangerously moreish, and I often have to ask for it to be taken out of my reach. Apart from this one type, I usually buy pecorino from producers local to us, due to the premium you pay when buying it from the smart shops in Pienza – as well the conspiracy theories pointing out the discrepancy between the number of sheep in the area and the amount of pecorino di Pienza for sale in the world.

When I was at primary school in our local village, Buonconvento, one of my best friends was a boy called Giovanni Chironi. He would often come up to Arniano, and we would play, or – more specifically – 'go on adventures'. There is a black-and-white photo, taken by some sneaky adult, of Giovanni and I setting off on one of these expeditions, dressed in our 'adventure' gear, which featured cowboy hats and chaps. In the picture, Giovanni seems to have confused matters by adding a cape to the ensemble. I would also go for lunch at Giovanni's house, a farm on the other side of Buonconvento, towards Montalcino.

His family were one of the first to arrive in Tuscany from Sardinia in the middle of last century. By the 1960s, it was no longer possible to make a living through cheese production on that impoverished island, and Tuscany experienced a large influx of Sardinian shepherds, who came here in search of better prospects. Giovanni's grandfather arrived in the area in 1963, having made the heartbreaking decision to leave Sardinia with his family, travelling for three days to reach the port where he could make the crossing to Talamone in southern Tuscany, accompanied by two small sons, 200 sheep and several sheepdogs.

That was the decade that saw Tuscany's native tenant farmers flocking to Italy's industrial cities in search of better-paid jobs. Many of the beautiful farmhouses that are dotted throughout the countryside – so coveted today – had been completely abandoned in favour of work in city factories. Giovanni's grandfather bought one of these houses, where the family still live today. Fifty years on, Giovanni joined forces with his two brothers and his father to carry on their family's cheese-making tradition; over the past ten years, the Chironis have been producing some very fine pecorinos on their organic farm, Fior di Montalcino.

I used to love going to Giovanni's house for lunch after school. Their home was cosy, and his family so kind to me as a fellow 'outsider', with the warmest smiles. Their farm was exciting: there were sheep and cows, and his mother used to make the famous Sardinian flatbread, *carasau*. I was also fascinated by his parents' accent, so different from that of Tuscany, where everyone drops their 'c's (Italians from other parts of the country will gleefully ask Tuscans to say 'Coca Cola', which invariably comes out as 'Hoha hola').

The atmosphere of the family-run farm still has not changed since I was seven years old. To get there from Arniano, you drive towards the hilltop town of Montalcino, forever a presence in our landscape. Arriving at the farm involves driving along a dirt track, past a wonderful avenue of cypress trees; by the time you get halfway down the drive, you are more than likely to bump into Giovanni's brother Pietro heading off to Buonconvento on his tractor, or their eldest brother Francesco and his children as they play with their favourite donkey. On reaching the farmhouse and parking your car, you are welcomed by many dogs and the sound of bleating sheep in the barns.

What was once the open terrace where we did our homework as children is now Giovanni's cheese room, with Willy Wonka-scale equipment. On entering, you are swept up by Giovanni's irrepressible enthusiasm, as abundant now as it was when we were at primary school. The room has huge windows, which allow Giovanni to look upon the glorious surrounding countryside as he singlehandedly produces 150 cheeses a day, his only company a blasting radio – and, occasionally, Rosa, who makes the yoghurts and panna cottas that are shipped out to many a boutique hotel throughout Tuscany.

The farm is fully organic, and zero waste. They produce all the grains, oats, hay and wheat that their sheep eat. I have watched Giovanni put these principles into action as he makes a soft cheese, retaining the excess whey to make ricotta, and feeding anything that is left over to the pigs.

Unlike family-run farms in many parts of the world, the Chironis' story is one of slow but incremental growth and prosperity. They seem to need to expand this family business every two years or so, with Giovanni converting rooms in the house to accommodate his ever-expanding production. He recently created a whole new aging room, cavernous and lined with specially constructed wooden shelves, which he has designed himself to store, aerate and mature the cheeses. The old barn is being turned into a beautiful tasting room, where tourists will be able to come and sample products, all the while looking out towards the farm's amazing view.

---

**A FEW PECORINO TOSCANO RECIPES:-**

- Broad beans and pecorino (p. 89)
- Ricotta, black olive and basil tart (p. 153)
- Pear, rocket, pecorino and walnut salad (p. 175)

*Torta salata di ricotta, olive e basilico*

# RICOTTA, BLACK OLIVE AND BASIL TART

**PREPARATION:- 20 minutes**
**COOKING:- 40 minutes**

**SERVES 6**

1 rectangular sheet of ready-rolled shortcrust pastry

500 g ricotta

1 tablespoon olive oil

45 g parmesan, finely grated

Salt

Freshly ground black pepper

¼ whole nutmeg, finely grated

150 g pitted black olives, drained and roughly chopped

A handful of basil leaves, roughly torn

3 eggs

40 g semi-matured pecorino, finely grated, as topping for the tart

Preheat the oven to 220 °C/200 °C fan-forced.

Butter or line a 25 cm tart tin and place the pastry sheet in the tin, trimming off any excess pastry. Line the pastry case with baking parchment that you have scrunched in your hand and then flattened out. Fill the lined pastry with baking beads, dried beans or rice, and then blind bake for 15 minutes. Take the tin out of the oven, remove the beads and baking parchment, and bake the pastry for a further 5 minutes, until the bottom of the pastry case has completely dried out and is uniformly golden.

Remove the pastry from the oven and set it aside to cool while you make the filling. Turn the oven down to 180 °C/160 °C fan-forced.

Put the drained ricotta in a large metal bowl and break it up with a fork. Using the fork, beat in the olive oil until it is fully incorporated with the ricotta. Add the parmesan, salt, pepper and finely grated nutmeg, and combine thoroughly. Mix in the chopped olives and basil leaves. Taste for seasoning, adding more salt, pepper or nutmeg as preferred, then beat in the eggs, one by one.

Once you have prepared the pastry case and the ricotta filling, you can keep them in the fridge for up to a day before assembling the *torta*.

Pour the ricotta mixture into the cooled pastry shell, spreading it evenly and smoothing it with the back of a spoon. Top with the grated pecorino. Bake for 25–30 minutes, until the top of the tart starts to brown and there is still a gentle wobble at its centre.

Remove the tart tin from the oven and place it on a wire cooling rack. When it is cool enough to handle, transfer the tart to a plate, ready to serve.

**DELICIOUS WITH:-**

On a blistering summer's day, serve at room temperature with an array of salads such as Grated carrots with lemon and basil (p. 245), Courgette carpaccio (p. 134) and a plate of velvety prosciutto dolce. When the weather is a little less sweltering, serve warm with Baked endive and radicchio (p. 259), Peppery green salad (p. 244) and maybe some Charred roast potatoes with lemons (p. 265).

*Gelato al lime e basilico*

# LIME AND BASIL ICE CREAM

This flavour is one that used to be served at my favourite *gelateria* in Florence. My mum and I loved it so much, and found it so unusual, that we bought a few tubs of it (driving hell for leather the hour and a half home, while it melted in the back of the car) and spent the next two days trying to recreate it perfectly, using shop-bought vanilla ice cream and adding lime zest and basil leaves. I've found that the homemade custard base gives a richer and more indulgent feel and is the perfect vehicle for this unlikely but fabulous flavour combination. I don't have an ice-cream maker, so I just pop the gelato in the freezer and take it out twenty minutes before serving – I always find it to have a lovely texture and flavour. But if you do have an ice-cream maker, by all means, churn away!

PREPARATION:– About 2 hours, plus 3 hours freezing
COOKING:– 30 minutes

**MAKES 1 LITRE OF ICE CREAM, ENOUGH TO SERVE 6**

800 ml double cream

250 ml full-fat milk

2 vanilla pods

8 egg yolks

180 g caster sugar

Zest of 5 limes and juice of 2 limes

45 g basil leaves, finely chopped with a sharp knife

Put the cream and milk in a saucepan (choose one with a lid). Halve the vanilla pods lengthways and scrape the seeds into the pan, discarding the pods. Set the pan over a medium heat and remove from the heat just as the cream and milk mixture is about to come to the boil. Set aside to cool a little.

Put the egg yolks and sugar into a large bowl, then whisk using an electric mixer or hand-held electric beaters until the mixture is very thick and pale.

Bit by bit, pour the warm cream and milk into the sugar and egg mixture, stirring with a wooden spoon as you go. Once it is thoroughly combined, return the mixture to the saucepan. Set the pan over a medium heat, stirring constantly. The mixture will begin to thicken as the eggs start to cook. Once it is on the edge of coming to the boil, remove the custard from the heat and move the pan to a cool surface. Stir the custard constantly for about 5 minutes to ensure it stays smooth.

Cover the pan with the lid and allow the custard to cool down for about 15 minutes, stirring frequently. Add the lime zest and juice, and the chopped basil leaves, and stir them through. Cover the custard again, then set it aside for 1–2 hours to cool completely. During this time the flavours will develop and amalgamate.

Transfer the cooled custard to a shallow container, making sure the basil is evenly distributed. Put it in the freezer for at least 3 hours. Or, if you have an ice-cream maker, churn as instructed before putting it in the freezer.

Twenty minutes before serving, take the ice cream out of the freezer to soften a little. Scoop it into individual bowls and eat with a teaspoon.

*Insalata di mele, cioccolato e menta di Rossana*

# ROSSANA'S APPLE, CHOCOLATE AND MINT SALAD

Rossana has been the housekeeper at Arniano since my parents bought the house in 1989. Her main job when I was little was to take care of guests during the summer, when we would visit family in England and the house would be rented out. Rossana would make breakfast for the renters and generally make sure everything looked lovely. She has been both a steward of our family and caretaker of Arniano during our long periods of absence in the years since my father died. She invented this salad one summer morning when everyone was too hot to speak. I often make this as a dessert in summer, as it's crunchy, a little sweet and very refreshing.

**PREPARATION:- 10 minutes**

**SERVES 6**

3 crunchy apples

120 g dark chocolate

10 mint leaves

300 g Greek yoghurt, to serve

1 tablespoon runny honey, to serve

Peel, quarter and core the apples, then slice them thinly. On a round serving plate, arrange the apple slices in a pattern of concentric circles, slightly overlapping the slices.

Finely grate the chocolate over the apples and dot with the mint leaves. Serve this dessert on its own, or with a dollop of Greek yoghurt and runny honey.

*Pesche al forno con alloro e crema al Grand Marnier*

# ROAST PEACHES WITH BAY AND GRAND MARNIER CREAM

**PREPARATION:- 10 minutes**
**COOKING:- 30 minutes**

**SERVES 6**

**FOR THE PEACHES:-**
60 g blanched almonds

200 ml Grand Marnier

60 g brown sugar – plus extra, for roasting the peaches

25 ml olive oil

25 ml maple syrup or runny honey

6 peaches, ripe but firm

4 bay leaves

**FOR THE CREAM:-**
1 tablespoon Grand Marnier

250 g double cream

Preheat the oven to 200 °C/180 °C fan-forced.

Spread the almonds on a baking tray and toast them in the oven for 10 minutes, until they just start to brown. Remove from the oven and set aside to cool completely.

Put the Grand Marnier and sugar in a small pan and set over a medium heat, stirring to dissolve the sugar. Bring to the boil and allow to bubble for 5 minutes to burn off some of the alcohol. Remove the pan from the heat and stir in the oil and maple syrup.

Cut each peach in half and remove the stone. Place the peach halves cut side up in an ovenproof dish and add the bay leaves. Pour the Grand Marnier syrup over the peaches, then sprinkle them with a little more sugar. Bake in the oven for 25 minutes, or until the liquid is bubbling and the tops of the peaches are browning. Baste the peaches with the cooking liquid halfway through roasting.

In the meantime, mix the Grand Marnier and double cream in a bowl, and keep in the fridge until ready to serve. Roughly chop the cooled almonds.

Remove the peaches from the oven. Serve warm or at room temperature, with a spoonful of their sweet and sticky cooking liquid, a sprinkling of roasted almonds and a dollop of Grand Marnier cream.

# SUMMER MENU

## A FEW FAVOURITE INFORMAL SUMMER LUNCHES

### MENU 1

Fusilli with Sicilian almond pesto . . . p. 140

Cherry tomatoes with burrata

Peppery green salad . . . . . . . . . . . . . p. 244

Courgette carpaccio . . . . . . . . . p. 134

Lime and basil ice cream . . . . . . . . . . . . . p. 154

*(Serve all at once, for everyone to help themselves)*

### MENU 2

Peach, mozzarella and mint salad . . . p. 133

A plate of prosciutto San Daniele

Grated carrots with lemon and basil . . . p. 245

Trofie with pesto and cherry tomatoes . . . p. 138

Rossana's apple, chocolate and mint salad . . . p. 157

### MENU 3

Cherry tomato, thyme
and mascarpone tart
. . . . . . . . . . . . . . . . . . . p. 148

Peppery green salad
. . . . . . . . . . . . . . . . . . . p. 244

Fennel and orange salad
. . . . . . . . . . . . . . . . . . . p. 256

A plate of finocchiona
and prosciutto

Roast peaches with bay
and Grand Marnier cream
. . . . . . . . . . . . . . . . . . . p. 158

### MENU 4

Linguine with lemon, ricotta
and basil . . . p. 143

Peach, mozzarella and mint salad
. . . p. 133

Peppery green salad . . . . . . . . p. 244

A bowl of cherries,
with coffee and dark chocolates

## A FEW FAVOURITE SUMMER DINNERS

**MENU 1**

**TO START**

*Acqua di pomodoro* with buffalo mozzarella . . . . . . . p. 130

**TO FOLLOW**

Grilled chicken breast with lemon and thyme . . . . . . . . . . . p. 147

Roast potatoes with garlic and rosemary . . . . . p. 262

Grilled aubergine with summery green sauce (without the mozzarella) . . . p. 137

**TO FINISH**

Roast peaches with bay and Grand Marnier cream . . . . . . . . . . . p. 158

**MENU 2**

**TO START**

Fried courgette flowers, sage leaves and mini mozzarellas with lemon zest . . . p. 128

**TO FOLLOW**

Spaghetti with datterini tomatoes and basil . . . . . . . . . . . p. 141

Buffalo mozzarella with grilled aubergine and summery green sauce . . . p. 137

Baked fennel with white wine . . . . . p. 260

Peppery green salad . . . p. 244

**TO FINISH**

Lime and basil ice cream . . . p. 154

**MENU 3**

**TO START**

Peach, mozzarella and mint salad . . . . . . . . . . . p. 133

**TO FOLLOW**

Ricotta, black olive and basil tart . . . p. 153

Charred roast potatoes with lemons . . . p. 265

Mama's roast cherry tomatoes . . . p. 251

**TO FINISH**

Flourless chocolate, almond and chilli cake . . . . . . . . . . . p. 115

**MENU 4**

**TO START** Penne with cherry tomatoes, onions and ricotta . . . p. 144

**TO FOLLOW** Grilled chicken breast with lemon and thyme . . . . . p. 147

Slow-roasted San Marzano tomatoes . . . . . . . . . . . . . . . . . . . p. 250

Balsamic-glazed lentils with pancetta and cloves . . . p. 249

Peppery green salad . . . . . . . . . . . . . . . . . . . . . . . . . . . . . . . p. 244

**TO FINISH** A bowl of cherries, with coffee and chocolates

# AUTUMN

AUTUNNO

The transition from summer to autumn is often abrupt. One moment you are eating dinners outside without giving a thought to the temperature, meeting friends at specifically cool times of day to avoid going out in the most vicious moments of summer heat, and then – all of a sudden - outdoor dining takes on a decided chill in the evening. It's still possible, but a warm shawl or a jumper needs to be worn, and there is a 'goodbye to summer' feeling in the air. In this area, that is because the next three months will be about hard work, turning the fruition of Tuscany's bounty into lucrative exports: wine (Brunello being the most lucrative), olive oil, mushrooms and white truffles.

*La vendemmia*, the wine harvest, doesn't have an exact date – the grapes are harvested when they are ready, and very clever *enologi* (oenologists) are paid fortunes to pinpoint that moment – but roughly speaking, it is in the second half of September. When I was at school here, every year we would be taken on a class trip to 'help' with the harvest. Picking grapes is fun for the first few hours, but after that it is such hard work that I am amazed as an adult that tourists come and pay to participate. Perhaps it is just that the novelty of the practice wore off for me many years ago.

More interesting to me is the olive harvest, also hard work (though less so than grape picking), but yielding one of my favourite things: peppery, fluorescent-green, new season's oil. I can happily spend hours among the olives, drawing the fruit away from the branches with my hands to cascade down onto the nets that we've laid on the ground. After which we weigh our bounty, before taking the olives to the *frantoio* (olive press) to be pressed and turned into oil.

And there are mushrooms to be foraged. The rich and meaty porcini that grow in the woods attract many a mushroom hunter at this time of year – you will see them stomping about in wellies with their walking sticks, carrying wicker baskets in which to bring home their spoils. There is a specific etiquette to mushroom picking: you have the right to search for them and pick them in your own *comune*, or municipality, but in order to cross into another *comune*'s woods, you need to have a permit from the mushroom pickers' co-op, which can be obtained by Tuscan residents for the princely sum of €25 p.a.

Then, of course, there is the hallowed white truffle. This earthy, magical truffle is famous throughout the world, and its season here in Tuscany runs from around mid-October to the last day of December. *Tartufai*, or truffle hunters, own truffle reserves in the woods surrounding Arniano – more specifically, in the area's valleys, as the white truffle likes to grow in damp and dark conditions. The weather throughout the preceding twelve months will determine whether it will be a 'good'

– A corner of the sitting
room. The benches along
the wall were converted from
old feeding troughs from
the days when the house
was a farm. The painting by
David Marrian depicts the
nearby church of Sant'Antimo
(as described on page 274) –
though set in a Kenyan
landscape, oddly enough.

or 'bad' year for these subterranean fungi, or indeed a 'fantastic' or 'terrible' year – the likelihood of any of these scenarios is a hot topic of conversation among the Tuscans during this time.

Aside from all of the aforementioned excitements that autumn brings, this season is often spectacularly beautiful. The sunshine is much more reliable from September until the end of November than it is in April or May, and if you dare dip a toe in the sea, it will be warmer than in the spring, having been heated by the sun throughout the summer. It was for this reason that we began offering painting courses in October – the colours of the landscape are glorious, and lunch outside is possible more often than not. It has been a joy to watch our painters' autumnal colour palettes develop, and I love being able to prepare dishes with the bounty that the area brings.

I remember first realising that November was my favourite month in Tuscany when I was eighteen. I was with my dad, and we were visiting the truffle fair in San Giovanni d'Asso, which is held in mid-November. The sky was cornflower blue, the sunlight low – but warm and bright – and I remember feeling complete contentment looking out across the valley at the woods, a riot of canary yellow and umber leaves, as I ate tagliolini with truffle from a plastic plate, bought for €15 at one of the stalls.

November remains my favourite month in Tuscany. When I picture November, I picture picking olives with our friends Carolina and Nicola, and having lunch outside in the sunshine as the yellow leaves of the lime tree outside the kitchen fall around us – eating crunchy crostini topped with porcini that Nicola nipped into the woods to pick as we were harvesting the olives, and drinking wine carefully chosen by Carolina (whom I met on our first day at primary school), now a sommelier at a nearby winery. November is her moment of rest after a busy summer and an even busier *vendemmia*. We chat and laugh, feeling lucky and full under the autumnal skies, downing a quick coffee before heading back to the olives to crack on with the picking.

The recipes in the following pages reflect the energy of autumn. These dishes are what I feel like eating throughout the season, and in some cases they champion ingredients that are only available at this time of year.

# SIDECAR COCKTAIL

This simple but rewarding cocktail is adapted from *The Savoy Cocktail Book*, a copy of which lives permanently on the bar at Arniano. Our version adds egg whites, and it's always a hit with our painters. Matthew's favourite game when serving is to ask those unfamiliar with this cocktail to guess the main ingredients. Hardly anybody can believe that it is 50 per cent brandy. This is why I think it is such a good cocktail: the individual ingredients blend seamlessly together to create a completely new flavour, such that no single component stands out. Adding fresh egg white gives a nice frothy finish.

PREPARATION :- **10 minutes**

**MAKES 4**

**100 ml fresh lemon juice**

**100 ml Cointreau**

**200 ml brandy**

**2 egg whites**

Fill a 500 ml cocktail shaker with ice. Pour in the lemon juice, Cointreau, brandy and egg whites, put the lid on and shake well. Strain into cocktail glasses, removing the lid to spoon some of the froth left in the shaker onto the cocktail.

In terms of ratios, the rule is 25 per cent lemon juice, 25 per cent Cointreau, 50 per cent brandy, plus as much egg white as you like – I like my cocktails nice and frothy, and so include plenty.

*Crostini con porcini al rosmarino e prosecco*

# CROSTINI WITH PORCINI, ROSEMARY AND PROSECCO

**PREPARATION:- 10 minutes**
**COOKING:- 15 minutes**

**SERVES 6**

**350 g fresh porcini**

**6 large slices of white sourdough (preferably a little stale), cut 1 cm thick**

**2 tablespoons olive oil – plus extra, for cooking mushrooms and to serve**

**20 g unsalted butter**

**1 garlic clove, peeled and crushed**

**Salt**

**A large handful of rosemary leaves, finely chopped**

**150 ml dry prosecco**

Preheat the oven to 120 °C/100 °C fan-forced.

Clean the porcini, using a clean brush or tea towel to rub away any dirt. Cut away any roots. (This may have been done for you by the time you buy them.) You should be left with about 300 g once cleaned and prepped. Dice the mushrooms into 1 cm cubes and set aside.

Place the pieces of bread on a baking tray and toast in the oven for about 5 minutes, until golden. Flip each piece over and toast the other side for another 3–5 minutes, until the bread is completely dry and crunchy.

Put the oil, butter, garlic and a pinch of salt in a wide, heavy-based pan over a medium heat, allowing the butter to melt slowly. Once the butter starts sizzling, add half the rosemary and gently fry for 5 minutes. Add the mushrooms, along with the rest of the rosemary and another glug of olive oil. Stir to make sure that all the mushrooms are evenly coated in the oil and butter, and leave to cook for 2–3 minutes. Resist the temptation to stir too much, as the mushrooms will lose their texture and become slimy.

Pour the prosecco over the mushrooms, stir, and increase the heat to high. Shaking the pan occasionally, allow 5 minutes for the alcohol to evaporate and the mushrooms to cook, then remove the pan from the heat.

Drizzle some good-quality olive oil onto each of the crostini, sprinkle with a pinch of salt, then spoon the cooked porcini onto the bread. Serve immediately.

*La fettunta*

# CROSTINI WITH THE NEW SEASON'S OLIVE OIL AND GARLIC

The simplest way to show off *olio nuovo* – new oil – this dish will appear in most restaurants in Tuscany in November. Its name combines the word for 'slice', *fetta*, with the term for 'oily' or 'fatty', *unta*. Made at the right time of year, this humble 'oily slice' is a total pleasure.

**PREPARATION:- 7 minutes**

**SERVES 6**

**6 large slices of white sourdough (preferably a little stale), cut 1 cm thick**

**1 garlic clove, peeled**

**100 ml new season's olive oil**

**Sea salt**

Preheat the oven to 120 °C/100 °C fan-forced.

Place the pieces of bread on a baking tray and toast in the oven for about 5 minutes, until golden. Flip each piece over and toast the other side for another 3–5 minutes, until the bread is completely dry and crunchy.

Remove the crostini from the oven and transfer to a serving plate. Lightly rub each piece with the garlic clove. Drizzle liberally with the new season's oil – its vibrant green colour will contrast beautifully with the golden, toasted crostini. Sprinkle with a little sea salt and eat immediately.

*Insalata di pere, rucola, pecorino e noci*

# PEAR, ROCKET, PECORINO AND WALNUT SALAD

This is a delicious salad, made up of various textures. The pear and walnut make it quite rich, so it is perfect as a starter, or as part of a wider feast of salads and pasta. You can prepare all the separate elements ahead of time and assemble when ready to serve.

**PREPARATION:– 15 minutes**

**SERVES 6**

2 pears, ripe but firm

Juice of ½ lemon – plus extra, to stop pear discolouring

50 ml olive oil

Salt

Freshly ground black pepper

250 g rocket

60 g walnuts, roughly chopped

75 g pecorino *semi-stagionato*, shaved (use a potato peeler to shave thin slices from a piece of pecorino)

Quarter and core the pears. Place each quarter cut side down on a chopping board and slice lengthways into four or five very thin slices. Put the slices in a bowl and toss with a squeeze of lemon to stop the pear from discolouring.

In another bowl, make the dressing by mixing the lemon juice and olive oil with a pinch of salt and a few grinds of black pepper.

Put the rocket in a large salad bowl, add the dressing and toss together. Add the walnuts and toss again. Mix in the pears and top the salad with the pecorino shavings. Serve immediately.

*Prosciutto e fichi*

# PROSCIUTTO WITH FIGS

A joy of late summer and early autumn, I find prosciutto with figs to be even more delicious than its very famous counterpart, *prosciutto e melone* (ham and melon). Figs are more subtle and mellow in their sweetness than melon, and I find they pair beautifully with the almost velvety savouriness of a good prosciutto. The silky, high-quality fat on a prosciutto from Parma or San Daniele obviates the need for oil or any accompanying fat. Everything you need is present in these two ingredients - though if you do feel like drizzling over a little good-quality olive oil, it will, of course, still be delicious.

**PREPARATION:- 5 minutes**

**SERVES 6**

500 g (about 12 slices) prosciutto dolce (Parma or San Daniele)

6 figs

Peel off each slice of prosciutto and arrange on a serving platter. Try to 'drape' the slices on the plate, giving them a little height so that they don't look like they were plonked there straight from the packet.

Slice the figs into quarters, dot them over the plated prosciutto and serve immediately.

*Zuppa di ceci e rosmarino*

# CHICKPEA AND ROSEMARY SOUP

Whenever I make this, I think of Marcella Hazan, who always stresses that the most important part of any dish is its base – essentially, what you do in the first few minutes of cooking. In this recipe, the base is formed by infusing the olive oil with a sprig of rosemary, before gently frying the onions. This is the stage one must never rush, as what happens at this point will dictate the depth of flavour that develops later. It is such a helpful way to look at the process of building up flavour, particularly with soups.

*Zuppa di ceci* is also delicious cold and even tastier the next day. You can make it ahead of time and keep it in the fridge for up to six days, heating it up as and when you need to – just add 50 ml water to loosen it.

**PREPARATION:-** 15 minutes
**COOKING:-** 35 minutes

**SERVES 6**

150 ml olive oil – plus extra, to serve

1 whole rosemary sprig (leaves and stalks)

2 red onions, diced

Salt

Leaves from 4 large rosemary sprigs, finely chopped

5 x 400 g tins chickpeas

300 ml water or vegetable stock

2 x 400 g tins peeled plum tomatoes

Parmesan, to serve

**FOR THE ROSEMARY OIL:-**

100 ml olive oil

1 large rosemary sprig

Begin by heating half the olive oil with the whole sprig of rosemary in a heavy-based pan over a low heat. Using a wooden spoon, move the rosemary around the bottom of the pan for a minute or so until it starts to gently sizzle. Leave to sizzle for 5 minutes, swirling the pan occasionally. You do not want the oil to get so hot that it fries the rosemary.

Turn up the heat to medium, remove the sprig of rosemary, and add the onions and a pinch of salt. Cook until the onion softens and starts to look translucent (this should take just under 5 minutes). Add the chopped rosemary, mixing it in before adding the drained chickpeas. Stir to make sure everything has a good slick of oil over it, then turn down the heat and cook for a few minutes before adding the water or vegetable stock and another pinch of salt. Allow to bubble away over a medium heat for 5 minutes, stirring occasionally, during which time the flavours will amalgamate. Add the tomatoes and cook for a further 20 minutes.

Remove the pan from the heat, add the rest of the olive oil and taste to check the seasoning. If the soup needs it, don't be afraid to add a generous pinch of salt.

Allow the soup to cool for 5 minutes before ladling it into a blender or food processor. Pulse until it reaches a thick, textured consistency, but avoid blending so much that it becomes a smooth purée. You could blend it in two batches so you are more in control. Return to the pan and set aside until serving.

To make the rosemary oil, gently warm the oil and rosemary sprig in a pan over a low heat, and infuse as described above.

Serve each bowlful with a generous sprinkling of parmesan and a drizzle of rosemary olive oil.

**VARIATION:-**

To make *pasta e ceci*, add some cooked pastina or broken-up pieces of spaghetti.

**DELICIOUS WITH:-**

If you and your co-diners are feeling hungry, a basic bruschetta is an excellent addition to this meal - use it to scoop up your soup. To make the bruschetta, toast a piece of bread in the oven, lightly rub the top with a peeled garlic clove and drizzle with olive oil.
This soup is also a wonderful main after Pear, rocket, pecorino and walnut salad (p. 175) or as a starter before Roast chicken with grapes (p. 188).

*Le mie 'penne alla Bettola'*

# MY PENNE 'ALLA BETTOLA', WITH TOMATO AND VODKA

**DELICIOUS WITH:-**

This dish is very rich. Precede with a plate of Crostini with porcini, rosemary and prosecco (p. 172) or Prosciutto with figs (p. 176). Finish off with some Cardamom poached pears (p. 232), Berry clafoutis with Amalfi lemon cream (p. 199) or *affogato* - vanilla ice cream 'drowned' in coffee (p. 200).

This dish is my imitation of the famous house dish of creamy tomato penne cooked with vodka that is served at Alla Vecchia Bettola, a fabulous restaurant in Florence. I devised this recipe in a fit of desperate craving - at a time when I was not in Florence and unable to go to the restaurant.

What's unusual and delicious about the Alla Vecchia Bettola dish is the use of 'smooth' penne lisce, meaning that there aren't any ridges for the sauce to cling to. For that reason, the final stage of cooking the penne happens *in* the sauce, so that the pasta soaks up the tomato, chilli and vodka. For the pasta to be al dente, it's vital that you only cook the penne in boiling water for two-thirds of the time recommended on the packet, before transferring it to the pan with the sauce for the last third of the cooking process. For instance, De Cecco penne will take 11 minutes to cook al dente; I would therefore cook the pasta in boiling water for 7-8 minutes and transfer the penne to the sauce for the last 2-3 minutes.

**PREPARATION:- A couple of minutes to organise the ingredients**
**COOKING:- 1 hour**

**SERVES 6**

½ tablespoon chilli flakes

1 clove garlic, peeled and crushed

60 ml olive oil

1 bottle (680–700 g) tomato passata

Salt

120 ml vodka

200 ml single cream

500 g penne lisce (smooth) or penne rigate (ridged)

60 g parmesan, grated – plus extra, to serve

A handful of flat-leaf parsley leaves, roughly chopped, to serve

In a large frying pan, gently heat the chilli flakes and garlic in the oil for 3–5 minutes over a medium heat. Allow the garlic to infuse, but do not let it brown. Add the bottle of passata to the chilli and garlic, together with a generous pinch of salt. Half-fill the bottle with water, swish it around to pick up any remaining passata and pour the tomatoey water into the pan. Cook for 25 minutes, stirring occasionally, until the liquid has reduced by a third.

Put a large pan of well-salted water on to boil.

Pour the vodka into the reduced liquid, stir and then increase the heat to high. Allow to bubble for 5 minutes, so that the alcohol evaporates, then reduce the heat to medium-low and cook for another 15 minutes, stirring occasionally. Stir in the cream and switch to a low heat while the pasta cooks.

Once the pasta cooking water is at a lively boil, add the penne. After the pasta has been cooking for 8 minutes, use a slotted spoon to transfer the pasta from the water to the tomato sauce. Add a ladleful of the starchy pasta cooking water if the sauce looks like it needs help to fully coat the pasta. Turn up the heat and allow to bubble and cook for a further 3 minutes, then stir in the parmesan.

Remove the pasta from the heat and transfer to a serving bowl. Top with a little chopped parsley and some freshly grated parmesan. Serve immediately.

*Sformato di ricotta con pomodoro e basilico*

# BAKED RICOTTA WITH OLIVE OIL, TOMATO AND BASIL

A *sformato* is a cross between a soufflé and a savoury flan. Made of ricotta and eggs, it doesn't contain beaten egg whites, making it less airy than a soufflé - but then again, there is no need to worry about it collapsing. As served in restaurants, a *sformato* will often contain a vegetable purée. I've had them with asparagus, spinach, broad beans and even aubergine, usually smothered in a rich béchamel sauce. This ricotta *sformato* recipe is a little lighter than some, and works particularly well with the sharp acidity of the tomatoes in the sauce. It is also good with a variety of other sauces, including ragù in winter, or fresh broad beans and mint in spring.

You will need a ring mould for this dish to be a proper show stopper - and for the drama of the tomato sauce running from the central well as you cut into the *sformato*. But you can of course also make it in whatever non-stick container you have to hand in your kitchen, and simply pour the tomato sauce over the top.

**PREPARATION:- 25 minutes**
**COOKING:- 30 minutes**

**SERVES 6**

**FOR THE TOMATO SAUCE:-**

1 garlic clove, left unpeeled, gently squashed with the edge of a large knife

90 g basil, leaves and stalks – plus extra leaves, to serve

2 tablespoons olive oil

Salt

500 g tomato passata

**FOR THE SFORMATO:-**

500 g ricotta

150 ml olive oil

Salt

Freshly ground black pepper

70 g parmesan, finely grated – plus extra, to coat the ring mould and to serve

½ whole nutmeg, finely grated

Zest of ½ lemon

3 large eggs

Preheat the oven to 170 °C/150 °C fan-forced.

Gently warm the garlic clove, basil and olive oil in a frying pan over a low heat for 2–3 minutes, allowing the garlic and basil to infuse into the oil. Add a pinch of salt, followed by the passata. Half fill the bottle with water, swish it around to pick up any remaining passata and pour the tomatoey water into the pan. Allow to bubble for 10–15 minutes, stirring occasionally and tasting as you go. Switch off the heat and set the sauce to one side. Fish out the clove of garlic and discard.

Put the drained ricotta in a mixing bowl and break it up using an electric mixer or hand-held electric beaters. Slowly add the olive oil, bit by bit, whisking in between additions and allowing the ricotta to absorb the oil before adding more. Once you have a loose, velvety mixture, add two pinches of salt, a generous grind of black pepper and all the other *sformato* ingredients except the eggs, and whisk well. Taste and adjust the seasoning as required, before whisking in the eggs, one by one.

Butter a 20 cm ring mould. Sprinkle a little parmesan into the mould, tilting it to ensure that the sides and base are evenly coated. Pour the *sformato* mixture into the mould, levelling it out with the back of a spoon. Bake for 25–30 minutes, until a cake tester comes out clean(ish). Remove the baked ricotta from the oven and set aside for a few minutes to cool a little. Gently reheat the tomato sauce.

Place a serving plate over the mould and invert the baked ricotta onto the plate. Fill the centre with the reheated tomato sauce. If any excess liquid gathers at the base of the baked ricotta, dab it with kitchen paper. Sprinkle with grated parmesan and arrange some basil leaves on top for decoration before serving.

**DELICIOUS WITH:-**

*Sformato* is a wonderful starter before Roast beef with green sauce (p. 109), or in fact any meat dish. It can also be served as part of a wider feast, which might include Radicchio, cannellini bean and hazelnut salad (p. 246), Baked endive and radicchio (p. 259), a plate of prosciutto dolce or finocchiona, and Grated carrots with lemon and basil (p. 245).

**VARIATION:-**

You can fill the baked ricotta with any sauce you like – for instance, ragù in the winter – but a wonderful spring alternative is to fill the centre with broad beans, cooked and dressed as described in Crostini with broad beans, mint and ricotta (p. 86).

# OLIO NUOVO

 Go into any restaurant in Tuscany in late October and early November, and you will notice that the diners are divided into two groups. I don't mean physically. But some share a secret that the others don't. The first group are those who are happy with the standard bottle of olive oil left for them on the table, alongside the usual salt cellar, pepper grinder and basket of unsalted Tuscan bread. They are usually mostly interested in ordering, or having a look at the wine list, oblivious to the fact that there is a superior product available to them if only they knew to ask. The second group are those who eye up the bottle of olive oil left for them, and judge it wanting. These people will call the waiter over to their table and demand '*Olio nuovo*,' saying the words as though they were a password. Restaurants rarely dole out the new season's olive oil unless it is specifically asked for – why waste this precious, emerald-coloured nectar on people who are indifferent? A few moments will pass before the waiter returns, presenting these in-the-know diners with a labelless bottle of dark-green liquid – at times so vividly coloured it is almost neon – accompanied by a conspiratorial look. This bottle will be sniffed, and the contents poured with great interest onto a plate. The diners will then observe its colour and consistency, before scooping it up with bread or some raw vegetables, exclaiming as to its potency, colour, pepperiness and flavour.

---

**A FEW OLIO NUOVO RECIPES:-**

- Crostini with the new season's olive oil and garlic (p. 173)
- Breadless ribollita (p. 212)
- Blood orange and olive oil upside-down cake (p. 235)

New oil, which is pressed between late October and mid-December, is revered stuff to Tuscans, and is certainly not the oil you would pop in the pan to cook with. Its consistency is thicker than the olive oil you buy in the supermarket, and when just pressed it has a lively colour and peppery flavour; both of these qualities mellow over the course of the year, and the oil becomes the sweeter, paler stuff we are used to. Tuscans like to make the most of the short-lived moment when the new oil's flavour and colour are at their best. Restaurants celebrate new oil with two dishes in particular: *fettunta*, stale toasted bread, rubbed with garlic and dressed in liberal amounts of new oil; and *pinzominio*, a selection of raw vegetables (artichoke, fennel, radishes) beautifully chopped and presented alongside a bowl of new oil and a mound of salt.

With most things in Italy, different regions will proclaim that their version of anything is the best. In Liguria, the olive oil is famous for its mellow, subtle flavour, whereas in Tuscany the olive oil is hardy and robust, making it well suited to the meaty and bean-heavy dishes so typical of the area. This is partly due to the fact that Tuscans harvest their olives much earlier in the season than most areas of Italy, as they love the acid-green colour, and the peppery, bitter and almost fiery oil this yields.

Alessandro Nannetti runs our local *frantoio* (olive press), 4 kilometres down the road, where my father always took our olives to be turned into olive oil. He says the reason Tuscan oil is so special is that you taste so such more than just the bitterness: 'Tuscan olive oil carries a million shades and nuances in its flavour. Part of that is the way that we structure the olive groves, the soil and the harvest. But it is also due to the entire ecosystem of the area. In Tuscan olive oil you can taste not just the bitter olive, but the grass where it was grown; there is a hint of artichoke, and all the other flowers and plants that the pollinators carry. It's not a monoculture, but a whole variety of factors that influence the flavour.'

Olive oil is so ubiquitous in Mediterranean cooking that it is easy to forget that olives are fruits, grown in orchards, which are cared for, tended and harvested when perfectly ripened – though there is much debate as to when that moment is. Olive groves aren't made up of just one variety of olive tree, but will usually have three or four, contributing to the oil's rich flavour and aiding cross-pollination. The Correggiola olive is responsible for the oil's green colour; the Leccino grows a blacker olive, packed full of flavour and a little bitter; Moraiolo olives are fresh and sweet; and those of the Frantoio cultivar are slightly astringent and add a hint of artichoke. Tuscan olive oil is usually a blend of the fruits of all of these different trees, which contribute to the million shades and nuances that Alessandro describes.

The harvesting period is one of intense busyness for *frantoie* throughout Italy and the rest of the Mediterranean. Frantoio Etrusco is no exception, as can be attested by the relentless whir of activity surrounding the building when we drive past to buy the paper or on our return from a late dinner with friends. A large, unassuming tin warehouse, the *frantoio* sits just off the main road at the foot of a pretty hill on the outskirts of our local village. Between October and December, it hums with industry, pressing olives by appointment 24 hours a day.

Drive up to Frantoio Etrusco, and you will see the hustle and bustle of pick-up trucks coming and going, their khaki-clad owners unloading their homegrown olives, picked that morning or the day before at the most. Everyone clamours to press their olives as quickly as possible, and all are on the alert for queue barging, or – disaster of disasters – their olives being mixed in with someone else's.

The clientele is a mixture of farmers who wish to press their olives in order to sell their oil commercially, and families – like us – who have just enough olive trees to yield them just enough oil to last them the year. Not using sauces or butter in their cooking as the French do, most families in Tuscany get through 1 or 2 litres of olive oil a week (well, ours certainly does). Provided you have few enough olive trees that you don't need to employ anyone to help you pick them, growing olives for your own use – or to share with friends – can be cost efficient.

For an olive oil to be considered 'extra virgin' – as it is when pressed at Frantoio Etrusco – it must be cold-pressed, including both the pulp and pip of the olive and never exceeding a temperature of 27 °C at any point during pressing. When you bring your olives to the *frantoio*, they will be loaded onto a conveyor belt, and a blower will be used to separate the fruit from the much lighter stems and leaves. The olives are then rinsed in cold water, and sent to a large machine made up of six chambers – each one containing a different client's olives. Every client's batch will differ slightly in colour, depending on the maturity and variety of their bounty. Within these chambers, the entire olive is mechanically crushed and churned for 45 minutes, kept constantly in motion so that the pulp separates from the oil. The air in the room is heady and thick, the bitter but beguiling scent of oil hitting you in the back of the throat and making you long for a piece of bread drenched in the stuff. At the end of the pressing and extraction process, the water and the solid parts of the olives are discarded, and a vivid green liquid emerges from a tap. The olive oil is ready. It is caught in 30-litre stainless-steel barrels, and each client's quantity will either be delivered to their home (in its entirety) to be decanted as and when needed, or will be bottled by one of Alessandro's team.

In order to book a slot for your olives to be pressed you pay a small fee per kilo of olives – you must have a minimum of 150 kilograms of freshly picked olives for pressing. This is about the amount that we grow at Arniano on our forty-odd trees. Our olives take two people two full eight-hour days to pick. The amount of oil this will yield varies year to year, but generally we get about 25 litres. Needless to say that in a region where olive groves are everywhere, 150 kilograms is considered a measly amount. Most locals bring a few *quintali* (1 *quintale* being 100 kilograms) in a good year, and book every one of the six chambers in the press; the olives will be crushed in batches, the machines sometimes operating through the night.

In the season of 2020, the *frantoio* broke its record and pressed 12,000 *quintali* (over a million kilograms) of olives. The previous record of 9000 *quintali* had been set twenty years ago. In November of 2020, it took me 45 minutes to get Alessandro's attention in order to pay my bill, with his phone constantly ringing off the hook. Everyone was inundated with olives. Alessandro hadn't seen a season so bountiful in over thirty years working at the *frantoio*. Consequently, all the presses in the surrounding area were booked solidly, and people from as far away as the other side of Siena were ringing and begging him to give them a slot in the presses, so they wouldn't miss the perfect moment to pick their olives. Thankfully for Alessandro and his wife, this intense period is, as always, followed by nine months of calm, when the olive press stands closed. During this time, the family pop in to man the office and sell the olive oil they have pressed during the season, as well as selling *nocciolino* – the extracted and dried-out olive pips, which can be used as a fuel for heating stoves.

Alessandro's father-in-law set up the village *frantoio* in the late 60s. At that time, it was a much smaller enterprise, run from a workshop in the heart of the town, pressing the olives grown by local farmers and families. In 1975, he started to build the presses that stand today. Things went well for the next ten years, before the infamous Grande Gela (the Great Frost) of 1985, which killed off about 90 per cent of Tuscany's olive groves (including my father's, at my parents' house in Greve). The frost of that year saw many farmers needing to rethink and take stock, as they tried to salvage their plants. For the next half a decade, Tuscany failed to produce even a tenth of its usual olive harvest, and Alessandro's family *frantoio* was closed for almost five years. I can only imagine the conversations taking place among Tuscans throughout the region each autumn in the late 80s, concern on wise old faces, locals shaking their heads bitterly and sighing resignedly at the lack of olives.

When the *frantoio* reopened in 1989, Alessandro and his wife joined the family business to try to help reinvigorate the mill. They decided to invest, to update the machines and expand the premises, renaming themselves Frantoio Etrusco. This was a nod to the Etruscan settlements – famous for their olive oil – that have been discovered in the area, and to the Etruscan archaeological museum in the local hamlet of Murlo.

Reopening was slow work. Many Tuscans had chopped the seemingly dead trees right back, hoping that new shoots would regrow. Thankfully, in many cases they did, although a great number of centuries-old trees were lost. With their elusive silver colour, gnarled trunks and long elegant branches and leaves, olive trees might be strikingly distinctive – but they are a plant like any other and consequently, nearly forty years on from the Grande Gela, they still have good years and bad years. Sometimes absolutely terrible years, during which the price of good oil skyrockets and it is very difficult to get hold of any substantial quantity (2018 and 2019 were two such seasons). Given the international popularity of Italian olive oil, the olive harvest and its resultant product will always be a hot topic of conversation in Tuscany during the autumn.

Conversely, when I lived in the UK I discovered that it was possible to feel removed from the source of the olive oil that is used for cooking and for dressing salads. Seeing the oil neatly packaged up, sitting on supermarket shelves, it is easy to forget that it is the result of a harvest, and that it is not everlasting (olive oil should, in fact, be stored with its lid firmly on, in a dark, cool place, as it is sensitive to light, air and heat). I would also sometimes forget that you should never use olive oil more than eighteen months on from when it was pressed. If you have ever cooked with oil that has been sitting in the back of the cupboard for a long time, the resulting meal will attest to the veracity of this golden rule. Rancid oil does not a good base for a meal make!

*Pollo arrosto con uve bianche*

# ROAST CHICKEN WITH GRAPES

This was the first dish I ever learned to cook, and such is its simplicity that from the age of twelve I was allowed to make it unsupervised. My mother was taught it by Josefa, a Catalan woman who knew my family in Spain. When I was at university, I would make roast chicken with grapes for large gatherings in our apartment in Edinburgh, where it went down incredibly well - people I haven't spoken to since graduating in 2012 still text me occasionally and ask for the recipe.

If you are any more than four people, I recommend roasting two chickens (as in this recipe) and feasting on the leftovers throughout the week. If you are four or fewer, roast one chicken and halve the quantities of the other ingredients.

**PREPARATION:- 5 minutes, plus 1 hour 10 minutes resting**
**COOKING:- 1 hour 20 minutes**

**SERVES 6-12**

**2 large (about 2 kg each) free-range chickens**

**Salt**

**500 g white grapes**

**50 ml olive oil**

Preheat the oven to 200 °C/180 °C fan-forced.

Remove the chickens from the fridge 40 minutes before cooking. Generously season the chickens all over with salt and put them in a large roasting pan. Cover and set aside for 40 minutes, to allow the chickens to come up to room temperature.

At the end of this time, arrange the grapes around the chickens and then pour the oil evenly over the top of the birds and the fruit.

Roast the chickens for 20 minutes, then remove the pan from the oven and check them – they should have a little colour on them, and the grapes should be starting to turn brown. Pour 150 ml water over the chickens and the grapes.

Return the pan to the oven and roast for another 40 minutes, basting the chickens two to three times during the roasting process. Use a large serving spoon to scoop up some of the cooking liquid, and pour this carefully over the chickens (gently lift up one side of the roasting pan to make it easier to collect the pan juices). If the pan dries out as the chickens are cooking, add more water as necessary. After 40 minutes, remove the chickens from the oven and check that the meat has cooked through thoroughly: there should be no pink meat, and the juices should run clear. If the chickens aren't cooked, return them to the oven for a further 15–20 minutes, always keeping an eye on them.

Leaving the grapes in the pan, transfer the chickens to a plate or chopping board, cover them in foil and allow to rest for 30 minutes. Taste the cooking liquid – it should be a wonderful balance of sweet and savoury, the flavours amalgamated and not at all watery, like a sweet gravy. If it is still a little watery, put the pan over a medium heat on the stovetop, and allow the grapes and cooking liquid to bubble away and reduce for about 5 minutes.

Remove the foil and carve the chickens, arranging the pieces on a serving platter. Pour the gravy over the meat, top with the grapes and serve.

**DELICIOUS WITH:-**

Chickpea and rosemary soup (p. 178) is a wonderful starter ahead
of this dish. This chicken also makes a perfect meal served with
Balsamic-glazed lentils with pancetta and cloves (p. 249) or Roast
potatoes with garlic and rosemary (p. 262), along with Peppery
green salad (p. 244) and Mama's roast cherry tomatoes (p. 251).

*Arista al forno con prugne e pinoli*

# ROAST PORK LOIN WITH PRUNES AND PINE NUTS

**PREPARATION:-** 15 minutes, plus 1½ hours resting
**COOKING:-** 1 hour 45 minutes

**SERVES 6**

**700 g organic boneless pork loin (ask your butcher to remove any excess fat or crackling)**

**2 cloves garlic, left unpeeled, gently squashed with the side of a large knife**

**1 whole rosemary sprig (leaves and stalks)**

**Salt**

**250 g pitted prunes, roughly chopped**

**Leaves from 2 rosemary sprigs, finely chopped**

**100 ml olive oil**

**50 g pine nuts**

---

**VARIATION:-**

Apply the process and ingredients (wine and herbs) used for Roast beef (p. 109) to the pork loin, but cook for the same amount of time as the recipe here.

---

One hour before cooking, remove the pork loin from the fridge. If necessary, trim away any excess fat or any layer of fat intended for crackling. Sit the pork on top of the crushed garlic and the whole rosemary sprig in a roasting pan. Lightly spread a layer of salt all over the meat, then cover the pork with a clean tea towel and allow it to rest in its salt coating for 1 hour. Put the pan in the fridge if it's a hot day.

Preheat the oven to 200 °C/180 °C fan-forced.

In a bowl, mix together the prunes, rosemary leaves and a pinch of salt.

Once the meat has rested, use a sharp knife to carefully make incisions all over the pork loin, about 1 cm wide and deep. Take care not to cut straight through the pork to the bottom of the pan, as the meat juices will run out during roasting. Stuff each of the incisions with as much of the prune and rosemary mixture as will fit. Reserve any leftover mixture to add to the pan before roasting.

Put 2 tablespoons of the olive oil in a large, heavy-based frying pan and bring the heat up to high. When the oil is piping hot, brown the pork all over.

Scatter the rest of the prune and rosemary mixture into the roasting tray, leaving the garlic and rosemary sprig in the pan. Place the browned pork back on top and drizzle with the rest of the oil.

Put the pan in the oven and cook for 20 minutes. Remove the pan, pour 250 ml water over the pork, then cover the pan in foil and roast in the oven for a further hour, checking and basting occasionally. Use a large serving spoon to scoop up some of the cooking liquid and pour this carefully over the pork (gently lift up one side of the pan to make it easier to collect the pan juices). If the pan dries out as the pork is roasting, add more water as necessary.

Gently toast the pine nuts in a dry frying pan over a medium heat for 2 minutes, shaking the pan occasionally. Set aside until serving.

Remove the pork from the oven and allow to rest for at least 20 minutes before serving.

Slice the pork as thinly as you can. Arrange the slices on a serving dish, then pour the cooking liquid over the meat. Scatter the roasted prunes over the pork and top with the toasted pine nuts.

---

**DELICIOUS WITH:-**

The pork itself is very rich, so I usually wouldn't serve a starter for this dish, but an abundance of sides makes for a delicious meal. Additions could be Roast potatoes with garlic and rosemary (p. 262), Slow-roasted San Marzano tomatoes (p. 250), Baked endive and radicchio (p. 259) or Greens 'in the pan' with garlic and chilli (p. 258). Maria's marmalade, mascarpone and almond tart (p. 196) would be the perfect end to this meal.

*Tiramisù ai cachi della Chiara*

# CHIARA'S PERSIMMON TIRAMISÙ

Our friend Chiara is the proprietor of Trattoria Cammillo, which serves the best food in Florence. The secret to Cammillo's success lies not only in the wonderful atmosphere and the impeccable service (delivered by waiters in black bow ties, headed by the irrepressible Alan), but also in Chiara's skill in coming up with fascinating new dishes, using whatever's in season, instead of falling back on the usual Tuscan fare. She has a genuine love of food and ingredients, and when not in the kitchen is out scouring Florence and the rest of Italy for the very best suppliers.

The recipe below, which Chiara has kindly shared with me, is typical of her imagination. She takes a classic pudding like tiramisù and elevates it by substituting the usual coffee with lightly blended persimmon (a fruit only briefly in season). I have halved Chiara's quantities, as she is usually cooking for a restaurant full of hungry diners.

**PREPARATION:-** 15 minutes, plus at least 3 hours chilling

**SERVES 12**

150 ml Zibibbo sweet wine or muscat

3 ripe persimmons

100 g caster sugar

750 g mascarpone

1 pack (about 200–250 g) sponge finger biscuits (preferably pavesini, which are lighter than savoiardi)

**DELICIOUS WITH:-**

A wonderful way to end a meal of Roast pork loin with prunes and pine nuts (p. 192) or My penne 'alla Bettola', with tomato and vodka (p. 181).

Mix the Zibibbo and 150 ml water together in a shallow bowl, which should be wide enough to dip the biscuits into. Set to one side until you are ready to assemble the tiramisù.

Quarter the persimmons and use a spoon to gently scoop the flesh from the skin. Discard the skin and transfer the flesh to a large bowl. Using a hand blender, briefly blend the fruit until you have a loose, vibrantly orange-red purée. You don't want it to be completely smooth. Set it to one side.

Using hand-held electric beaters, whisk the sugar and mascarpone together in a large bowl, then gradually begin to add the persimmon purée, bit by bit. Keep back about a third of the purée, for serving. Continue whisking for about 3 minutes, until the purée is fully incorporated with the mascarpone and the mixture becomes light and airy.

Begin assembling the tiramisù. You will need a large, deep serving dish to hold the persimmon mascarpone mixture and the biscuits.

Briefly dip each of the sponge fingers into the Zibibbo and water mix, placing the biscuits in the serving dish as you go. Dip and place as many biscuits as will fit next to one another in one layer in the base of the dish, breaking some up to stuff into any empty nooks as necessary. Spoon half the persimmon mascarpone over the biscuits, spreading it evenly using the back of the spoon. Repeat with another layer of biscuits and cover with the remaining persimmon mascarpone. Cover the tiramisù with tin foil or cling film and put it in the fridge to set for at least 3 hours, or leave in the fridge overnight and consume the next day.

Serve in individual portions with a little of the remaining persimmon pulp on top for decoration.

*La crostata di Maria, all'arancio, mascarpone e mandorle*

# MARIA'S MARMALADE, MASCARPONE AND ALMOND TART

**PREPARATION:-** 1½ hours, plus 2 hours chilling
**COOKING:-** 25 minutes

**SERVES 6-10**

**FOR THE PASTRY:-**

2 egg yolks

2 tablespoons ice-cold water

60 g caster sugar

Salt

240 g '00' flour

140 g unsalted butter, chilled and diced

**FOR THE FILLING:-**

60 g chopped blanched almonds

150 g cream cheese

150 g mascarpone

300 g orange marmalade

**DELICIOUS WITH:-**

The citrusy marmalade and creamy notes of this dessert make it a fabulous finish to most meals, but I particularly love it after Baked ricotta with olive oil, tomato and basil (p. 182) or Roast chicken with grapes (p. 188).

**MAKING THE PASTRY**

Use a fork to gently mix the egg yolks with the ice-cold water in a small bowl. Keep the yolk mixture in the fridge until ready to use.

Mix the sugar and a pinch of salt into the flour. If you are using a food processor, blitz the flour and the diced butter until the mixture resembles breadcrumbs. With the processor running, add the chilled egg yolk and water mixture.

Alternatively, put the flour and butter in a bowl, and rub in the butter using your fingertips. Your hands should be cool and dry when you do this. Once the butter is thoroughly rubbed into the flour and no large lumps remain, add the egg yolk mixture, using a fork or a knife to combine.

Once a roughly unified dough starts to form, tip it out onto a lightly floured surface. Gently bring the large lumps of dough together with your hands, kneading once or twice. Form the ball of dough into a disc shape, wrap it in cling film and leave it to rest in the fridge for 30 minutes to 1 hour.

Preheat the oven to 200°C/180°C fan-forced. Grease a 25 cm tart tin and line the bottom with a disc of baking parchment.

Once the dough has rested, lightly flour the work surface again and start rolling out your pastry. Turn it 90 degrees after each roll, to prevent it from sticking to the surface and to ensure you are rolling it out to an even thickness.

Roll out the pastry until it is about 5 mm thick, then loosely fold the pastry around your rolling pin and gently transfer it to the tart tin. Trim off any excess pastry with a sharp knife and prick the bottom all over with a fork. Put the tin in the freezer for at least 20 minutes, until the pastry is firm to the touch – this will stop the pastry shrinking in the oven.

Retrieve the chilled pastry case from the freezer and line with baking parchment that you have scrunched in your hand and then flattened out. Fill the lined pastry with baking beads, dried beans or rice, and then blind bake for 15 minutes. Take the tin from the oven, remove the baking parchment and beads, and bake for a further 10–15 minutes, until the bottom of the pastry case has completely dried out and is uniformly golden. Remove from the oven and allow it to cool completely in the tin.

**MAKING THE FILLING**

Put the chopped almonds onto a baking tray and toast for 10 minutes, until lightly golden. Remove the nuts from the oven and leave to cool.

Beat the cream cheese and mascarpone together in a mixing bowl. Spoon the mixture evenly into the cooled pastry case, smoothing it out using the back of the spoon. Put the filled tart in the fridge for 1 hour, until the cream cheese layer has set, then gently spread the marmalade over the top. Sprinkle with the chopped almonds. Return the tart to the fridge until you are ready to serve.

*Clafoutis con frutti di bosco e crema al limone*

# BERRY CLAFOUTIS WITH AMALFI LEMON CREAM

While clafoutis is not strictly an Italian dish, this fruity baked pancake always reminds me of a restaurant on the Amalfi coast where I was once served a glorious lemon soufflé. The waiter cracked the soufflé open with a spoon at the table, before pouring a lemony custard into the well that he'd created. This *made* the dish, the cold, citrusy cream pairing perfectly with the hot, steaming dessert. I immediately went home and made a cheat's version, substituting a mixture of ice cream and crème fraîche for the custard, which I poured over a hot clafoutis straight from the oven. If you need to double the quantities given here, make sure to divide the clafoutis mixture between two roasting dishes, otherwise the dessert will be too thick and stodgy. The baking time works well if you remember to put the clafoutis into the oven just as you are about to sit down to eat the first part of your meal.

**PREPARATION:-** 20 minutes
**BAKING:-** 35 minutes

**SERVES 6**

**FOR THE CLAFOUTIS:-**

2 large eggs

90 g caster sugar – plus 1 tablespoon, for sprinkling over the berries

Zest and juice of 1 lemon

75 g '00' flour

200 ml full-fat milk

150 g blackberries or blueberries

**FOR THE LEMON CREAM:-**

150 g vanilla ice cream, softened

100 g crème fraîche

Zest of 1 lemon

Juice of ½ lemon

Preheat the oven to 200 °C/180 °C fan-forced. Butter a 25 cm ovenproof ceramic dish.

Whisk together the eggs and sugar until the mixture becomes thick and pale. Add the lemon zest and flour, and mix together with a wooden spoon until fully combined. Bit by bit, add the milk and lemon juice, whisking as you pour, to amalgamate the liquid. Put the mixture in the fridge for 15 minutes to rest.

While the clafoutis mixture is resting, make the lemon cream. Mix together all the ingredients in a bowl until fully combined. Cover and put in the freezer until ready to serve.

Arrange the berries evenly over the bottom of the buttered ovenproof dish and sprinkle them with a tablespoon of sugar. Pour the clafoutis mixture over the berries. Put the clafoutis in the oven and bake for 35–40 minutes, or until the top is golden and a cake tester comes out clean.

When the clafoutis is ready, remove it from the oven and serve immediately. Spoon each portion into a bowl and top with a spoonful of the half-frozen lemon cream. The cold, citrusy cream will start to melt on top of the hot clafoutis – making this is a heavenly and indulgent dessert.

# Autumn menu

## A FEW FAVOURITE INFORMAL AUTUMN LUNCHES

*(Serve all at once, for everyone to help themselves)*

### MENU 1

Baked ricotta with olive oil, tomato and basil . . . p. 182

Radicchio, cannellini bean and hazelnut salad . . . . . . . . . p. 246

A plate of prosciutto San Daniele, topped with artichokes preserved in oil

Crostini with the new season's olive oil and garlic . . . . . . . . . . . . . . . . . . . . . . . p. 173

Maria's marmalade, mascarpone and almond tart . . . p. 196

### MENU 2

Crostini with cavolo nero and ricotta . . . p. 210

Chickpea and rosemary soup . . . p. 178

Prosciutto with figs . . . p. 176

Grated carrots with lemon and basil . . . . . . . . . . . . . . . . . . p. 245

Peppery green salad . . . p. 244

*Affogato* (vanilla ice cream 'drowned' in coffee) -
to make, pour a freshly brewed shot of espresso over a scoop of vanilla ice cream

### MENU 3

Crostini with porcini, rosemary and prosecco . . . p. 172

My penne 'alla Bettola', with tomato and vodka . . . p. 181

Peppery green salad . . . p. 244

Chiara's persimmon tiramisù . . . . . . . . . . . . . p. 195

### MENU 1

**TO START**

Crostini with cavolo nero and ricotta . . . . . . . p. 210

**TO FOLLOW**

Roast chicken with grapes . . . . . . . . . . p. 188

Balsamic-glazed lentils with pancetta and cloves . . . . p. 249

Mama's roast cherry tomatoes . . . p. 251

Peppery green salad . . . p. 244

**TO FINISH**

Berry clafoutis with Amalfi lemon cream . . . p. 199

### MENU 2

**TO START**

Crostini with porcini, rosemary and prosecco
. . . p. 172

**TO FOLLOW**

Roast pork loin with prunes and pine nuts
. . . p. 192

Roast potatoes with garlic and rosemary
. . . p. 262

Baked endive and radicchio
. . . p. 259

**TO FINISH**

Flourless chocolate, almond and chilli cake
. . . p. 115

### MENU 3

**TO START**

Pear, rocket, pecorino and walnut salad
. . . p. 175

**TO FOLLOW**

Roast beef with green sauce . . . p. 109

Baked fennel with white wine . . . . . p. 260

Polenta . . . . . . p. 266

**TO FINISH**

Blood orange and olive oil
upside-down cake . . . . . . . . p. 235

# WINTER

INVERNO

Because Arniano was our base and home for so long during the years when my sister and I were at school, it is well designed for winter. The kitchen and sitting room are cosy and comfortable, and so the prolonged hours of darkness are less of a hardship than they might otherwise be, affording an excuse to spend many hours in the kitchen. In the winter months, this is where you want to be holed up with friends when they are here for lunch or dinner – or when they come to stay as house guests. Whether you are rolling malfatti, making fresh pasta or sitting around prepping artichokes together to make risotto, what better distraction from the cold, dark and short days than chatting and cooking with friends?

Menus at this time of year are never too elaborate, usually consisting of one central dish in one pot, but the actual cooking of it will be a slow process – a long, gentle roast or stew, or something that requires a few pairs of hands to prepare. At this time of year, I love to make the most of hardy Tuscan cooking, which was developed with these months in mind. Stews, soups, broths and lots of beans – dishes that can be cooked in one pan and accompanied by polenta or celeriac mash, the very things you crave after a brisk walk in the cold, the wind or, indeed, the rain. In short, food that is warming, earthy and comforting.

Although the landscape can look bleak, the choice of ingredients is anything but: bitter leaves, red and pink radicchio, cavolo nero, fennel, brussels sprouts, cardoons and artichokes (with their season extending into spring). Then, just as the darkest days of January set in, Nature sends us bright and zesty citrus fruits to cheer us up: jewel-red blood oranges, plump little clementines, pomegranates bursting with juice, and vivid yellow lemons from the Amalfi coast. The recipes in the following pages represent this mood, the slow cooking of winter veg and fruit, made into warming meals that lift the spirits.

The fires at this time of year are always roaring – from necessity, as well as an attempt at cosiness. Whoever is up first to put on the coffee will take on the duty of lighting the fires, so that the laborious task of warming the large, high-ceilinged rooms gets underway as early as possible. The house is made of stone and so really is designed to keep itself cool in summer, which makes keeping it warm in winter a full-time job. Life therefore tends to revolve around the kitchen fire. Strangely, the temperature often reflects the mood of the house – and when it is full of people, it naturally warms itself, encouraging us to congregate with friends and spend our short weekend days walking and chatting, before settling in to an afternoon and evening in the kitchen after an early sunset. I have vivid memories of winter parties, weekends and dinners hosted by my parents when I was a child, and I always saw them as both cosy and glamorous. Everyone looked fabulous, the fires were lit, the food was wintry and there were candles everywhere. This is how my sister and I endeavour to make them today. When we are here with friends to see in the new year, we spend the morning arranging candles and foraging in the woods for greenery to dress the table, and the afternoon slowly stewing whatever is on the menu for dinner.

Winters are biting but mercifully short in Tuscany, and the cold can be easily combated with a vigorous walk in the hills, followed by a hot bath laced with some delicious unguent. It is also one of my favourite times of year to be in Florence, especially in the run-up to Christmas, when the city is decorated with absurdly tasteful lights and abuzz with the festive spirit. As you cross the Ponte Santa Trinita, you can often see a thick layer of white snow capping the mountains at Abetone in the distance, luring one away for a bracing day's skiing. More often than not, though, I stick to the more sybaritic pleasures – a glass of prosecco and a truffle sandwich at Procacci, a historic wine bar on the fashionable Via dei Tornabuoni, famous for its year-round truffled-cream sandwiches.

At Arniano, the mood is no less lively than in the city, as we put on loud music and decorate the house with candles and olive branches. Looking out at the view, we are lucky that so many trees here are evergreen. Cypress, beech, ilex and Roman pines – all retain a muted green colour, not as vibrant as in the spring and summer months, but more uplifting than the sad, empty branches of other trees. Olives, also, never lose their silvery green leaves, and add a comforting bushiness to our surroundings. On frosty mornings, the garden looks as though it has been scattered with sparkling diamonds, and spiders' webs glisten like giant snowflakes.

Looking towards Montalcino, you can almost feel how much windier and colder it is up there; behind it, Monte Amiata will have a sprinkling of snow, its four ski runs glowing white against the black mass of the mountain's forests. Very occasionally, only once every few years, we will wake up to snow at Arniano, and the whole valley from here to Amiata will be cloaked in a deep, white silence. We know then that we are trapped, not going anywhere, as we do not keep a four-wheel-drive car for these rare occasions. But on those days, so long as the larder is stocked and we have wood for the fires, there is nowhere else in the world I would rather be.

OPPOSITE

– My mum's collection of knick-knacks. The table is from her furniture shop, which she had for many years in the local village; she probably sourced it from a junkyard and restored it to something special, as with much of the merchandise in the store. The tapestry was a gift from my dad's uncle, Desmond Guinness, who bought it in the 40s for his room at Oxford. Before he gave it to my parents in 1992, it lived in Castletown House in Kildare, Ireland – saved from demolition by the Irish Georgian Society, which he founded.

# BELL-AMI COCKTAIL

This cocktail is named after the house mixologist, my husband, Matthew Bell. He is a journalist, and before Matthew and I were married he worked in London and would spend most evenings in Soho at a writers' club called The Academy. That was where, one winter's evening, he came up with this cocktail, which is essentially a Negroni without the bitters. The house barmaid, Lucy, gave it the name 'Bell-Ami', a play on both Matthew's name and the novel by Maupassant – whose hero is also a rackety journalist. He has since fine-tuned the recipe to make it slightly less potent, and I prefer the Arniano Bell-Ami. I give both recipes here, so you can decide.

**PREPARATION:– 15 minutes**

# THE SOHO BELL-AMI

**SERVES 4**

200 ml gin

200 ml red vermouth

1 slice of orange, lightly squeezed

4 shavings of orange peel, to serve

Chill a martini glass or cocktail glass in the freezer. Combine all the ingredients in a cocktail shaker with lots of ice. Shake, then strain into a glass and top with a shaving of orange peel.

---

# THE ARNIANO BELL-AMI

**SERVES 4**

100 ml gin

100 ml red vermouth

100 ml Cointreau

100 ml freshly squeezed lemon juice

Chill a martini glass or cocktail glass in the freezer. Combine all the ingredients in a cocktail shaker with lots of ice. Shake, then strain into a glass.

*Crostini con cavolo nero e ricotta*

# CROSTINI WITH CAVOLO NERO AND RICOTTA

**PREPARATION:–** **10 minutes**
**COOKING:–** **10 minutes**

**SERVES 6**

**6 large slices of white sourdough (preferably a little stale), cut 1 cm thick**

**150 g cavolo nero, woody stalks removed**

**70 ml olive oil**

**Salt**

**Freshly ground black pepper**

**250 g ricotta**

**Chilli flakes**

**2 garlic cloves, peeled**

**Zest of 1 lemon**

Preheat the oven to 170 °C/150 °C fan-forced.

Place the pieces of bread on a baking tray and toast in the oven for 5–7 minutes, until golden and completely dry. Turn the slices over halfway through, so that they dry evenly. Remove the crostini from the oven and set to one side until ready to serve.

Chop the cavolo nero widthways across the leaf, to create thin ribbons. Wilt the leafy ribbons with 150 ml water in a wide saucepan (choose one with a lid) over a low heat. Increase the heat to medium, put the lid on the pan and cook for 8–10 minutes. If the pan is drying out, add more water as necessary. The cavolo should be wilted and tender, but not charred.

Drain the cavolo and wring it out in a clean tea towel to get rid of any excess moisture, then roughly chop into small pieces and transfer to a bowl. Drizzle the cavolo with a tablespoon of the oil, toss with a pinch of salt and a little pepper, and set to one side to cool.

In a separate bowl, use a fork to combine the drained ricotta with some salt and pepper, and a pinch of chilli flakes.

Rub each of the crostini with a garlic clove and drizzle with a little of the oil. Place a heaped tablespoon of ricotta on each crostini and top with the chopped cavolo. Drizzle with the last of the olive oil, sprinkle with a generous amount of lemon zest and serve immediately.

*Bruschetta alla tartufaia*

# HOT TOAST WITH TRUFFLED BUTTER

Our local family of truffle hunters, the Bernis, really know how to enjoy their truffles, even teaching me to shave them onto hazelnut ice cream - a ridiculous indulgence, which is in fact fabulous in its luxuriant absurdity. They also taught me one of the simplest ways to eat white truffle: a breakfast of kings (or truffle hunters), which in their family is known as *bruschetta alla tartufaia*. This is what the family patriarch, Gianfranco, has eaten for breakfast during the truffle season for over fifty years, and it is a way to make the most of every last shard of white truffle after you have shaved it over your pasta or eggs. You take the last tiny pieces and crumble them into a generous knob of butter, seal this in an airtight container overnight, and the next day simply slather it over hot toast. What a fragrant and warming way to start your day.

I have tried to recreate this in England, with truffle oil. Although most truffle oil is made with a synthetic flavouring, it can do the trick if used sparingly and will give you a sense of what a white truffle tastes like. Another delicious combination is to pair truffle oil with sweet prosciutto di Parma and grilled baby artichokes preserved in oil.

CHILLING:- Overnight
COOKING:- 10 minutes

**SERVES 6**

50 g unsalted butter, not too cold and hard

5–10 g fresh white truffle, crumbled, or 1 teaspoon truffle oil

6 large slices of white sourdough (preferably a little stale), cut 1 cm thick

Salt

Put the butter in a bowl and mash it with a fork. Add the fresh truffle or truffle oil and mash together thoroughly. Spoon the mixture into an airtight container, seal and keep it in the fridge overnight.

Preheat the oven to 170 °C/150 °C fan-forced.

Place the pieces of bread on a baking tray and toast in the oven for 5–7 minutes, until golden and completely dry. Turn the slices over halfway through, so that they dry evenly.

Remove the toasted bread from the oven and immediately spread liberally with the truffled butter and a pinch of salt. Eat hot.

*Ribollita senza pane*

# BREADLESS RIBOLLITA

This is one of my favourite soups. Hearty and filling, it is essentially a vegetable and bean stew - the ultimate comfort food. Traditionalists would insist a true ribollita should contain bread, as the dish was invented as a way of using up old vegetables and stale bread; *ribollita* literally means 're-boiled'. While ribollita is delicious with bread, I find that the cannellini beans (an essential ingredient in this soup) make it hearty enough.

PREPARATION:- 40 minutes
COOKING:- 50 minutes

**SERVES 6
(10 IF YOU ADD
STALE BREAD)**

**FOR THE SOFFRITTO:-**

½ red onion

50 g celery

50 g carrots

A handful of flat-leaf parsley leaves

4 tablespoons olive oil

Salt

**FOR THE RIBOLLITA:-**

500 g carrots

400 g celery, leaves included

1 head (about 200 g) cavolo nero or kale

A large handful of flat-leaf parsley leaves

4 tablespoons olive oil – plus extra, to serve

Salt

1 x 400 g tin peeled plum tomatoes

2 x 400 g tins cannellini beans

Parmesan, finely grated, to serve

### PREPARING THE VEGETABLES

The process of making this soup benefits from chopping all your vegetables before you begin. For the *soffritto*, chop the onion, celery stalks, carrots and parsley as finely as you can. Put all of the chopped *soffritto* vegetables into one bowl and set them aside until you are ready to fry them in olive oil (which will create the base flavour of your ribollita).

I have a particular method for chopping the bulkier vegetables that are added to the ribollita after you have cooked the *soffritto*. These vegetables will be added to the ribollita at different times, so put them in separate bowls. For the carrots: if they are small, chop them into 1 cm discs; if large, cut them lengthways down the middle, then cut them into half-moons. For the celery: chop into 1 cm pieces, starting at the top of the head of celery; include any leaves as well, as they add flavour. For the cavolo nero: chop the cavolo (including the stalk) widthwise into 2 cm strips, working from top to bottom; discard the last 5–10 cm of the stalk, where it is very thick and woody.

Roughly chop the large handful of parsley for the ribollita and set aside in a separate bowl.

### COOKING THE RIBOLLITA

Pour the olive oil into a wide, high-sided pan (choose one with a lid), enough to lightly coat the bottom of the pan. Set the pan over a medium heat, then add the *soffritto* mix of onions, celery, carrots and parsley, together with a pinch of salt. Allow the *soffritto* vegetables to soften for about 5 minutes, stirring occasionally.

Put two-thirds of the large pieces of carrot, celery and parsley in the pan (the cavolo nero will be added later in the process). Use a wooden spoon to mix the vegetables in with the softened *soffritto*, adding another drizzle of oil as you stir. Allow to cook for 5–10 minutes, stirring occasionally. Once the vegetables have cooked for a few minutes, add two generous pinches of salt, 250 ml water and the tinned tomato. Fill the empty tin with water, swirling it around to pick up all of the remaining tomato, and add the tomatoey water to the pan. Mix well, then simmer the soup over a low heat for about 5 minutes while you prepare your cannellini beans.

Drain one tin of cannellini and blitz the beans in a blender or food processor (I use a NutriBullet) with 100 ml water and a pinch of salt, until smooth and creamy. Add the puréed beans to the soup along with the remaining carrot, celery and parsley, the cavolo nero and another good drizzle of olive oil. Taste to check the seasoning and adjust as necessary. Cook over a low heat for 40 minutes with the lid half on, stirring occasionally. Drain the second tin of cannellini beans and add to the soup.

Serve the soup with a drizzle of the best olive oil you can find and a grating of parmesan.

This ribollita is even better the next day. To reheat, add 50 ml water and a drizzle of oil to the soup, then gently simmer over a medium heat for a few minutes.

DELICIOUS WITH:-

This soup makes for a fabulous starter as a small portion before Roast chicken with grapes (p. 188) or can be served as a hearty and filling vegetarian main. It's mainly vegetables, so if this is the main event, be sure to have a greedy dessert to finish.

# PENNE WITH CAVOLO NERO AND PANCETTA

**PREPARATION:- 10 minutes**
**COOKING:- 40 minutes**

**SERVES 6**

**400 g cavolo nero**

**75 ml olive oil – plus extra, to fry the pancetta and to finish the sauce**

**200 g unsmoked pancetta slices, cut into strips about 1 cm wide**

**Chilli flakes**

**2 garlic cloves, peeled and crushed**

**Salt**

**50 g unsalted butter**

**Freshly ground black pepper**

**500 g penne rigate**

**80 g parmesan, finely grated – plus extra, to serve**

Chop the cavolo (including the stalk) widthwise into 5 cm strips, working from top to bottom. Discard the bottom 5–10 cm of the stalk, where it is very thick and woody (if the supermarket has done this for you, use all of the cavolo).

Drizzle a little olive oil in a wide, heavy-based frying pan or flameproof casserole dish (choose one with a lid, for use later in the cooking process) and gently fry the pancetta over a medium heat until crispy. Using a spoon, transfer the pancetta from the pan to a bowl and set to one side until serving. Discard any cooking fat that is left in the pan. Leave the pan to cool for a few minutes and wipe with some kitchen paper, but don't clean it completely.

Once the pan has cooled down, add half the olive oil, two pinches of chilli flakes, the garlic and a pinch of salt. Gently fry the garlic over a low heat for 1 minute – allow it to sizzle, but do not let it burn. Add the cavolo to the pan and stir, so that it is coated in a little oil. Increase the heat to medium and fry the garlic and cavolo for a few minutes before adding 150 ml water. Cover and cook at a gentle simmer for 10 minutes.

Meanwhile, put a large pan of well-salted water on to boil.

Add another 150 ml water to the cavolo, along with the butter, a pinch of salt, black pepper and the rest of the olive oil. Cover and cook for another 15 minutes, then take the pan off the heat. Taste some of the cavolo and cooking liquid, which should have amalgamated into a tasty sauce, and adjust the seasoning as necessary.

Once the pasta cooking water is at a rolling boil, add the penne and cook until al dente.

Halfway through the cooking time for the pasta, set the pan of cavolo over a high heat and add one ladleful of the pasta cooking water. Once the penne has cooked, use a slotted spoon to transfer it the pan of cavolo. Mix the pasta through the sauce, along with the pancetta, parmesan and a generous drizzle of fresh oil. Toss again and serve immediately.

If your pan or casserole dish is attractive, bring it straight to the table so that everyone can help themselves. Serve with a grind of black pepper and some grated parmesan.

**VARIATION:-**

You can easily make this a vegetarian dish by substituting the pancetta with a finely chopped white onion. Gently cook the onion with the garlic, then leave in the pan to cook with the cavolo nero.

**DELICIOUS WITH:-**

This pasta is rich and filling, so I wouldn't serve a starter. Cardamom poached pears (p. 232) or a slice of Maria's marmalade, mascarpone and almond tart (p. 196) would be a fabulous way to finish off this meal.

# PASTA 'ALLA SAVANNAH', WITH SPICY ITALIAN SAUSAGE

This recipe is a combination of the recipes written thirty years ago by my parents' dear friends, Adam and Cloe Alvarez. Adam and Cloe were immortalised by their great friends Rose Gray and Ruth Rogers in the River Cafe's first book, their characters reflected in their respective recipes for these two almost identical pasta sauces: Cloe's took twenty-five minutes, Adam's two-and-a-half hours. Adam and Cloe are no longer with us, but my dear friend, their daughter Savannah, has come up with a happy medium, combining their methods to create a sauce that takes an hour to prepare.

Always a crowd pleaser, this pasta is one to follow a hearty walk, or to be eaten with good friends on a cold night or on a sunny winter's day. It is best with Italian sausages - the texture is wonderful and crumbly, as they aren't too processed - but if you can't find any, buy the best-quality organic pork sausages available and add lots of freshly ground black pepper. I love to make this recipe with conchiglie, but you can use any dry short pasta with a cavity to scoop up the sauce, such as penne or Campania-style 'gnocchi' (as pictured).

**PREPARATION:- 15 minutes**
**COOKING:- 45 minutes**

**SERVES 6**

**2 tablespoons olive oil**

**1 red onion, finely chopped**

**Salt**

**6 Italian pork sausages, meat removed from the skins and crumbled**

**Leaves from 6 rosemary sprigs, finely chopped**

**3 bay leaves**

**1 teaspoon chilli flakes**

**250 ml hearty red wine (I use Rosso di Montalcino)**

**800 g tin peeled plum tomatoes**

**500 g conchiglie, or your preferred pasta shape**

**150 ml double cream**

**¼ whole nutmeg, grated**

**120 g parmesan, finely grated**

In a wide, heavy-based saucepan or flameproof casserole dish, heat the oil with the onion and a pinch of salt over a medium heat. Fry until translucent (about 5 minutes). Add the crumbled sausage meat, half the rosemary, and the bay leaves and chilli flakes. Stir, mashing the sausage meat with the end of your spoon. Cook the meat for 10–15 minutes, until evenly browned. Add the red wine, increase the heat and cook for another 5 minutes, until the alcohol has evaporated.

Put a large pan of well-salted water on to boil.

Add the tomatoes to the sauce, together with the rest of the rosemary. Bring the sauce to the boil and then immediately reduce the heat to medium. Simmer for 20 minutes, then remove the pan from the heat.

Once the pasta water is at a rolling boil, add the conchiglie and cook until al dente.

A few minutes before the pasta is done, stir the cream and nutmeg through the sauce. Drain the pasta and add it to the pan with the sauce, along with half the parmesan, stirring thoroughly to combine. Serve immediately, with the rest of the parmesan.

# TARTUFI BIANCHI

 The hallowed white truffle enjoys something of a cult status, and nowhere more so than in Tuscany. Growing abundantly in our area, the Creti Senesi, it is much rarer than the black truffle and can be an elusive creature, appearing only under certain conditions and in certain secret places. For this reason, it is almost as famous for its price tag as for its pungent, musky aroma.

The scent and flavour of these earthy jewels is very particular, and it is virtually impossible to feel lukewarm about them. You either love them or you hate them. If the former, you will eat them at every opportunity that your wallet will allow. If the latter, their rich, heady scent can be enough to ruin a meal. My friend Emily, an Italian travel expert who runs Bellini Travel, is the only person I know to have experienced a 180-degree change of position, going from hating to loving them. This conversion was admittedly born out of necessity, in the name of 'market research'. Emily and I were on a mission to find the best plate of pasta with truffles in Tuscany for one of her clients – to not grow to like them would have made it a torturous two days. And, sure enough, by the time we completed our trip, Emily had the zeal of the born-again truffle lover.

Personally, I adore truffles. I love their intoxicating fragrance and unique earthy flavour. Whenever I am lucky enough to get a waft of one, I immediately want to shave it over a plate of hot, buttery pasta, or over fried eggs. Their pungency (and expense) means that fresh white truffles are best used sparingly over uncomplicated dishes that allow the truffle to dominate. They are shaved using a special gadget that allows you to take the little gnarled ball and serve it in gossamer-thin, translucent slices over whatever dish you are pairing it with.

So all-pervasive is the scent of white truffle that if it is not sealed properly in an airtight container in the fridge, it will tinge all the other food in there with its flavour. This can be a wonderful trick if you are planning to eat your truffle with eggs: simply place the truffle in a jar or Tupperware box with the eggs overnight, and its scent will make its way through their porous shells, infusing the yolks. Your 'truffled' fried or scrambled eggs, topped with freshly grated truffle, will be all the more magical. This tendency is less enjoyable when it comes to food you do not wish to taste of truffle. On one occasion, when I was eating a tiramisù at a friend's restaurant, I felt compelled to ask her: 'Is this meant to be a truffle dessert?' At my words, her face fell – and she immediately bounded into the kitchen, shouting at the chefs for not having correctly sealed the box containing that week's truffles, thereby infusing all the puddings for that night's service.

The price of a white truffle can be prohibitive in many restaurants. While they are still expensive in our area, they are not prohibitively so, and don't carry the same cost as truffles from Piedmont, or any that you will eat in London or New York. During their season, which in Tuscany runs from mid-October to the last day of December (the best month being November), my philosophy is to eat them at any opportunity I get, counterbalancing the expense by living on cheap vegetable stews for the rest of the week. A plate of *tagliolini con tartufo* at Trattoria Cammillo in Florence, or at Locanda Il Paradiso in Chiusure when I am at Arniano, is worth every *centesimo*, and I highly recommend you take advantage if you are ever in the area at this time of year.

The commercialisation of white truffles is a fairly new phenomenon. As I speak with Gianfranco Berni, now nearly seventy, who has been a *tartufaio* (truffle hunter) for fifty-eight years, he recalls that the truffles he collected in his youth were for the family – to have over their evening frittata, or to eat with buttered toast while they were working on the farm. Gianfranco was born and brought up in a farmhouse in the woods in the prime truffle-land near Asciano. The house had no electricity or drinking water, and he scoffs at the idea of his children and grandchildren being able to survive there for one week. Back then, though, these conditions were the norm. One upside was that he could find truffles just outside his front door, giving him plenty of opportunity to learn about the landscape and weather needed to encourage truffles to grow.

There was little market for white truffles when Gianfranco was young, and none for summer's black truffles. A few of the white variety were bought by a client who owned a few local restaurants – but, generally speaking, the idea of packaging them up for export was considered ludicrous. Even in Siena, only 18 miles away, restaurants didn't regard truffles as 'local' enough to be included on their menus. And there simply wasn't the gastronomic tradition around them that we have now.

Before the 1970s, it was *tartufai* from outside Tuscany who really understood the commercial potential of truffles, and it was one such group of men, from Le Marche on the east coast of Italy, who taught Gianfranco to cultivate and search for truffles in the 60s. The following decades saw the development of new dishes featuring white truffles, along with an emerging competitive trade, eventually leading to the international market we know today. While understanding that this popularity is a blessing, Gianfranco also holds it partly responsible for the increase in *tartufai* who don't know the basics. 'They don't even know how a truffle grows and regenerates,' he complains. 'They know nothing about truffle cultivation.' He often argues this at conferences on truffle conservation. 'No resource is inexhaustible,' he says, and if you 'don't take care of it, and don't understand it, you risk that the land will simply stop producing it.' While there have been attempts to create artificially cultivated truffle farms, the topic is hotly debated. Gianfranco is very much a believer in understanding how truffles occur naturally, and he is adamant that the tending of woodland by *tartufai* is the best way of encouraging nature to do its thing.

Truffles are the underground fruiting bodies of a fungus, which grows in the form of a threadlike web of subterranean filaments, collectively known as mycelium; these are so fine that they are invisible to the naked eye. The fungus grows among the roots of certain species of trees, and will begin to generate fruit at the base of its host trees between May and June. The summer will determine how many truffles 'take' – as with most things in nature, extreme weather is no help. Truffles like temperate, cool weather, as well as the dark and damp: conditions that are not too wet and not too hot.

Truffles are harvested from well-kept areas of woodland known as *tartufaie*, 'truffle reserves'. In order to create the best conditions for truffle formation, *tartufai* will spend much of early spring clearing the woodland, to ensure that the ground isn't overcrowded with large tree trunks and roots. These reserves are carefully safeguarded, either by the *tartufai*, who own and tend to the reserve privately, or by the Associazione di Tartufai Senesi.

The trouble with the high value of white truffles is that younger *tartufai* are often reluctant to forgo 10 grams of truffle – and its cargo of spores – for the sake of regeneration. To get to those last 10 grams, they might remove everything from the earth, digging such a wide hole that even the mycelium is damaged.

When I have been on a truffle hunt with Gianfranco, the greatest care is taken to dig the smallest hole possible, so as not to 'tear' the invisible net. 'With my sons and grandchildren, one of the first things I taught them when foraging is to leave the earth how you found it,' he says. 'If you disturb the roots too much or destroy the web of mycelium so that it can't repair itself, our territory will stop producing truffles. I always leave a small amount of truffle in there, it helps it to regenerate.' The trouble can be that a young truffler might come by an hour later and dig up what he has left – for the sake of an extra 5 grams to sell on.

My favourite of the truffle hunts I have been on throughout Tuscany have always been with Gianfranco and his family. They have a beautiful truffle reserve near us, and make fantastic wine as well. The Bernis bought I Loghi in 1992 and have been expanding the enterprise and land ever since. A walk through their woodland with Gianfranco and his trusted truffle dog, Dora, is like being led down a path from folklore – a *tartufaio* and his relationship with his dog is something to behold. The dogs are so attuned to the scent of truffles that they can smell them up to a metre underground. They will pat the spot with two paws if they know it is a good truffle, and with only one paw if it has gone bad.

When I was young I believed that people used pigs to forage truffles, but the Bernis tell me that this is nonsense. A pig would never be able to resist gobbling the truffle for itself, whereas a dog has the sensibility and intelligence not to do so.

It's a thrill when Dora bounds to the foot of a tree, excitedly sniffing and patting the ground with both of her front paws, with Gianfranco encouraging: '*Vai, vai, vai Dora. Vai!*' Dora will then scratch the top layer of earth away, before allowing Gianfranco to take over with a narrow spade designed for the purpose; I am instantly intoxicated by the scent that permeates the air as dog and *tartufaio* between them gently lift the pale, honey-coloured pebble from the ground. Truffles aren't always perfect – sometimes they crack during harvesting. And the tastiest truffles are not the largest. It's the ones that weigh between 50 and 70 grams that are the most flavoursome and sought after.

---

**A FEW TARTUFI BIANCHI RECIPES:-**

- Hot toast with truffled butter (p. 211)
- Tagliolini with white truffles (p. 222)

*Tagliolini con tartuffi bianchi*

# TAGLIOLINI WITH WHITE TRUFFLES

**PREPARATION:- 1½ hours**
**COOKING:- 10 minutes**

**SERVES 6**

**FOR THE PASTA:-**

600 g '00' flour – plus extra, for dusting and for coating the pasta

6 large eggs

Semolina, for coating the pasta

**FOR THE SAUCE:-**

80 g white truffles

200 g unsalted butter

Salt

50 g parmesan, finely grated

Freshly ground black pepper

Make the pasta dough and prepare the sheets following the instructions for Homemade tagliatelle with spring peas (p. 98). Run your silky sheets of pasta through the tagliolini setting on your pasta machine.

Clean the truffles, using a damp cloth to rub away any dirt. *Don't* clean the truffles under running water.

Melt the butter, together with a generous pinch of salt, in a large, wide frying pan over a medium heat, then grate in 10 g of the truffles. Turn off the heat and leave the butter and grated truffle to infuse.

Fill an enormous pan with plenty of well-salted water and bring it to a lively boil. Cook the pasta in the boiling water for about 1 minute, stirring as soon as you put it into the water to stop the strands sticking to one another.

Using tongs, transfer the tagliolini to the pan of melted butter and toss through. Add half a mugful of the pasta cooking water to loosen up the mixture if it looks a little dry. Add the parmesan, some black pepper and another pinch of salt, and toss again.

Divide the pasta equally into six bowls, and spoon a little of the butter remaining in the pan over each one. Using a truffle slicer, or a potato peeler, gently slice about 10 g of white truffle over each bowl of pasta and serve immediately.

*Gobbi al forno con crema e parmigiano*

# CARDOON GRATIN

Cardoons are an odd vegetable – they look a bit like giant, pale celery and have a flavour that is somewhere between artichoke and celery, but with a meatier texture. I often make this dish as a main course with some fresh sides, but it also works as a side dish itself. The outer layer of the stalks is a bit stringy, so cardoons need peeling, but once prepared they are delicious, and their enticing and interesting flavour always reminds me of winter.

**PREPARATION:-** 20 minutes
**COOKING:-** 45 minutes

**SERVES 6**

½ **lemon**

1 kg **cardoons**

**Salt**

**Freshly ground black pepper**

250 ml **single cream**

60 g **parmesan, grated – plus extra, for topping**

½ **whole nutmeg, grated**

Preheat the oven to 200°C/180°C fan-forced.

Half-fill a pan (choose one with a lid) with cold water, squeeze the lemon into it and throw in the lemon shell as well.

Pull the cardoon stalks away from the heart, discarding the very woody outer stalks. Trim each end. Using a potato peeler or small paring knife, peel away the stringy outer layer of each stalk. Cut the stalks into four or five pieces, each roughly 6 cm in length. Put the chopped cardoon into the pan of lemony water as you go, to stop it discolouring.

Put the pan of cardoons and lemony water on the stovetop over a high heat, add a generous pinch of salt, then cover and bring to the boil. Reduce the heat, remove the lid and simmer for 15 minutes, until the cardoons are starting to become tender – while still retaining some 'bite'. Drain well, and toss with salt and pepper.

Butter an ovenproof dish and add the cardoons in one layer, packed in as tightly as possible. Mix the cream with the parmesan, grated nutmeg, a pinch of salt and some grinds of black pepper. Pour the cream mixture over the cardoons, then top with more grated parmesan.

Cook in the oven for 25 minutes, until bubbling and brown. Remove the gratin from the oven and leave to rest and cool down for 10 minutes before serving.

**DELICIOUS WITH:-**

This is a wonderful vegetarian main for a winter's night. As it is quite rich, it needs nothing more than a Peppery green salad (p. 244) – and maybe Slow-roasted San Marzano tomatoes (p. 250) or Mama's roast cherry tomatoes (p. 251) – to add some freshness and acidity. If you are serving cardoons as a side dish, they go beautifully with Grilled chicken breast with lemon and thyme (p. 147), Beef stew with gremolata (p. 227) and Roast beef with green sauce (p. 109).

*Risotto ai carciofi*

# ARTICHOKE RISOTTO

PREPARATION:- **40 minutes**
COOKING:- **30 minutes**

**SERVES 6**

8 large Sardinian spiny artichokes or 6 globe artichokes

1 lemon (1 half for lemony water, half for the artichoke leaves and stalks)

1 vegetable stock cube

50 g unsalted butter

60 ml olive oil

1 red onion, diced

Salt

2 garlic cloves, peeled and crushed

500 g arborio rice

200 ml white wine

80 g parmesan, finely grated – plus extra, to serve

Freshly ground black pepper

### PREPARING THE ARTICHOKES

Prepare the artichokes, following the instructions on page 91. Take about half of the prepared artichoke quarters and cut them lengthways into wedges. Slice each of the stalks into 5 mm discs and add them to the artichoke chunks. Finely slice the remaining prepped artichokes lengthways into pieces 5 mm thick, and then return them to the bowl of lemony water with the rest of the artichoke slices. You can do this a few hours in advance and leave the artichokes in the lemony water until you are ready to make the risotto.

### MAKING THE RISOTTO

Put 500 ml water on to boil in a pan over a high heat. Crumble the stock cube into the water, then add half of the lemony water that the artichokes are sitting in, making sure that enough water remains in the bowl to cover the artichokes.

In a wide, heavy-based skillet or frying pan, gently melt 25 g of the butter with all the olive oil over a medium heat. Once it starts to sizzle, add the onion, along with a pinch of salt. Cook until the onion is translucent (about 3–5 minutes), stirring occasionally, then add the garlic and continue to stir. Retaining the rest of the lemony water in the bowl, transfer all the artichoke pieces to the frying pan, mixing everything together so that the artichoke is coated with the oil and butter. Cook over a medium heat for 3–5 minutes.

While the artichoke is cooking, strain the rest of the lemony artichoke water through a sieve, discarding the lemon shell and any pieces of choke that have made their way into the water. Add this water to the boiling stock and leave to bubble over a high heat.

Add the rice to the artichoke, thoroughly mixing everything together, and increase the heat to high. The starchy outer coating of the rice will start to soften and disintegrate. When the rice begins sticking to the pan and making a cracking noise (usually after about 5 minutes of cooking), add the wine. Stir continuously until the alcohol has evaporated.

Add a ladleful of the stock and artichoke water to the rice. Stir until the rice has absorbed the liquid, then add another ladleful. Repeat this process for 15 minutes, until most of the liquid has been absorbed. Try the rice: it should be cooked but still have a little bite (although it shouldn't be chalky), and the artichoke should be tender. Add the rest of the butter and the parmesan and stir through. Turn off the heat, grind lots of black pepper over the risotto and stir for another minute or so. Bring to the table and serve with extra parmesan.

**DELICIOUS WITH:-**

This is a rich main course, so I wouldn't usually make a starter, but a heavenly way to finish the meal would be with Cardamom poached pears (p. 232) or Maria's marmalade, mascarpone and almond tart (p. 196).

*Pollo e verdure bollite con salsa verde*

# POACHED CHICKEN AND VEGETABLES WITH GREEN SAUCE

This is a perfect winter dish in my eyes, warming, delicious and with a little kick from the accompanying green sauce. It's also versatile, as you can eat it like you would a roast dinner: chicken and veg at the centre, with a little of the green sauce, saving the warming broth for some other use at a later date - or indeed, serving the broth as a starter before the chicken. If you are in need of a culinary hug, you can simply place torn pieces of the chicken along with the vegetables in a bowl of broth and top with the green sauce.

**PREPARATION:- 1 hour**
**COOKING:- 1½ hours**

**SERVES 4**

1 whole chicken (about 2 kg)

Salt

5 large carrots, cut into half-moons

½ small red onion

2 celery stalks, halved

¼ teaspoon whole black peppercorns

1 bay leaf

A handful of flat-leaf parsley, leaves roughly chopped, stalks removed and saved for poaching

8 new potatoes, whole, or 4 small potatoes, quartered

½ fennel bulb, finely sliced

Olive oil

Green sauce (p. 254), to serve

Take the chicken out of the fridge about an hour before you start cooking. Put it in a deep-sided saucepan (choose one with a lid) that will be large enough to hold the chicken and veg and enough water to submerge them.

Season the chicken with salt, cover the pan with a tea towel and set to one side to allow the chicken to come up to room temperature.

Add two of the carrots, the onion, celery, peppercorns, bay leaf and parsley stalks to the pan. Pour 2 litres cold water into the pan, to completely cover the chicken and vegetables. The amount of water required may vary, depending on the size of the chicken and your pan. Cover the pan with the lid and bring the water to a boil over a high heat. Once the water is boiling (usually after 15 minutes), reduce the heat to low and adjust the lid so that the pan is only partially covered. Simmer for 1 hour, occasionally checking the pan. If any froth forms on the top, skim it off using a slotted spoon and discard.

After 1 hour of simmering, add the potatoes, the remaining carrots and the fennel. Simmer uncovered for a further 20 minutes, until the second batch of veg is tender. The carrots and celery that you put in at the beginning will be so soft that they are almost disintegrating, but don't worry about this.

Transfer the chicken to a large serving dish and arrange the vegetables around it. Pour a ladleful of the broth over the chicken and vegetables, drizzle with some oil and sprinkle with the chopped parsley. Serve immediately in a shallow bowl, with a ladleful of broth over the top and a dollop of green sauce.

## MAKING THE CHICKEN BROTH

Once you have removed the chicken and vegetables from the broth, discard the peppercorns, parsley stems and bay leaves and strain the broth through a sieve. Allow it to cool down before putting it in the fridge. After an hour in the fridge, a layer of fat will have formed on top of the broth – skim this off before reheating. You can also freeze the broth at this stage. Use it within a month.

**DELICIOUS WITH:-**

Serve with a piece of really good bread, to scoop up the broth and green sauce. And to finish - a warm and comforting Berry clafoutis with Amalfi lemon cream (p. 199).

*Spezzatino con gremolata*

# BEEF STEW WITH GREMOLATA

This recipe reminds me of school-night suppers by the fire in winter, when my mother would make us this hearty, tasty and warming stew – which, as it is cooked in one pan and can be prepared ahead of time, is also perfect for serving a crowd. Its rich, deep flavour is transformed and elevated by a small amount of gremolata, which is sprinkled on the dish just before serving. Gremolata is a dry seasoning of garlic, parsley and lemon zest; used sparingly, its tart, acidic flavour provides a real contrast and boost to the meatiness of the stew.

One of the joys of stews is that they are easy to make, since you essentially chuck all your ingredients into a pan and leave them to cook for four hours. But it's still important to stir occasionally, checking to make sure there is enough liquid for the meat to tenderise in. Most important of all, be generous with that vital ingredient – time. Whenever I have tried to rush the process by cooking on a higher heat and adding more herbs and seasoning to speed up the emergence of the flavours, it has never been as good. The stew also benefits from resting and reheating, allowing the flavours to amalgamate and develop. If you can, make it the day before.

PREPARATION:- 30 minutes, plus at least 1–2 hours resting
(the stew can be rested overnight)
COOKING:- 2 hours 45 minutes

DELICIOUS WITH:-

Beef stew is almost a self-contained meal in itself, but I do love it with buttery Polenta (p. 266) or earthy and creamy Celeriac mash (p. 267). A heavenly finish to the meal would be Hazelnut, almond and pear tart (p. 231).

**FOR THE SOFFRITTO:-**

1 red onion, finely chopped

1 carrot, finely chopped

1 celery stalk, finely chopped

1 garlic clove, peeled and crushed

Salt

**FOR THE STEW:-**

800 g beef, diced (I prefer 2.5–3 cm cubes)

1 tablespoon plain flour

4 tablespoons olive oil

4 bay leaves

1 teaspoon of whole black peppercorns

Leaves from a handful of thyme sprigs

Salt

1 bottle hearty red wine (I use a Rosso di Montalcino)

½ head garlic (sliced horizontally)

4 carrots, cut into discs about 1 cm thick (or half-moons, if using large carrots)

4 celery stalks, cut into half-moons about 1 cm thick

500 g new potatoes, halved

300 g whole shallots, skins removed

Freshly ground black pepper

**FOR THE GREMOLATA:-**

Zest of 2 lemons

2 garlic cloves, peeled and very finely chopped

2 handfuls of flat-leaf parsley leaves, very finely chopped

## PREPARING THE INGREDIENTS

Start by chopping all your ingredients. If your beef has come pre-chopped, check that the chunks have been diced to a size of your liking. If you think they are too big, cut them into smaller pieces, remembering that they will shrink slightly while cooking.

### MAKING THE STEW

Put the beef into a large bowl with the flour. Shake the bowl vigorously, making sure that the meat is coated lightly and evenly. You can also do this by putting the flour and meat in a freezer bag – remember to seal it, to stop any flour escaping and creating mess.

Pour half the olive oil into a wide, heavy-based casserole dish (choose one that has a lid) – enough to lightly coat the bottom of the pan. Heat the oil over a medium heat, then brown the cubes of beef, making sure each side is well sealed. You may need to do this in batches. Once the beef is browned (with some parts a dark, rich brown), remove it from the pan and set to one side in a bowl.

Using the same pan, and without removing any of the bits of flour that might have stuck to the bottom, pour in the rest of the oil and reduce the heat to low. Add your *soffritto* of onion, carrot, celery and garlic, along with a pinch of salt, mixing everything together with a wooden spoon to make sure that all the vegetables are covered with a slick of the beef's cooking fat. Cook gently for about 5 minutes, stirring occasionally, allowing the vegetables to soften.

Put the beef back into the pan, stirring to mix with the vegetables. Add the bay leaves, peppercorns, thyme and a generous pinch of salt. Cook for a couple of minutes so that all the flavours begin to come together. Add half the wine and 500 ml water, then add the halved head of garlic and another generous pinch of salt.

Turn the heat right down, partly cover the pan and allow the stew to bubble away for 1½ hours. Keep an eye on it during this time, stirring occasionally to make sure it doesn't dry out or stick to the bottom. If too much liquid evaporates and the stew begins to look a bit dry, add a little more water.

At the end of the simmering time, add the rest of the wine and another 500 ml water, along with the chunky pieces of carrot and celery, the halved potatoes and whole shallots. Taste the liquid to check the seasoning and add salt and pepper if you think they're needed. Cover the pan with the lid and cook over a very low heat for 1 hour.

Once it is cooked, leave the stew to rest for at least 1–2 hours (or, even better, overnight) before reheating and serving with a sprinkling of gremolata.

### MAKING THE GREMOLATA

Chop the lemon zest as finely as you can. Put the zest in a bowl, add the finely chopped garlic and parsley, mix and then set aside ready for sprinkling over the stew. I sprinkle it over the *spezzatino* in the serving dish, and leave a small bowl on the table so people can add more if they like.

*Crostata di nocciole, mandorle e pere*

# HAZELNUT, ALMOND AND PEAR TART

**PREPARATION:- 30 minutes**
**BAKING:- 30 minutes**

**SERVES 6**

100 g blanched hazelnuts

1 packet ready-rolled puff pastry

1 small egg, for egg wash

80 g unsalted butter, softened

75 g caster sugar

50 g demerara sugar

Zest of 2 lemons

1 large egg

2 large pears, ripe but firm

Juice of 2 lemons, to prevent pears from discolouring

50 g flaked almonds

Crème fraîche or vanilla ice cream, to serve

Preheat the oven to 200 °C/180 °C fan-forced.

Toast the hazelnuts on a baking tray in the oven for 5 minutes, or until they start to smell nutty and are turning golden brown. Remove them from the oven and leave to cool completely.

While the nuts are still in the oven, unroll the puff pastry and lay it flat on a baking tray lined with baking parchment. Using the tip of a knife, and being careful not to cut right through, score a line 1 cm in from the edge of the pastry, all the way around – a neat, raised crust will form as the pastry cooks. Using a pastry brush, egg-wash the pastry and then prick it all over with a fork. Keep the pastry in the fridge until you are ready to assemble and bake the tart.

Put the cooled hazelnuts in a food processor and pulse until coarsely chopped.

Using hand-held electric beaters, cream together the butter, both sugars and the lemon zest until the mixture becomes thick and pale. Mix the chopped hazelnuts with the creamed butter and sugar, using a wooden spoon, then add the egg. Set the frangipane mixture to one side until you are ready to assemble the tart for baking.

Peel, quarter and core the pears. Cut each of the pear quarters into four juicy slices. Set the pears aside in a bowl as you go, adding a squeeze of lemon to stop them discolouring.

Retrieve the pastry from the fridge. Spoon the frangipane onto the pastry, spreading it out evenly within the 1 cm border and smoothing it using the back of the spoon. Lay the pear slices on top, in neat, slightly overlapping rows, gently pressing the slices down into the frangipane. Sprinkle with the flaked almonds.

Bake for 25–30 minutes, until golden. Remove the tart from the oven and serve hot or at room temperature with crème fraîche or a scoop of ice cream.

*Pere con vino rosso e cardamomo*

# CARDAMOM POACHED PEARS

My mother always made these poached pears on cold winter nights. I love to serve them following a heavy meal - the fruit provides a sweet and mellow finale to a feast, while the red wine sauce makes this a robust and comforting winter dessert.

**PREPARATION:- 10 minutes**
**COOKING:- 40 minutes**

**SERVES 6**

Juice of 2 lemons

6 pears, ripe but firm

1 bottle hearty red wine

300 g brown sugar

Juice of 2 oranges

Seeds from 20 g cardamom pods (crack the pods to remove the seeds)

2 bay leaves

Crème fraîche, double cream or vanilla ice cream, to serve

Add half the lemon juice to a bowl large enough to hold all the pears.

Put 200 ml water and all the ingredients except for the pears into a large pan. Gradually bring to the boil over a medium heat, stirring to ensure that the sugar dissolves completely. Once the poaching liquid is boiling, reduce the heat and allow to gently bubble away for 5 minutes, so that the alcohol evaporates.

Peel the pears (leaving the stems on), and trim 5 mm from the bottom of each one so that it can stand up. Put each prepared pear in the bowl of lemon juice as you go, coating it in the juice to stop it turning brown.

Holding each one by its stem, gently lower the pears into the poaching liquid, then add the bowlful of lemon juice and bring the liquid to a simmer. Cover the pears with a sheet of baking parchment, pushing it down flat to the level of the liquid and pears. Simmer for 20 minutes. Remove the parchment paper and transfer the cooked pears to a plate, standing them upright on their trimmed base. Set to one side.

Continue to simmer the poaching liquid, uncovered, for another 15 minutes, or until the liquid has reduced by half. Strain the poaching liquid through a sieve, discarding the cardamon seeds and bay leaves, and then return it to the pan. Add the pears to the pan and coat them in the thickened sauce.

Serve the pears warm. Place a tablespoon of your cream of choice in the centre of each serving bowl, before standing the pear on the dollop and drizzling with some of the sauce.

*Torta rovesciata all'olio e arance rosse*

# BLOOD ORANGE AND OLIVE OIL UPSIDE-DOWN CAKE

Nature has a charming way of providing a burst of colour just when we need it most. In the darkest days of January, the ruby red of blood oranges arrives to lift our spirits. I love pairing them with this oil-based sponge, which has an almost savoury-sweet quality, deriving from the olive oil. For the sliced oranges that sit on top of the cake when it is inverted, I try to find the bloodiest of oranges, cooking them in syrup beforehand to make the skins palatable. If this isn't for you, feel free to peel your oranges before slicing.

**PREPARATION:- 20 minutes, plus 20 minutes cooling**
**BAKING:- 55 minutes**

**SERVES 6**

**FOR THE TOP OF THE CAKE:-**

2 blood oranges, peel on, finely sliced into discs

70 g caster sugar

**FOR THE CAKE BATTER:-**

2 large eggs

220 g caster sugar

Zest of 2 blood oranges

Juice of 1 blood orange

100 ml olive oil

100 ml full-fat milk

200 g self-raising flour

Crème fraîche or double cream, to serve

**PREPARING THE ORANGE SLICES**

You will need a frying pan that is wide enough to hold all the orange slices laid flat. To make the syrup, add 100 ml water and the caster sugar to the pan and set it over a medium heat, stirring until the sugar has dissolved. Reduce the heat to low and allow the syrup to bubble gently for another 5 minutes. Once it is bubbling and caramelising, add the orange slices in a single layer. Simmer for 5 minutes, occasionally lifting the pan by the handle and swirling the contents around. Use tongs to turn the oranges over halfway through simmering. Remove the pan from the heat and transfer the orange slices to a plate lined with greaseproof paper. Allow to cool completely.

**MAKING THE CAKE**

Preheat the oven to 180 °C/160 °C fan-forced. Butter a 24 cm cake tin and line the base with baking parchment.

Use hand-held electric beaters to beat the eggs, sugar and blood orange zest in a large bowl until the mixture is very thick and pale (usually 3–5 minutes). Mix the orange juice, oil and milk in a measuring cup or jug. Bit by bit, add the orange juice mixture to the eggs and sugar, beating well to make sure each addition is incorporated before adding more.

Using a hand whisk, mix the flour into the wet ingredients until you have an amalgamated batter.

Lay the orange slices in one layer on the bottom of the lined cake tin. Pour the batter over the orange slices.

Bake for 40 minutes. At the end of this time, cover the top of the cake with foil and bake for a further 15 minutes. The cake is done when it is golden brown on top and is coming slightly away from the sides.

Remove the cake from the oven and leave it to cool in its tin for 15–20 minutes. If the cake has risen too much, slice the top off using the sides of the cake tin as a guide. Invert the cake onto a cooling rack and gently peel away the baking parchment.

Allow the cake to cool completely before transferring it to a serving plate. Serve with a dollop of crème fraîche or double cream.

# WINTER MENU

## A FEW FAVOURITE INFORMAL WINTER LUNCHES

*(Serve all at once, for everyone to help themselves)*

### MENU 1

Poached chicken and vegetables with green sauce . . . p. 226

Crostini with the new season's olive oil and garlic . . . . . . . p. 173

Maria's marmalade, mascarpone and almond tart . . . . . . . . . . . . p. 196

### MENU 2

Penne with cavolo nero and pancetta . . . p. 217

Baked fennel with white wine . . . p. 260

Artichoke, parmesan and rocket salad . . . p. 90

*Affogato* (vanilla ice cream 'drowned' in coffee) . . . . . . . . . . . . . . p. 200

### MENU 3

Crostini with cavolo nero and ricotta . . . p. 210

Artichoke risotto . . . p. 224

Blood orange and olive oil upside-down cake . . . . . . . . . . p. 235

### MENU 4

Breadless ribollita . . . p. 212

Crostini with the new season's olive oil and garlic . . . p. 173

Flourless chocolate, almond and chilli cake . . . p. 115

**MENU 1**

TO START  Pea and mint soup . . . . . . . . . . . . . . . p. 92

TO FOLLOW  Pasta 'alla Savannah', with spicy Italian sausage . . . . . . . . . . . p. 218

Peppery green salad . . . . . . . . . . . . . . . . . . . . . . . . . . . . . . . . . . . . . . . . . p. 244

TO FINISH  Cardamom poached pears . . . . . . . . . . . . . . . . . . . . . . . . . . . p. 232

**MENU 2**

TO START

Cardoon gratin . . . p. 223

TO FOLLOW

Breadless ribollita . . . p. 212

TO FINISH

Berry clafoutis with Amalfi
lemon cream . . . p. 199

**MENU 3**

TO START

Crostini with cavolo nero and ricotta . . . p. 210

TO FOLLOW

Beef stew with gremolata . . . p. 227

Polenta . . . p. 266

TO FINISH

Hazelnut, almond and pear tart . . . p. 231

**MENU 4**

TO START

Hot toast with truffled butter . . . . . . . . . . . . . . . . . . . . . p. 211

TO FOLLOW

Roast chicken with grapes . . . . . . . . . . . . . . p. 188

Charred roast potatoes with lemons . . . . . . . . . . . p. 265

Mama's roast cherry tomatoes . . . . . . . . p. 251

Peppery green salad . . . . . . p. 244

TO FINISH

Hazelnut, almond and pear tart . . . p. 231

❦❦❦

# SIDES

AND

# STAPLES

FOR

# ALL

# SEASONS

I hesitate to say that these are the most important recipes in the book, but they are certainly the most essential to me and the ones I turn to most frequently. These are the side dishes, salads and vegetables that have come to be my best friends when cooking for lots of people, and I keep them in the toolbox year-round.

The following recipes use vegetables that are, on the whole, available in every season, and I often make two or three for any given lunch, allowing people to indulge in the pleasure of having lots of choice and being able to have a little bit of everything. Most of these dishes can be made ahead of time, or are very quick and easy to prepare, which is useful if you are going to invest time in making something more fiddly as the main course. All of them immediately add colour, freshness and texture to the broader, smorgasbord-style feast.

Whether I am cooking in the first flourish of spring, or as the days begin to shorten and the light from the sun shines lower in the sky, I know that a seemingly ordinary meal will immediately be enlivened with the addition of one of these dishes.

*Insalata di rucola*

# PEPPERY GREEN SALAD

I generally reach to make this salad before giving any thought to other side dishes. The bitter freshness of rocket cuts through anything rich, and I find this salad always elevates and balances a meal. This is the simplest way to make it, but I am including another way I frequently dress rocket leaves in the box below.

**PREPARATION:- 5 minutes**

In a large salad bowl, toss the rocket with the olive oil, lemon juice and a generous pinch of salt. Serve immediately.

**SERVES 5**

200 g rocket

75 ml olive oil

Juice of 1 lemon

Salt

**VARIATION:-**

I frequently add 1 tablespoon of balsamic glaze and 100 g of chopped walnuts to this salad, which makes it a sweeter and more robust side.

*Carote grattugiate con limone e basilico*

# GRATED CARROTS
# WITH LEMON AND BASIL

Undoubtedly one of my staples in summer (and year-round, come to think of it). I eat this on its own by the bowlful. When I was at school in the local village, this was the vegetable we had on Tuesdays, and I would always ask for seconds and thirds. It goes beautifully as part of a picking lunch made up of lots of dishes, or you can add a ball of mozzarella and have it as a starter.

**PREPARATION:– 10 minutes**

**SERVES 6**

8 large carrots, tops and bottoms chopped off

50 g basil, leaves roughly torn

Juice of 1 lemon

75 ml olive oil

Salt

Grate the carrots using the side of your box grater with the largest holes, so that you are left with orange-coloured shards. Put the grated carrot in a serving bowl, add the torn basil leaves and toss together. If making this salad ahead of time, set the carrot and basil aside in the fridge until you are ready to add the dressing.

To make the dressing, mix the lemon juice and olive oil with a generous pinch of salt. Pour the dressing over the carrots and basil, mix thoroughly and serve immediately.

*Insalata di radicchio, cannellini e nocciole*

# RADICCHIO, CANNELLINI BEAN AND HAZELNUT SALAD

An aesthetically pleasing and substantial salad, which I often serve with lots of other vegetarian dishes.

**PREPARATION:- 5 minutes**
**COOKING:- 10 minutes**

**SERVES 6**

**FOR THE SALAD:-**
100 g blanched hazelnuts
2 large heads red radicchio
1 x 400 g tin cannellini beans

**FOR THE DRESSING:-**
50 ml olive oil
Juice of ½ lemon
3 tablespoons balsamic glaze
Salt
Freshly ground black pepper

Preheat the oven to 170 °C/150 °C fan-forced.

Spread the hazelnuts on a baking tray and toast them in the oven for 10 minutes, or until they start to smell nutty and are turning golden brown. Remove them from the oven and allow to cool completely.

Prepare the radicchio by first removing any damaged outer leaves. Tear off the inner leaves one by one, keeping them as intact as possible, and put them in a large salad bowl.

Drain the cannellini beans in a colander over the sink, rinse them in cold water and set aside.

Make the dressing by mixing together the olive oil, lemon juice and balsamic glaze, along with a pinch of salt.

Roughly chop the cooled hazelnuts, so that you have nice chunky pieces.

Add the cannellini beans and hazelnuts to the radicchio leaves. Toss with the dressing and sprinkle with a generous pinch of salt and pepper. Taste a leaf for seasoning and adjust as necessary. Serve immediately.

*Lenticchie con balsamico, pancetta e chiodi do garofano*

# BALSAMIC-GLAZED LENTILS WITH PANCETTA AND CLOVES

This is my family's number one go-to side dish to serve a crowd. It has been on the menu of any family function ever given, at which my mother usually cooks. Whether you are four or fifty, the time it takes to prepare doesn't really vary - and it is even better when made ahead of time and served the next day. Scaling the recipe up is as simple as buying more packets of lentils and chopping a few more sprigs of parsley and pieces of pancetta. For a vegetarian version, omit the pancetta and add an extra tablespoon of olive oil and balsamic glaze.

**PREPARATION:- 5 minutes**
**COOKING:- 35 minutes**

**SERVES 6, WITH LOTS OF LEFTOVERS**

1 red onion, whole

15 g whole cloves

500 g puy lentils or mignon lentils

A small handful of sage leaves

120 ml olive oil – plus 2 tablespoons, to serve

3 garlic cloves, peeled and crushed

300 g sliced pancetta, cut into strips about 1 cm wide

100 ml balsamic glaze

Salt

Freshly ground black pepper

A handful of flat-leaf parsley leaves, roughly chopped

Cut the top off the onion and peel away the outer skin and first inner layer of flesh. Pierce the onion all over with the cloves, then put it in a deep saucepan with the lentils and sage. Add enough cold water to the pan to just cover the onion and lentils, bring to the boil over a medium heat, then reduce the heat and gently simmer for 20–25 minutes, or as instructed on the packet. If the pan starts to dry out, add more water as necessary. The lentils are done when they are tender but still have a little bite. Drain, discard the clove-studded onion and sage, and set the lentils to one side.

Drizzle a tablespoon of the oil into a frying pan and add the crushed garlic and pancetta. Gently fry the garlic and pancetta over a low heat, stirring occasionally, until the pancetta is cooked but not crispy. Add the rest of the oil and the balsamic glaze, then stir for 1–2 minutes, until the mixture is sizzling and the ingredients have amalgamated. Add the lentils, along with a generous pinch of salt and a few grinds of black pepper. Toss the lentils through, then taste for seasoning and adjust as necessary. Set to one side until ready to eat.

Transfer the lentils to a serving dish. Drizzle with the olive oil, add the parsley and taste again for seasoning. This side is delicious at room temperature or reheated.

**DELICIOUS WITH:-**

Roast beef with green sauce (p. 109), Roast chicken with grapes (p. 188), Slow-cooked lamb shoulder with garlic, herbs and lemon (p. 112) and Mama's roast cherry tomatoes (p. 251). Or on its own, with Baked fennel with white wine (p. 260) and Peppery green salad (p. 244).

*Pomodori San Marzano al forno*

# SLOW-ROASTED SAN MARZANO TOMATOES

This method for slow-roasting tomatoes is delicious, and the sugar and salt give it a lovely savoury-sweet note. This recipe is very useful year-round. It even brings out the best of their flavour in the dark winter months, a time of year when you wouldn't dream of eating a tomato raw - not only because of the cold weather, but also because it's almost impossible to find a good tomato.

**PREPARATION:- 5 minutes**
**COOKING:- 1½ to 2 hours**

**SERVES 6**

**8 San Marzano tomatoes, or any firm plum tomatoes you can find**

**2 teaspoons Maldon salt**

**1 teaspoon brown sugar**

Preheat the oven to 170 °C/150 °C fan-forced.

Cut the tomatoes in half lengthways and put them on a baking tray lined with baking parchment. The tray should be large enough to hold all the tomatoes, cut side up, in one layer. Combine the salt and sugar in a small bowl and sprinkle evenly over the tomatoes.

Put the tomatoes into the oven and roast for 1½ to 2 hours. Once the tomatoes look as though they are drying out and are becoming a little charred around the edges, they are done.

Remove the tomatoes from the oven and transfer them to a serving dish. I arrange mine in a pattern of concentric circles, on a round plate. The tomatoes will now be ready to pluck from the plate as a delicious and sweet accompaniment to your main.

**DELICIOUS WITH:-**

These tomatoes can transform and elevate any lunch, but I particularly love them with Potato and onion frittata (p. 110), Roast chicken with grapes (p. 188) and Lemony aioli (p. 255).

*Pomodorini al forno*

# MAMA'S ROAST CHERRY TOMATOES

Not only beautiful, this side dish also balances out most rich mains with its sweet acidity. It has always been a staple of my mother's repertoire, and I find myself adding it to most meals.

**PREPARATION:-** **A few minutes**
**COOKING:-** **40 minutes**

**SERVES 6**

**800 g cherry tomatoes on the vine**

**Olive oil**

**Salt**

Preheat the oven to 200°C/180°C fan-forced.

Put the tomatoes in an ovenproof dish, drizzle with a little oil and sprinkle with salt. Roast for 40 minutes, until the tomatoes begin to char and shrivel.

Remove the tomatoes from the oven and transfer them to a serving dish, or serve them directly from the ovenproof dish.

**DELICIOUS WITH:-**

Balsamic-glazed lentils with pancetta and cloves (p. 249), Roast chicken with grapes (p. 188), Roast beef with green sauce (p. 109) or Ricotta, black olive and basil tart (p. 153).

*Salsa verde*

# GREEN SAUCE

*Salsa verde* is a hugely useful sauce. Verdant and punchy, it will cheer up even the simplest roast vegetable. I often dollop a spoonful on roast cauliflower - in fact, it can be served with any roast vegetable. And it is of course fabulous with poached chicken, roast beef or veal, or in a bowl of plain broth. Here in Italy, there are almost (but perhaps not quite) as many recipes for green sauce as there are for tomato sauce; in Florence, the flavour is predominantly anchovy. Some recipes use white wine vinegar and no lemon, and others feature a wider variety of herbs - parsley being the central herb, no matter the recipe. This sauce is the one my mother has always made, and I love its fresh, citrusy notes and the umami flavour that the anchovies bring - more of a sensation than a dominant flavour. For the chopping, I use a very useful tool called a *mezzaluna* (half-moon), which is a curved knife with a handle at either end. The *mezzaluna*'s seesaw motion means that finely chopping a large bunch of herbs takes half the usual time and is also quite mesmeric, but a normal heavy chopping knife will do the trick too. And by all means, feel free to use a machine for this task.

**PREPARATION:- 15 minutes**

**SERVES 10**

A large handful of flat-leaf parsley leaves

A large handful of basil leaves

A small handful of mint leaves

2 garlic cloves, peeled and crushed

1 tablespoon capers, finely chopped and gently squashed with the side of a knife

1½ teaspoons Maille dijon mustard

2 teaspoons anchovy paste, or 30 g anchovy fillets finely chopped and squashed with the side of a knife

100 ml olive oil

Juice of ½ lemon

Chop the parsley, basil and mint as finely as you can on a chopping board, or blitz them in a food processor.

Put the chopped herbs in a bowl, together with the garlic. Add the capers, mustard and anchovy paste, and mix roughly together using a spoon. Stir in the olive oil and the lemon juice, then taste for seasoning and adjust as necessary. (Does it need more acidity? Add lemon. More salt? Add anchovies.) If it seems a bit dry, add a drizzle more oil. Cover and set aside until serving.

*Aioli con limone*

# LEMONY AIOLI

There is nothing quite like homemade aioli (with garlic) or mayonnaise (no garlic). Serving a bowl of this bright-yellow substance alongside a home-cooked meal always seems to fill everyone's hearts with joy, particularly when you can spoon it onto your plate with abandon. At the start of a painting course - or when I know we have people coming over for a meal or to stay - I will often make a jar of aioli, to serve alongside a frittata, with roast chicken, or simply to have on toast with slow-roasted tomatoes.

**PREPARATION:- 15 minutes**

**MAKES I JAR**

3 egg yolks

Salt

1 garlic clove, peeled and crushed

1 teaspoon Maille dijon mustard

100 ml sunflower oil

100 ml extra virgin olive oil

Juice of ½ lemon

Put the egg yolks, a large pinch of salt, the garlic and mustard in a clean, dry bowl. Combine by briefly whisking with hand-held electric beaters.

Mix together the sunflower oil and olive oil in a measuring cup or jug.

With your electric beaters on a low setting, and whisking constantly, slowly drip the oil into the egg yolks, bit by bit. Watch carefully to make sure that the oil is absorbed into the yolks and emulsified. Once the mixture starts to thicken, whisk in the lemon juice. Keep going until all the oil has been incorporated and you have a nice, thick aioli. If you feel it is too thick, or has split, add a tablespoon of hot water and mix it through with a fork – this should loosen the aioli should it be too thick, or bring it back together if it has split.

Cover and set to one side until needed. The flavours will be enhanced if you let the aioli sit for an hour or so, and it can be left in a jar in the fridge for up to 3 days.

**VARIATION:-**

If you would like something more mellow, omit the crushed garlic to make a basic lemony mayonnaise.

*Insalata di finocchi e arance*

# FENNEL AND ORANGE SALAD

Strictly speaking, the ingredients in this salad are of the winter variety. However, as both fennel and oranges are readily available year-round – and because I love the combination in this classic salad so much – I throw it together whenever the temperature rises and I crave something fresh. If you do happen to be serving it between January and March, it is all the more beautiful for being made with ruby-red blood oranges from Sicily; otherwise, any good oranges will do. I also love a plain fennel salad, dressed in the same way but omitting the oranges and nuts, but I would say this version is infinitely more joyous.

**PREPARATION:- 15 minutes**

**SERVES 6**

50 g blanched hazelnuts

2 large fennel bulbs

2 oranges

30 ml olive oil

Juice of ½ lemon

A handful of mint leaves, roughly chopped

Salt

Preheat your oven to 170 °C/150 °C fan-forced.

Spread the hazelnuts on a baking tray and toast them for 10 minutes, or until they start to smell nutty and are turning golden brown. Remove them from the oven and allow to cool completely.

Prepare the fennel bulbs by tearing off any outer layers that are damaged or brown. Using a paring knife, peel away the woody bottom part of the bulbs, but don't remove the fennel tops and fronds. Very finely slice the fennel bulbs lengthways. If you have a mandolin or a meat slicer, this step will be much easier and you will end up with gossamer-thin fennel ribbons, which not only are attractive but also have a lovely texture.

Peel the oranges and remove any pith, before using a very sharp knife to slice them into discs.

Roughly chop the cooled hazelnuts.

In a salad bowl, gently toss the fennel and oranges with the oil, lemon juice, mint and salt. Top with the chopped hazelnuts. Serve immediately.

**VARIATION:-**

To make this fresh and citrusy salad creamier and more indulgent, top with a whole ball of burrata, allowing everyone to tear away some of the cheese as they help themselves to the salad.

**DELICIOUS WITH:-**

This crunchy salad is a great starter, or it can be served as a side dish accompanying Grilled chicken breast with lemon and thyme (p. 147), Cherry tomato, thyme and mascarpone tart (p. 148), Courgette carpaccio (p. 134), Peach, mozzarella and mint salad (p. 133) or Buffalo mozzarella with grilled aubergine and summery green sauce (p. 137).

# GREENS 'IN THE PAN' WITH GARLIC AND CHILLI

This is one of my favourite *contorni*. It is always available in Italian restaurants. Whenever I order it, I ask if they have 'something green *in padella*'; depending on the season, the restaurant will have spinach, chard, cavolo nero or chicory. I have not put a specific green here, as you might want to choose yours depending on what's in season. The cooking is almost exactly the same for all leafy greens – the only variation being that cavolo nero needs to be blanched longer than more delicate leaves such as spinach.

PREPARATION:- 5 minutes
COOKING:- 10–15 minutes

**SERVES 6**

500 g of your leafy green of choice (for example, spinach, chard or cavolo nero)

50 ml olive oil – plus extra, to serve

2 garlic cloves, peeled and crushed

Chilli flakes

Salt

½ lemon

Chop your greens into 5 cm strips. If you are using chard, separate the stalks and the leafy tops. If you are using cavolo nero, discard the woody part of the stalks.

Blanch or steam the greens: 5 minutes for spinach or chard; 10 minutes for cavolo nero. Drain and set aside.

Heat the oil, garlic, a pinch of chilli flakes and a pinch of salt in a large frying pan over a medium heat for about 5 minutes. Don't allow the garlic to brown – it simply needs to infuse into the oil. If you think the oil is getting too hot, add another tablespoon of oil to cool it down.

Once the oil is gently sizzling, add the greens and toss with the oil and garlic mixture. Sprinkle with a little more salt, toss again and cook over a medium heat for a further 5 minutes.

Transfer to a serving dish. Squeeze the lemon over the greens and drizzle with a little more oil. Serve hot, or at room temperature.

**DELICIOUS WITH:-**

Beef stew with gremolata (p. 227) and Polenta (p. 266), Roast chicken with grapes (p. 188) or Potato and onion frittata (p. 110).

*Endivie e radicchio al forno*

# BAKED ENDIVE AND RADICCHIO

I often eat this on its own as a main course with a ball of mozzarella, but it is also a fabulous side. You can omit one or other of the vegetables, depending on preference or what you have available. The endive is buttery and almost creamy once baked, while the radicchio is slightly bitter and retains a little crunch.

PREPARATION:- 5 minutes
COOKING:- 25 minutes

**SERVES 6**

**3 heads white endive or chicory**

**2 heads red radicchio**

**4 tablespoons olive oil**

**Salt**

**30 g unsalted butter, diced**

Preheat the oven to 200 °C/180 °C fan-forced.

Cut the endive in half lengthways (if very large, cut in half again). Quarter the radicchio lengthways.

You will need a roasting pan large enough to hold all of the vegetables in one layer. Put the vegetables in the pan and toss with the oil and a generous pinch of salt, so that they are evenly coated. Arrange the endive and radicchio in the pan in one layer, cut side up. Dot with the cubes of butter, tucking some into the folds of the leaves and leaving others on top of the vegetables.

Put the vegetables in the oven and cook for 15 minutes. Remove the pan from the oven and turn the endive and radicchio so they are cut side down. Cook for a further 10 minutes. Serve hot.

DELICIOUS WITH:-

Roast pork loin with prunes and pine nuts (p. 192),
Roast chicken with grapes (p. 188) or Ricotta, black olive
and basil tart (p. 153).

# BAKED FENNEL WITH WHITE WINE

**PREPARATION:- 5 minutes**
**COOKING:- 35 minutes**

**SERVES 6**

4 fennel bulbs

3 tablespoons olive oil

A small handful of sage leaves

Leaves from 1 thyme sprig

Salt

Freshly ground black pepper

100 ml white wine

Preheat the oven to 200 °C/180 °C fan-forced.

Finely slice the fennel bulbs lengthways, leaving the fennel tops and fronds on the bulb. Put the fennel in a roasting pan, drizzle with the olive oil and add the sage leaves, thyme, a generous pinch of salt and a few grinds of black pepper. Toss the fennel in the oil and seasonings so the slices are evenly coated, then add the wine.

Cover the pan with foil and roast the fennel for 15 minutes. Take the pan out of the oven, remove the foil and then return the fennel to the oven for 20–25 minutes, until it starts to brown and the ends start to curl. Serve hot.

**VARIATION:-**

If you would like to serve the fennel as a main or a more substantial side, add parmesan and breadcrumbs. After you remove the foil, cover the fennel with 60 g finely grated parmesan, then top with 40 g (good-quality) store-bought or homemade breadcrumbs and a pinch more salt. Cook as instructed above until the top is bubbling and golden.

# ROAST POTATOES WITH GARLIC AND ROSEMARY

My go-to roast potato dish – because it's easy, salty, garlicky and aromatic; everything I want from a carbohydrate. These potatoes work well as a side to most mains, but I usually make them as a side to another roasted dish, as the oven will already be on, cooking the pork, chicken or beef. You can chop your potatoes ahead of time and keep them in a bowl of cold water to stop them from browning.

**PREPARATION:–** 10 minutes
**COOKING:–** 40 minutes

**SERVES 6-8**

**1.5 kg potatoes, skin on**

**100 ml vegetable oil**

**6 garlic cloves, peeled and crushed**

**Salt**

**Leaves from 2 rosemary sprigs, finely chopped**

Preheat the oven to 220 °C/200 °C fan-forced.

Quarter the potatoes into wedges – you won't be parboiling them, so they need to be a bit smaller than normal roast potatoes. Put them in a large bowl of cold water as you go, to stop them turning brown.

Using a slotted spoon, transfer the potatoes to a roasting pan that is large enough to hold all the wedges in one layer. Don't worry if a little water comes with them. Add the oil to the pan. Toss the potatoes with the oil until they are evenly coated. Add the garlic to the potatoes, sprinkle with a generous pinch of salt and the rosemary, then toss the potatoes again to make sure they are evenly coated.

Put the potatoes in the oven for 40 minutes at 220 °C/200 °C fan-forced, or 50 minutes at 200 °C/180 °C fan-forced, depending on how hot you need the oven for anything else you might be roasting. Halfway through the cooking time, remove the pan from the oven and toss the potatoes to make sure they don't stick. The potatoes will be done when they are soft in the middle and crispy and golden brown on the outside.

Remove the potatoes from the oven and transfer to a serving bowl. Eat immediately.

**VARIATION:–**

This recipe also works very well if you peel the potatoes, cut them into larger pieces, parboil them for 10 minutes and then roast for 10 minutes less than described above.

**DELICIOUS WITH:–**

Roast chicken with grapes (p. 188), Roast pork loin with prunes and pine nuts (p. 192), Roast beef with green sauce (p. 109) or Baked fennel with white wine, topped with parmesan and breadcrumbs (p. 260).

*Patate nuove con carciofi*

# NEW POTATOES WITH BABY ARTICHOKES

Artichokes have a wonderfully long season, from mid-October to late May, so while this is not strictly speaking a year-round side dish, I feel that I make it in enough months of the year to warrant it being in this section. If you can't find baby artichokes, you can use full-size artichokes, or any you can get your hands on. The long roasting with the potatoes will still result in a wonderful combination of flavours. If you can only get larger artichokes, simply quarter instead of halve them.

**PREPARATION:– 15 minutes**
**COOKING:– 45 minutes**

**SERVES 6**

**500 g new potatoes, skin on**

**500 g baby artichokes or 4 artichokes**

**75 ml olive oil**

**Salt**

**6 bay leaves**

Preheat the oven to 220°C/200°C fan-forced.

Slice the potatoes in half lengthways, and put them in a large roasting pan.

Prepare the artichokes as described on page 91. Cut into quarters if using large artichokes, and in half if using baby ones. Put the artichoke pieces in the pan with the potatoes, then add the oil, a generous pinch of salt and the bay leaves, and mix everything together using your hands or a large spoon.

Roast for 45 minutes until the potatoes are sizzling and golden, and the artichoke pieces are a dark green with charred edges. Serve hot.

**DELICIOUS WITH:–**

Roast beef with green sauce (p. 109), Slow-cooked lamb shoulder with garlic, herbs and lemon (p. 112) or Ricotta and asparagus tart (p. 106).

*Patate al forno con limone*

# CHARRED ROAST POTATOES WITH LEMONS

**PREPARATION:-** 5 minutes
**COOKING:-** 40 minutes

**SERVES 6**

1 kg small potatoes, skin on

2 lemons

4 garlic cloves, peeled and crushed

2 garlic cloves, left unpeeled, gently squashed with the edge of a large knife

1 whole rosemary sprig (leaves and stalks)

50 ml olive oil

50 ml vegetable oil

Salt

Preheat the oven to 240 °C/220 °C fan-forced.

Cut the potatoes into thin discs, about 1.5 mm thick (roughly the thickness of an English penny). If the potatoes are very large, cut each one in half horizontally before slicing.

Slice the whole lemons into discs, the same thickness as the potato slices.

Gently toss the potatoes with the crushed garlic cloves.

Place the whole garlic cloves, half the lemon discs, the rosemary sprig and the combined oils in a roasting pan. Put the pan in the oven to heat up for 5 minutes.

Gently toss the remaining lemon slices with the potatoes and two generous pinches of salt.

Once the oil is sizzling, remove the pan from the oven, discard the whole garlic cloves and rosemary, and add the potatoes and lemons. Toss the potatoes in the oil, return the pan to the oven and roast for 20 minutes. Take the pan from the oven, shuffle the potatoes, lower the heat to 220 °C/200 °C fan-forced and roast for another 15 minutes. After this time, turn the oven function to grill and grill the potatoes for 5 minutes until golden and charred.

**DELICIOUS WITH:-**

Slow-cooked lamb shoulder with garlic, herbs and lemon (p. 112) or Artichoke and béchamel pie (p. 101).

# POLENTA

COOKING:– 15 minutes

**SERVES 6**

1 vegetable stock cube

350 g instant polenta
(*polenta rapida*)

60 g unsalted butter

60 g parmesan, grated –
plus extra, to serve

Salt

Add 1 litre water to a large pan, crumble in the stock cube and bring to the boil. Once the water is boiling, pour in the polenta slowly and carefully, stirring constantly with a whisk. Reduce the heat to medium and stir for 8 minutes to stop any lumps forming. When the polenta starts spitting, reduce the heat to low and carefully carry on stirring.

Stir in the butter and parmesan, together with a generous pinch of salt. You should have a nice smooth, buttery polenta.

Transfer to a serving bowl and top with a little more parmesan. Serve immediately.

**DELICIOUS WITH:–**

Beef stew with gremolata (p. 227) or Roast chicken with grapes (p. 188). You can also serve it as a vegetarian main, topped with Baked fennel with white wine (p. 260), accompanied by a side dish of Balsamic-glazed lentils with cloves (p. 249) – simply omit the pancetta.

*Purè di rape*

# CELERIAC MASH

**PREPARATION:–** 15 minutes
**COOKING:–** 30 minutes

**SERVES 6**

**Salt**

**2 celeriac (about 500 g total), peeled and roughly chopped into cubes**

**2 large baking potatoes (about 700 g total), peeled and roughly chopped into cubes**

**75 g unsalted butter**

**2 tablespoons olive oil**

**Freshly ground black pepper**

Bring a large pan of water to a lively boil, then add a fistful of salt.

Add the celeriac and boil for 10 minutes, then add the potato and boil for a further 15 minutes. Once you can easily pierce the celeriac and potato with a knife, remove the pan from the heat, retaining a mugful of the cooking water before you drain the vegetables.

Return the drained celeriac and potato to the pan with the butter, olive oil, a pinch of salt, some grinds of black pepper and a drizzle of the cooking water.

Mash the potato and celeriac until smooth (alternatively, use hand-held electric beaters). Add more of the cooking water if the mixture seems a bit dry, and blend or mash again. Taste for seasoning and adjust as preferred.

> **DELICIOUS WITH:–**
>
> Beef stew with gremolata (p. 227).

# END
# THOUGHTS

# UNNOTICED TREASURES: DAY TRIPS FROM ARNIANO

Growing up near the 'Via Francigena', a famous and ancient pilgrim's route leading to Rome, I always took it for granted that we were spoilt for ancient cultural sites. Arniano is surrounded by beautiful monasteries and towns that grew because pilgrims were constantly passing by on their way down south. Because these places were on our doorstep, visits were always laidback and stress free – and were usually combined with lunch. These jaunts were often for a special occasion: midnight mass on Christmas Eve, for example, to see and hear the monks celebrate vespers in Gregorian chant at the Abbazia di Sant'Antimo; or a hot and sticky summer's day spent watching the Palio in Siena. Now they have become favourite places to take family, friends and our painters.

## ABBAZIA DI MONTE OLIVETO

Our favourite – and most visited – spot has always been the Abbey of Monte Oliveto Maggiore, a working Benedictine monastery built on a promontory in the heart of the Creti Senesi. This fossil-rich area, which millions of years ago was a sea bed, is also known as the Accona Desert, due to the barren, almost lunar, nature of the landscape.

The drive up to the monastery is a big part of the attraction. It leads you up from the valley where our local town of Buonconvento sits, and you gradually ascend along a winding road that crests a ridge, with beautiful fields and woodland falling away on either side – eventually giving way to grey, moonlike craters. In the distance, perched on top of a hill, sits the town of Chiusure, a favourite spot for lunch at Locanda Il Paradiso. This perfect, low-key trattoria is run by a contemporary of mine, Pamela, who has taken over from her parents. The views and unfussy food are unbeatable. As you gaze up towards Chiusure, to your right, beyond a crevasse, you can see a spire and turrets rising up from a patch of forest – the abbey, seemingly floating on its promontory.

When you finally arrive, you are welcomed by a medieval castle, where there is another fun restaurant (and part of the reason why we visit Monte Oliveto so often), Ristorante La Torre, so named as it sits in the turret of the castle. It has a sunny outdoor area, and the food is homely, greedy and local. My father, sister and I would often go on a winter's day after school to sit in the dark interior, hoping to catch sight of a monk surreptitiously watching the football. Before or after lunch, we would always visit the abbey, which you have to approach on foot. It truly does feel as though you have stepped back in time as you wander down an ancient cobbled path, before arriving at a large, beautiful building made up of a church, cloisters, pharmacy and elegant library.

Monte Oliveto is famous for the frescoes in its Great Cloister, representing the life of St Benedict. Parts of the frescoes were painted by Luca Signorelli from about 1495, and they were later completed by Antonio Bazzi, known as Il Sodoma, who began work in 1505. You can distinguish which artist painted which panel, as Il Sodoma loved painting animals, and in his depictions St Benedict is surrounded by badgers, geese and other creatures. I love the colours and patterns in the frescoes, which feel very familiar after a lifetime of slow, meandering visits.

## ABBAZIA DI SANT'ANTIMO

In the sitting room at Arniano, there are two large canvases painted in the style of the Renaissance. These depict buildings local to us, but there is something incongruous about them, which is that the surrounding landscape doesn't seem very Tuscan. In fact, it doesn't seem all that European, but rather looks like the savannah of Africa. That is because the paintings are by an artist friend of my parents who lives in Kenya. When the paintings arrived in large rolled canvases to be remounted, my mother felt they seemed far too shiny and new. So, with her restoration background, she immediately set to work with some sheets of sandpaper, rubbing them down to age them. The buildings, although set in an African landscape, are in fact very familiar and local.

The painting of which I am most fond is of the Abbey of Sant'Antimo. This beautiful 12th-century church – with links that go even further back, to the time of Charlemagne – is nestled in a glade atop a mountain on the other side of Montalcino. Unlike Monte Oliveto, which appears like a surprise from the trees as you approach it, Sant'Antimo is visible from afar as you drive towards it, standing in a picturesque meadow, which in spring is dotted with wildflowers, glorious among the surrounding centuries-old olive trees. I remember being awed by the size of the olives there when I was a child – they had trunks as wide as my leg was long – and my parents explaining how many hundreds of years ago they would have been planted.

The monastery was unused for a long time until, in the early 1990s, a group of French Benedictine monks came to inhabit it. They soon made the church famous for the Gregorian chants that they performed during services. We often went on Christmas Eve to the candlelit midnight mass, which was very atmospheric – though I must admit that the dour chanting wasn't exactly filled with the Christmas jollity of Protestant carols. There are no longer any monks at Sant'Antimo, as the order was consolidated with that of Monte Oliveto. But the church is so beautiful, and the setting so picturesque, that it is most definitely worth a visit. There is a charming osteria in Castelnuovo dell'Abate, and it happens to be minutes away from Tenuta Buon Tempo, one of our favourite wineries, who also offer wonderful wine tastings.

Siena is the capital of our province, and the closest town/city of any meaningful size. A medieval citadel, it was built between the 13th and 16th centuries, and is encircled by a high wall with seven ancient gates, through which you enter the city. The whole place seems poised for an impending attack. It is a labyrinth of winding alleys, with every building made from the same reddish brick; the colour of burnt sienna, mirroring the colour of the earth in the surrounding countryside.

Before internet shopping, Siena was where we would have to go to buy anything that wasn't available from our local village, and for me as a teenager it held the great excitement of having a CD shop – forget the culture. Nowadays, I love to visit the city cathedral, to my mind the most beautiful ever built. Clad in black-and-white marble stripes, it rises out of the red city and its rooftops. Although a little smaller than the Duomo in Florence, it is still enormous – despite the construction of a large extension being halted in the 15th century, due to the plague. I find that being a bit more compact makes it all the more mesmerising. The colours and details inside are exquisite: the marble inlay floor; the Piccolomini library, filled with ancient manuscripts surrounded by lovely frescoes; and my favourite – small blue-and-white diamond-shaped floor tiles with beautiful crescent moons.

I love to visit Siena in winter, when it's almost empty, and having been to the cathedral or one of the many other beautiful churches, to wander to the Campo, the conch-shaped square with the town hall at its centre. Soaring over the Campo is a skinny clock tower, which you can climb, though I wouldn't recommend it if you suffer from claustrophobia or vertigo. I long ago gave up clambering up all those steps. Instead, I like to sit in my favourite bar – Il Palio – and have a drink while watching the goings-on in the square.

In summer, the square changes dramatically when it is converted into a racecourse for the city's most famous and maddest tradition – the Palio, a horserace that has evolved from medieval jousting. Representatives of Siena's *contrade* (districts of the city) compete in the race, which takes place twice a year, in July and August. The enmities and alliances between the teams date back 500 years, and are as fraught today as they were back then. The jockeys ride the horses bareback, and there is a great deal of skulduggery and foul play. The Palio is wonderful and insane, not least because of the 'San Martino' corner on the north-east side of the square – essentially a right angle – which is taken simultaneously by all ten horses (only ten of the seventeen *contrade* are represented in each race; a ballot is taken to decide who gets to compete in each Palio). The race only lasts ninety seconds, which is the time it takes the horses to lap the square three times. The briefness of the race is made up for by hours of spectacle before and after, with dedicated residents dressed in medieval garb in their *contrada*'s colours, wandering around the square in regimented procession, some banging drums, playing trumpets or flag throwing, and others driving the bull and cart that carries the race's prize – a silk banner, known itself as 'the Palio', to be hung in the winning *contrada*'s own church. In Siena, the Palio is ever-present throughout the year. Wander down the streets on a cold day in February, and chances are you will hear the rumble of drums, making you feel that royalty must be approaching. Follow the thunder and you will be led to a back alley where a teenage boy will be practising with a younger brother for next summer's procession.

There are three ways to see the race. One is by cramming into the centre of the square, which is free of charge, and standing in the crowd inside the circuit, forgoing all shade or toilet access on a hot summer's day. Or you can watch from the specially erected steep stands, where you sit on a very narrow, uncomfortable bench. The most chic and comfortable way to watch the race is from a window of one of the *palazzi* surrounding the square, but it is also the most expensive. I think one feels most involved in the stands. A few years ago, I was sitting three rows back from the course, and a jockey was shoved by a rival and flipped over into the laps of the spectators sitting in front of me.

The ins and outs of this wonderful tradition are so numerous I could write a whole chapter about it, but I won't. If you are interested, there is a fabulous documentary by Cosima Spender named 'Palio' (2015), which explains more about the race.

While I adore visiting Siena for a drink, there aren't many restaurants that I love. I prefer to wander back to the car after my *aperitivo* and drive to Monteriggioni or Fonterutoli, two nearby villages, each equipped with a very good Tuscan *osteria*.

# WINES
# WE
# LOVE

According to my husband, I have very fixed tastes when it comes to wine, despite not knowing a huge amount about it. We are lucky to be surrounded by wineries that people cross the world to visit, and to be friends with some talented winemakers. Tuscany is dominated by the Sangiovese, a strong, punchy variety of grape. To the south of us lies Montalcino, home of some wonderful reds and the now world-famous Brunello (which I won't recommend here, as I find this wine prohibitively expensive – though if you do want to splash out, I would choose a Sesti Brunello di Montalcino 2015, made by my friend Elisa). And to the north is the Chianti region. I am usually a red wine drinker, as Tuscany is a little limited in its production of white wine. So, I will mostly be recommending reds. Read on for some of our favourite wines, which we serve to our friends and painters – and which all ship internationally, should you like to taste any of them.

While I am not an expert, it just so happens that one of my oldest friends, Carolina (whom I met and made friends with on our first day at primary school in the village), is now a sommelier. She runs the Millecento Wine Club at Castiglion del Bosco, a neighbouring 5000-acre estate, which was bought by Massimo Ferragamo in 2003 and is now a Rosewood Hotel. Carolina very kindly helps me figure out wine pairings when I am menu planning for the painting courses. On the following pages you will find her suggestions as to which dishes go best with our favourite Italian wines.

# PROSECCO

## VILLA MARCELLO PROSECCO MILLESIMATO BRUT (VENETO)

Coming in a very glamorous black-and-gold bottle, this is surprisingly refined and dry for a prosecco. It is a nicely balanced and super-refreshing glass of fizz: fruity, with an elegant structure and lovely acidity. We buy their beautiful magnums for the *aperitivo* hour – they look glorious on the bar and there is always plenty to go round.

Crostini with broad beans, mint and ricotta (p. 86)
Fried courgette flowers, sage leaves and mini mozzarellas with lemon zest (p. 128)
Prosciutto with figs (p. 176)
Crostini with porcini, rosemary and prosecco (p. 172)
A bowl of olives, some pecorino and good salami

# WHITES

## BELGUARDO VERMENTINO (TUSCANY)

Along with Vernaccia, Vermentino is one of only two noteworthy dry white wines that Tuscany and the Sangiovese kingdom have to offer. We love this Vermentino from Belguardo on the coast for its zesty and citrusy notes, which make it both structured and super refreshing. At our painting courses, as the bells chime midday in the distance, our painters' heads will snap up, and we know they are ready for a glass of refreshing Vermentino.

- Peach, mozzarella and mint salad (p. 133)
- Fusilli with Sicilian almond pesto (p. 140)
- Linguine with lemon, ricotta and basil (p. 143)
- Grilled chicken breast with lemon and thyme (p. 147)
- Artichoke risotto (p. 224)
- Ricotta and asparagus tart (p. 106)

## AZISA, ZISOLA (SICILY)

This is the most recent addition to our roster of house wines. It is particularly popular with our painters after a hot morning out in the sun at their easels. Although this wine is not made in Tuscany, it is made by Tuscans, the Mazzei family. It offers a slightly salty, fresh and fruity feel that is typical of Sicilian wines.

- Homemade tagliatelle with spring peas (p. 98)
- Potato and onion frittata (p. 110)
- Penne with cherry tomatoes, onions and ricotta (p. 144)
- Cherry tomato, thyme and mascarpone tart (p. 148)

# REDS

## ZISOLA NOTO ROSSO (SICILY)

From the same winery as Azisa. I first tried this while on holiday at the winery where it is made, on the edge of Noto, a Baroque town in south-eastern Sicily. It's impossible not to fall in love with this magical place – and with the wine that the Mazzei family make from vineyards surrounded by almond and orange trees, which flavour the palate of the wine. This light red has hints of citrus and dried fruit, which give it a refreshing acidity. It is quite translucent, and in the height of summer we keep it in the fridge to serve chilled.

- Pea and mint soup (p. 92)
- Grilled chicken breast with lemon and thyme (p. 147)
- Buffalo mozzarella with grilled aubergine and summery green sauce (p. 137)
- Artichoke and béchamel pie (p. 101)
- Spaghetti with datterini tomatoes and basil (p. 141)
- Fusilli with Sicilian almond pesto (p. 140)
- My penne 'alla Bettola', with tomato and vodka (p. 181)

## BUON TEMPO ROSSO DI MONTALCINO (TUSCANY)

Tenuta Buon Tempo sits in one of the most prized spots in the Montalcino region, to the south-east, just below Monte Amiata. It also sits in one of the prettiest spots, just beyond the Abbazia di Sant'Antimo, making a drive there a real treat. This is one of the best Rosso di Montalcino I have tasted; it has an inviting, deep ruby-red colour, and is much more layered in the nose than many of its counterparts from other wineries. It needs to be consumed with food to enhance the flavour and to balance its vibrant acidity, making it perfect to have with snacks, starters or throughout a meal.

- **A bowl of olives, some pecorino and good salami**
- **Ricotta, black olive and basil tart (p. 153)**
- **Penne with cavolo nero and pancetta (p. 217)**
- **Pasta 'alla Savannah', with spicy Italian sausage (p. 218)**
- **Roast chicken with grapes (p. 188)**

## SAN LEONE CASTELLO SONNINO (TUSCANY)

This is my favourite of the wines produced by the late Alessandro de Renzis Sonnino, who was my father's best friend and my sister's godfather. His wife, Caterina, designs their beautiful labels. San Leone is a lovely, full-bodied Tuscan blend of Merlot and Sangiovese, perfect for a special occasion. It works best with strongly flavoured dishes, meat dishes, or cheesy and rich vegetarian meals. Castello Sonnino also has a lovely *enoteca* (wine bar and shop), which is well worth a visit, and where the postage-stamp sized garden was designed by my father, Caterina and Alessandro.

- **Artichoke and béchamel pie (p. 101)**
- **Baked ricotta with olive oil, tomato and basil (p. 182)**
- **Roast pork loin with prunes and pine nuts (p. 192)**
- **Slow-cooked lamb shoulder with garlic, herbs and lemon (p. 112)**

## FONTERUTOLI CHIANTI CLASSICO (TUSCANY)

This winery is on the other side of Siena from us. The vineyards surround the beautiful hamlet of Fonterutoli, which belongs to our friends, the Mazzei family, whose ancestors have been making wine since 1435. This is a fabulous wine, with a beautiful complexity and robust structure, making it perfect for most meaty dishes, as well as for leaner vegetarian dishes. There is a lovely restaurant at Fonterutoli. I highly recommend that you visit if you are in the area, and take a wine tour of their amazing cellars.

- **Crostini with porcini, rosemary and prosecco (p. 172)**
- **Breadless ribollita (p. 212)**
- **Chickpea and rosemary soup (p. 178)**
- **Roast beef with green sauce (p. 109)**
- **Beef stew with gremolata (p. 227)**

## TENUTA PRIMA PIETRA – PRIMA PIETRA (TUSCANY)

This 'super Tuscan' wine is produced by our neighbours at Castiglion del Bosco, at Massimo Ferragamo's other vineyard, located near Riparbella, a pretty hilltop town. Tenuta Prima Pietra is apparently the highest vineyard along the Tuscan coast. This red sits at the upper range of what I would spend on a bottle of wine, but if you are in need of a special-occasion wine based on Cabernet Sauvignon and Merlot, this is fabulous. Deep, aromatic and satisfying to sip.

- **Penne with cavolo nero and pancetta (p. 217)**
- **Spinach and ricotta malfatti with butter and sage (p. 94)**
- **Roast beef and green sauce (p. 109)**
- **Beef stew with gremolata (p. 227)**
- **Slow-cooked lamb shoulder with garlic, herbs and lemon (p. 112)**

# CONVERSIONS

This book uses UK/US 15 ml (3 teaspoon) tablespoon measures.
Note that Australia uses 20 ml (4 teaspoon) tablespoon measures.

## LENGTH

| MM/CM | INCHES |
|---|---|
| 2 mm | ¹⁄₁₆ inch |
| 3 mm | ⅛ inch |
| 4 mm | ³⁄₁₆ inch |
| 5–6 mm | ¼ inch |
| 1 cm | ½ inch |
| 1.5 cm | ⅝ inch |
| 2 cm | ¾ inch |
| 2.5 cm | 1 inch |
| 3 cm | 1¼ inches |
| 4 cm | 1½ inches |
| 5 cm | 2 inches |
| 6 cm | 2½ inches |
| 10 cm | 4 inches |
| 18 cm | 7 inches |
| 20 cm | 8 inches |
| 23 cm | 9 inches |
| 24 cm | 9½ inches |
| 25 cm | 10 inches |
| 30 cm | 12 inches |

## WEIGHT

| G | OZ | LB |
|---|---|---|
| 15 g | ½ oz | |
| 30 g | 1 oz | |
| 55 g | 2 oz | |
| 85 g | 3 oz | |
| 115 g | 4 oz | ¼ lb |
| 140 g | 5 oz | |
| 175 g | 6 oz | |
| 200 g | 7 oz | |
| 225 g | 8 oz | ½ lb |
| 250 g | 9 oz | |
| 280 g | 10 oz | |
| 310 g | 11 oz | |
| 350 g | 12 oz | ¾ lb |
| 375 g | 13 oz | |
| 400 g | 14 oz | |
| 425 g | 15 oz | |
| 450 g | 16 oz | 1 lb |
| 680 g | 24 oz | 1½ lb |
| 900 g | 32 oz | 2 lb |

## LIQUID VOLUME

| ML/LITRES | FL OZ | CUPS |
|---|---|---|
| 15–20 ml | ½ fl oz | |
| 25 ml | ¾ fl oz | |
| 30 ml | 1 fl oz | ⅛ cup |
| 40 ml | 1¼ fl oz | |
| 45 ml | 1½ fl oz | |
| 55 ml | 1¾ fl oz | |
| 60 ml | 2 fl oz | ¼ cup |
| 70 ml | 2¼ fl oz | |
| 80 ml | 2½ fl oz | ⅓ cup |
| 100 ml | 3½ fl oz | |
| 115 ml | 3¾ fl oz | |
| 125 ml | 4 fl oz | ½ cup |
| 160 ml | 5 fl oz | ⅔ cup |
| 180 ml | 6 fl oz | ¾ cup |
| 200 ml | 7 fl oz | |
| 250 ml | 8 fl oz | 1 cup |
| 300 ml | 10½ fl oz | |
| 350 ml | 12 fl oz | |
| 400 ml | 14 fl oz | |
| 500 ml | 16 fl oz | 2 cups |
| 560 ml | 20 fl oz | 2¼ cups |
| 1 litre | 32 fl oz | 4 cups |

## OVEN TEMPERATURES

| °C | °F | GAS |
|---|---|---|
| 70°C | 150°F | ¼ |
| 100°C | 200°F | ½ |
| 110°C | 225°F | ½ |
| 120°C | 235°F | ½ |
| 130°C | 250°F | 1 |
| 140°C | 275°F | 1 |
| 150°C | 300°F | 2 |
| 160°C | 315°F | 2–3 |
| 170°C | 325°F | 3 |
| 180°C | 350°F | 4 |
| 190°C | 375°F | 5 |
| 200°C | 400°F | 6 |
| 210°C | 410°F | 6–7 |
| 220°C | 425°F | 7 |
| 230°C | 450°F | 8 |
| 240°C | 475°F | 8 |
| 250°C | 500°F | 9 |

## UK/US/AUSTRALIAN INGREDIENT TERMS

An online search will quickly clarify any variations in terminology, but alternative names for a few ingredients found in these recipes are worth listing here.

**aubergine** . . . . . . . . . . . eggplant
**bicarbonate of soda** . . . baking soda
**broad bean** . . . . . . . . . . fava bean
**cornstarch** . . . . . . . . . . . cornflour
**courgette** . . . . . . . . . . . . . zucchini
**double cream** . . . . . . . . thick cream
**plain flour** . . . . . . . all-purpose flour
**polenta** . . . . . . . . . . . . . cornmeal
**rocket** . . . . . . . . . . . . . . . arugula
**shallot** . . . . . eschalot/French shallot
**single (or pouring) cream** . pure cream
**tomato passata** . . puréed tomatoes
**topside (beef)** . . . . . . . . . top round

**A note about puff pastry:–**
If ready-rolled sheets of puff pastry are only available frozen, they will need to be thawed before use in these recipes.

# ACKNOWLEDGEMENTS

A huge amount of work has gone into bringing the story of Arniano to life in this book against all the odds thrown at it by the pandemic, and I am indebted to many talented and kind people.

Firstly, to my beloved, Matthew, without whose persistent persuasion, support and encouragement this book would never have been written. Thank you for always pushing me to make my dreams bigger, and for reading every iteration of the copy before it was sent off. I am hugely grateful to be married to such a wonderful person, writer and editor. To William Roper-Curzon, my second husband, friend and business partner: thank you for making the past seven years of painting courses so endlessly inspiring and fun. Thank you for making me laugh so often, and for your beautiful paintings which are the openers for each chapter.

My heartfelt thanks to Robyn Lea, who made this book possible, who believed in the project from the moment we spoke about it, and whose gorgeous photographs have brought the story of Arniano to life on the page. Thank you, Robyn, for going above and beyond for the book, and for throwing your immense talent and experience behind it. Thank you to Saghar Setareh for coming to Arniano in Robyn's stead when coronavirus made it impossible for her to be here in person, and for taking such breathtaking photos of Arniano in full spring. And to Alice Adams for styling them so beautifully. Thank you also to the talented Tara Rowse, whose photos grace the recipes for Baked ricotta with olive oil, tomato and basil, and Chiara's persimmon tiramisù.

To the whole team at Thames & Hudson, but in particular, to Kirsten Abbott, who is the driving force behind this book and whose flawless vision, taste and advice have made *A House Party in Tuscany* what it is. Thank you to my editor Diana Hill for bringing the text together so beautifully. To Ashlea O'Neill for designing a book lovelier than I could ever have imagined and for grappling with the lengthy text so skilfully. To my agent Laurie Robertson, and to Caroline Michel, for believing in the book from the first moment you heard about it, and for all the work behind the scenes to help and encourage me.

I would also like to thank my family and friends for their contributions, support and input: to my mum, endlessly, always. Hugo Guinness for his wisdom and for never pulling any punches. Tara Guinness of Tara Cookery for her wonderful and precise recipe-testing. To Claudia Guinness and Beata Heuman for their wonderful and less precise recipe-testing. To Grace Pilkington for all her professional advice, as well as being my dear friend – thank you, my darling Gramble. To Skye McAlpine for her words of encouragement and lovely words on the cover. My heartfelt thanks as well to Ruthie Rogers, Loyd Grossman and Emiko Davies for their hugely kind and generous quotes about the book.

To my Italian lockdown gang: Savannah Alvarez, Carolina Bracalente, Nicola Voltolini, Ben and Juliette Ashworth and Tom Richards. To Chiara and Massimo from Trattoria Cammillo for always feeding me, and for sharing Chiara's recipe for tiramisù. To Catherine, Georgie, Valentine, Sebastian and all my beloved cousins, uncles and aunts. To Virginia Loughnan, Nick and Olwen Bell, David Macmillan, Elliott Puckette, Ali and Jack Coleman, Liberty Nimmo, George Smith, Vanessa Garwood, Violet Day, Nicolas Niarchos, Lucy Boyd, Charles Pullan, Emily FitzRoy, Rossana Lippi, Daniele Zeddi, Grazia Floris, Andrea Lechner, Colin Brading, John Finlay, Bryan and Isaac Ferry, and Louise and Erskine Guinness. I love you all and cannot tell you what your enthusiasm and encouragement has meant throughout the whole process.

One of my biggest thanks is to all our painters, to everyone who has ever taken a chance on a holiday on a hilltop with our merry band. Thank you for planting the seed for this book with your chorus of 'What's the recipe for this?' and 'Please write a book' at the end of every meal, on every course, for the past seven years. We are so grateful to count you as friends. In particular, to those who keep coming back: Eva, Kerstin and Arvid, Pino, Bill and Susie, Kirsty, Ceri and David, Bill and Pam, Culley and the late, brilliant and much missed Sue Coulson.

My heartfelt thanks go to everyone who helped bring the imagery together through the loan of beautiful pieces of fabric, crockery, produce and flowers. To my dear friend Sue Townsend, to the whole team at Ortigia Sicilia, to Marta and Reona at Richard Ginori 1735, and to Luke Edward Hall for introducing us. To Lisa and Ida from Lisa Corti in Milan. To Robyn's assistant Carly Rowell, and Robyn's family – Issy, Freddie and Tim – who helped in ways large and small. To Deb Kaloper and Emma Roocke for their brilliant food styling. To Steven Maccora from Le Salon Aux Fleurs, Hilary Gwilim of Manon Bis, Sarah Hook from Fletcher Arts, Lily and Graham Geddes from Graham Geddes Antiques, Dani Dunlevy of Made & More, Priscilla and Chantel Giannarelli from Lusso Event Hire, Susan Sutton of &Sutton, and Trudie Cox and Chrissie Young from Eadie Lifestyle. Huge thanks also to Lara Dowd for contributing gorgeous freshly harvested produce, and to Penelope Scott and Daniela Mollica for volunteering their time and energy – I cannot stress how much it's appreciated. My deep gratitude also to Abby Cox and Phoebe Vile from PVPR who helped connect us with so many of this project's generous contributors.

Lastly, but by no means least, to the dear departed friends who made Arniano what it was and is, who are missed every day. To Mario Tinturini, Alessandro Pucci, Teddy Millington-Drake, Ingrid and Paul Channon, Tony Lambton and Claire Ward, Rob Hesketh, Matthew Carr, Lucy Birley, Rose Gray and Daisy Boyd, Adam and Cloe Alvarez, Alessandro de Renzis Sonnino, and of course, always, to Dada.

## IMAGE CREDITS

### PHOTOGRAPHY

*by Robyn Lea*

pp. 4–5, 10, 18–19, 22, 29, 33, 35, 46, 58–9, 64, 83, 99, 105, 108, 113, 125, 129, 131, 132, 135, 139, 145, 146, 152, 155, 156, 159, 166, 169, 174, 177, 180, 187, 189, 190–1, 193, 197, 198, 204, 207, 208, 213, 214–15, 216, 219, 225, 229, 230, 233, 234, 236–7, 242, 244, 248, 252–3, 257, 261

*by Saghar Setareh*

pp. 14, 15, 23, 26, 30, 38, 40–1, 44, 45, 48–9, 50, 52, 53, 54, 62, 68, 80, 82, 84, 87, 88, 91, 93, 95, 96, 97, 100, 107, 114, 117, 122, 126, 136, 142, 149, 160–1, 170, 179, 247, 268–9, 280–1

*by Tara Rowse*

pp. 183, 194

*by Juliette Pearce and Ben Ashworth*

p. 74

*by Amber Guinness*

pp. 111, 264

### PAINTINGS

*by William Roper-Curzon*

**Oil on gesso board**

**p. 8:** *Pink Olive trees at Arniano,* **p. 24:** *View of Hamlet from Arniano,* **p. 36:** *Clouds over Monte Amiata,* **p. 60:** *Tree and Pot at Arniano,* **p. 66:** *Still Life with Artichoke and Lemons,* **p. 78:** *Olive tree in landscape at Arniano,* **p. 120:** *Morning in the Olive Groves at Arniano,* **p. 164:** *Silver olive tree at Arniano,* **p. 202:** *Olive trees in evening light at Arniano,* **p. 240:** *Trees and ploughed field at Arniano,* **p. 270:** *Olive trees and Cypresses at midday at Arniano*

### ILLUSTRATED ICONS

*by Vanessa Garwood*

# INDEX

## A

Abbey of Monte Oliveto Maggiore 274
Abbey of Sant'Antimo 274
aioli, lemony 255
almonds
    flourless chocolate, almond and
      chilli cake 115
    fusilli with Sicilian almond pesto 140
    hazelnut, almond and pear tart 231
    Maria's marmalade, mascarpone
      and almond tart 196
anchovies
    about anchovy paste 71
    green sauce 254
apple, chocolate and mint salad,
    Rossana's 157
Arniano farmhouse 11–23
    landscape surrounding 31
    painting school 27–8, 32–5
artichokes
    about artichokes 104–5
    artichoke and béchamel pie 101–3
    artichoke, parmesan and
      rocket salad 90–1
    artichoke risotto 224
    boiled artichokes with prosciutto 76
    new potatoes with baby
      artichokes 263
asparagus
    ricotta and asparagus tart 106
aubergines
    aubergine parmigiana 70
    buffalo mozzarella with grilled
      aubergine and summery
      green sauce 137

## B

balsamic glaze 70
basil
    baked ricotta with olive oil, tomato
      and basil 182–3
    fusilli with Sicilian almond pesto 140
    grated carrots with lemon and
      basil 245
    green sauce 254
    lime and basil ice cream 154
    linguine with lemon, ricotta and
      basil 143
    spaghetti with datterini tomatoes
      and basil 141
    trofie with pesto and cherry
      tomatoes 138
béchamel 102
beef
    beef stew with gremolata 227–8
    roast beef with green sauce 109
berries
    berry clafoutis with Amalfi lemon
      cream 199
    custard and berry tart 116

blackberries
    berry clafoutis with Amalfi
      lemon cream 199
blood orange and olive oil upside-
    down cake 235
blueberries
    berry clafoutis with Amalfi lemon
      cream 199
bread
    about *pane toscano* 77
    crostini with broad beans, mint
      and ricotta 86
    crostini with cavolo nero and
      ricotta 210
    crostini with porcini, rosemary
      and prosecco 172
    crostini with the new season's olive oil
      and garlic 173
    hot toast with truffled butter 211
breadless ribollita 212–13
broad beans
    broad beans and pecorino 89
    crostini with broad beans, mint and
      ricotta 86

## C

cakes
    blood orange and olive oil upside-
      down cake 235
    flourless chocolate, almond and
      chilli cake 115
cannellini beans
    about cannellini beans 71
    breadless ribollita 212–13
    radicchio, cannellini bean and
      hazelnut salad 246
capers, about 72
cardamom poached pears 232
cardoon gratin 223
carrots
    beef stew with gremolata 227–8
    breadless ribollita 212–13
    grated carrots with lemon and
      basil 245
    poached chicken and vegetables
      with green sauce 226
cavolo nero
    breadless ribollita 212–13
    crostini with cavolo nero and
      ricotta 210
    greens 'in the pan' with garlic and
      chilli 258
    penne with cavolo nero and
      pancetta 217
celeriac mash 267
celery
    beef stew with gremolata 227–8
    breadless ribollita 212–13
    poached chicken and vegetables
      with green sauce 226
chicken
    grilled chicken breast with lemon and
      thyme 147
    poached chicken and vegetables
      with green sauce 226
    roast chicken with grapes 188–9

chickpeas
    about chickpeas 71
    chickpea and rosemary soup 178–9
chicory
    baked endive and radicchio 259
chilli
    about chilli flakes 70
    spaghetti with garlic, oil and chilli 70
chocolate
    flourless chocolate, almond and chilli
      cake 115
    Rossana's apple, chocolate and mint
      salad 157
clafoutis, berry, with Amalfi lemon
    cream 199
cocktails
    Arniano Bell-Ami, The 208–9
    'La Bomba' (watermelon cocktail) 127
    'Pink Wink' 85
    Sidecar 171
    Soho Bell-Ami, The 208–9
courgettes and courgette flowers
    courgette carpaccio 134
    fried courgette flowers, sage leaves
      and mini mozzarellas with lemon
      zest 128–9
crème pâtissière 116
crostini
    crostini with broad beans, mint
      and ricotta 86
    crostini with cavolo nero and
      ricotta 210
    crostini with the new season's olive
      oil and garlic 173
    crostini with porcini, rosemary and
      prosecco 172
    hot toast with truffled butter 211
custard and berry tart 116

## E

eggs, about 77
endive
    baked endive and radicchio 259

## F

fennel
    baked fennel with white wine 260
    fennel and orange salad 256
    poached chicken and vegetables
      with green sauce 226
figs, prosciutto with 176
finocchiona salami 76
flour, about 71
Fonterutoli 275
frittata
    potato and onion frittata 110–11
fritters
    fried courgette flowers, sage leaves
      and mini mozzarellas with lemon
      zest 128–9
fusilli with Sicilian almond pesto 140

## G

garlic
charred roast potatoes with
lemons 265
crostini with the new season's olive oil
and garlic 173
green sauce 254
greens 'in the pan' with garlic and
chilli 258
gremolata 228
lemony aioli 255
roast potatoes with garlic and
rosemary 262
spaghetti with garlic, oil and chilli 70
grapes, roast chicken with 188–9
Gray, Rose 16
green sauce 254
poached chicken and vegetables with
green sauce 226
roast beef with green sauce 109
greens 'in the pan' with garlic and
chilli 258
gremolata 227–8

## H

hazelnuts
fennel and orange salad 256
flourless chocolate, almond and chilli
cake 115
hazelnut, almond and pear tart 231
radicchio, cannellini bean and
hazelnut salad 246
hosting tips 51–2, 55–7

## I

ice cream
lime and basil ice cream 154

## L

lamb shoulder, slow-cooked, with garlic,
herbs and lemon 112
lemons
Arniano Bell-Ami, The 208–9
berry clafoutis with Amalfi lemon
cream 199
cardamom poached pears 232
charred roast potatoes with
lemons 265
gremolata 228
grilled chicken breast with lemon and
thyme 147
hazelnut, almond and pear tart 231
lemony aioli 255
linguine with lemon, ricotta and
basil 143
Sidecar cocktail 171
lentils
about Puy lentils 71
balsamic-glazed lentils with pancetta
and cloves 249
lime and basil ice cream 154
linguine with lemon, ricotta and basil 143
Locanda Il Paradiso 274

## M

malfatti
spinach and ricotta malfatti with
butter and sage 94–7
marmalade, mascarpone and almond
tart, Maria's 196
mascarpone
cherry tomato, thyme and
mascarpone tart 148
meat, tips for cooking 65
menus
autumn 200–1
tips on planning 47
spring 118–19
summer 162–3
winter 238–9
mint
green sauce 254
Rossana's apple, chocolate and mint
salad 157
Monteriggioni 275
mozzarella
aubergine parmigiana 70
buffalo mozzarella with grilled
aubergine and summery green
sauce 137
fried courgette flowers, sage leaves
and mini mozzarellas with lemon
zest 128–9
peach, mozzarella and mint salad 133
tomato 'water' with buffalo
mozzarella 130
mustard, Maille Dijon, about 72

## N

nutmeg, about 72

## O

olive oil
about new season's olive oil 184–6
about olive oil 69
blood orange and olive oil upside-
down cake 235
lemony aioli 255
spaghetti with garlic, oil and chilli 70
olives
about olives 72
ricotta, black olive and basil tart 153
onions
penne with cherry tomatoes, onions
and ricotta 144
potato and onion frittata 110–11
oranges
blood orange and olive oil upside-
down cake 235
cardamom poached pears 232
fennel and orange salad 256
Soho Bell-Ami, The 208–9
Owen, Sian Wyn 16

## P

painting at Arniano 32–5
pancetta
balsamic-glazed lentils with pancetta
and cloves 249
penne with cavolo nero and
pancetta 217
parmesan
about parmesan 75
artichoke, parmesan and rocket
salad 90–1
parsley
green sauce 254
gremolata 228
pasta
about dry pasta 72–3
fusilli with Sicilian almond pesto 140
linguine with lemon, ricotta and
basil 143
pasta 'alla Savannah', with spicy
Italian sausage 218
penne 'alla Bettola', my, with tomato
and vodka 181
penne with cavolo nero and
pancetta 217
penne with cherry tomatoes, onions
and ricotta 144
spaghetti with datterini tomatoes and
basil 141
spaghetti with garlic, oil and chilli 70
tagliatelle, homemade, with spring
peas 98–9
tagliolini with white truffles 222
trofie with pesto and cherry
tomatoes 138
pasta dough 98–9, 222
pastry 116, 196
peaches
peach, mozzarella and mint salad 133
roast peaches with bay and Grand
Marnier cream 158
pears
cardamom poached pears 232
hazelnut, almond and pear tart 231
pear, rocket, pecorino and walnut
salad 175
peas
pea and mint soup 92
tagliatelle, homemade, with spring
peas 98–9
pecorino
about pecorino Toscano 75, 150–1
broad beans and pecorino 89
pear, rocket, pecorino and walnut
salad 175
penne
penne 'alla Bettola', my, with tomato
and vodka 181
penne with cavolo nero and
pancetta 217
penne with cherry tomatoes, onions
and ricotta 144
persimmon tiramisù, Chiara's 195